For the grandchildren of David Brower:
Stephanie, David, Katy, and Rose

THE WILDNESS
WITHIN

THE WILDNESS WITHIN

REMEMBERING DAVID BROWER

Kenneth Brower

Heyday, Berkeley, California

Library of Congress Cataloging-in-Publication Data

Brower, Kenneth, 1944–
   Thee wildness within : remembering David Brower / Kenneth Brower.
     p. cm.
   ISBN 978-1-59714-186-4 (pbk. : alk. paper)—ISBN 978-1-59714-191-8 (google e-book)—ISBN 978-1-59714-196-3 (apple e-book)
    1. Brower, David Ross, 1912-2000. 2. Environmentalists—United States—Biography. 3. Conservationists—United States—Biography. I. Title.
   GE56.B79B76 2012
   333.72092—dc23
   [B]   2012002481

David Brower quotes throughout are © the Estate of David Brower. Ehrlich interview: excerpt on pages 15–16 from *The Population Bomb* (Sierra Club–Ballantine, 1968). Roper interview: excerpt on page 32 from *Camp 4* (Mountaineers Books, 1994); excerpt on page 34 from "Genesis," *Ascent*, 2011. Gilliam interview: excerpts on pages 43 and 44 from *Island in Time* (Sierra Club Books, 1962). Pesonen interview: letter on pages 57–63 is © Wallace Stegner.

Cover Photo: Arthur Schatz/Time & Life Pictures/Getty Images.
    Used with permission.
Cover Design: Lorraine Rath
Interior Design/Typesetting: Leigh McLellan Design
Printing and Binding: Thomson-Shore, Dexter, MI

Orders, inquiries, and correspondence should be addressed to:
   Heyday
   P.O. Box 9145, Berkeley, CA 94709
   (510) 549-3564, Fax (510) 549-1889
   www.heydaybooks.com

10 9 8 7 6 5 4 3 2 1

CONTENTS

INTRODUCTION

WHEN MY BROTHERS and sister and I were growing up in the fifties and sixties, classmates and teachers would occasionally ask what our father did for a living. "Conservationist," we would say. "He's a conservationist." The response from the citizenry was almost always the same. "A *conservationist?* What's that?"

It is easy to forget how young the environmental movement is, particularly in its modern incarnation.

On being hired in 1952 as the first executive director of the Sierra Club, our father, David Brower, became just the second full-time employee of the outfit. The first was Virginia Ferguson, a secretary. Back then the Club was essentially a hiking fraternity of just seven thousand members. In hiring David Brower, the organization doubled the size of its staff, but that still equaled only two.

In the nineteenth century, Thoreau, Muir, and George Perkins Marsh had argued eloquently for conservation, of course, but they were philosopher-writers with other concerns. In the first half of the twentieth, Teddy Roosevelt, Gifford Pinchot, and Aldo Leopold did brilliant conservation work, and they began to formulate, Leopold in particular, an ethic for the movement; but these men had government jobs with other duties. The citizen environmentalist we know so well today—the career activist employed by a nonprofit to advocate for wilderness, or wildlife, or wild rivers, or national parks, or clear air, or clean water, or efficient energy use—had yet to appear. In the early fifties there was Howard Zahniser at The Wilderness Society. There was my father at the Sierra Club. There must have been a handful of others, but the names don't come to mind.

Because he was among the first, in this dawn of his movement—the Archaeozoic of environmentalism, before specialization in the ranks—my father was forced to do a little of everything. He had no choice but to rise to the occasion. He became inexplicably good at a large number of things. He was a pamphleteer. He was a photographer. He was an executive. He was a grassroots organizer. He spoke or lectured to audiences large and small. He was a lobbyist. He testified regularly in Washington. (Great stacks of the *Congressional Record* piled up in our house. I skimmed these as a kid: you never saw such volumes of hot air distilled into print.) He was a magazine editor, recasting the *Sierra Club Bulletin*, which had been preoccupied with news of its mountaineering and outings programs, into a journal of advocacy. He was a filmmaker who wrote, directed, filmed, narrated, and produced sixteen-millimeter movies arguing for national parks in the Sierra Nevada and the North Cascades, and against ruinous dams in California and on the Colorado Plateau. (My siblings and I were pressed into service as child actors in several of these films. We were not paid at union scale; we were paid, in fact, nothing at all. We grumbled on being asked to repeat scenes, but we never staged a strike or sit-down—our father was nothing if not persuasive.)

He was an ad designer. He was a logistician, managing the Sierra Club's "High Trip" program and often leading the expeditions, mule-supplied forays by scores of Sierra Club hikers into the Sierra Nevada, the Cascades, the Tetons, and the Wind River Range. He organized Sierra Club river trips in order to build a constituency for the free-flowing rivers of the Southwest. He was a publisher who invented a genre, the large-format coffee-table book of nature photographs, of which he produced a thirty-volume series, along with smaller-format "battle books" and mountaineering manuals and guides.

"David dropped out of school before they could teach him what he couldn't do," my mother liked to say.

At sixteen my father had entered the University of California at Berkeley, but dropped out as a sophomore to go climbing. My mother, having stayed on at the same school to get her degree, knew how the college experience can trim a psyche down to size. Her unspoiled-by-academe theory of her husband has some merit, no doubt. But my own belief is that my father's renaissance tendencies owed less to what he escaped, in his flight from higher education, than to what he learned in his alternative, and more elevated, education up on the granite at 14,000 feet.

My father discovered himself in the mountains. He became one of the elite rock climbers of his generation, with many first ascents in Yosemite Valley and elsewhere in the Sierra Nevada. Among the peaks he found the love of wildness that would be the dynamo driving everything he later did. His initial preoccupation at the Sierra Club with wilderness preservation gave way, very soon, to the conviction that environmentalism had to embrace much more—pollution, pesticides, population, proliferation of nuclear weapons, just to name some Ps—yet love of wilderness always burned at the core. "Wilderness," he said, "is where the hand of man has not set foot." The definition was playful, but useful and apt. Wilderness is where the opposable thumb has not substantially transformed the landscape. The hand–foot distinction addresses a problem that critics of the wilderness idea always bring up: the fact that all wildernesses, save the Antarctic, have been inhabited by humans since the Stone Age.

Wilderness, indeed, is where we come from. *Homo sapiens* did not evolve in the Information Age, my father pointed out, or in the Space Age, or the Atomic, or the Industrial, or after the invention of agriculture. We evolved as hunter-gatherers in the wilderness of Mother Africa. We were fully human, entirely our present selves, long before domestication of the first seed. Natural selection tailored our every trait to life in wild country. Wilderness is home.

My father's climbing, his new marriage, and his career as an editor at the University of California Press were all interrupted by World War II and combat in Italy with the Tenth Mountain Division. I myself, his first child, was late in meeting him, for I was born while he was off fighting in the Italian Alps.

Kevin Starr, the dean of California historians, has suggested that the horrors of war were key to my father's resolve as an environmentalist, once he got home. This could be, but I am not so sure. In 1938, years before Pearl Harbor and his enlistment, he and Ansel Adams had led the Sierra Club campaign to establish Kings Canyon National Park, and by then he was regularly contributing articles on mountaineering and conservation to the *Sierra Club Bulletin*. He had already started down his road. David Brower was a man without a drop of bloodlust in him—he never hunted or even fished, preferring to leave his trout alive in the stream—but he proved a talented soldier. He thought outside the box as a battalion intelligence officer and won the bronze star for it. He was glad to have experienced war, he told his kids—no other experience resembles it—but he would never want to do it again. Hitler was not a necessary ingredient. Combat in the Tenth Mountain Division did not form him; just plain mountains were enough.

There are climbers frozen in the "gnarly, dude!" stage of development, long-in-tooth, grizzled men you can find hanging out at Camp 4 or the foot of the Tetons. There is a second, larger group who spend their footloose years up in the mountains, then grow up, come to their senses, and descend to begin an unrelated Book II of their lives. There is a third group in which something more interesting happens. The mountaineer-photographer Galen Rowell, the mountain-gear entrepreneur Yvon Chouinard, the wildlands philanthropist Douglas Tompkins, the park creator Kristine McDivitt Tompkins, the hospital builder Edmund Hillary, the prophet Moses, are people who bring something transformative down from the mountains and go on to do great things.

My father belonged to the latter group, the Moses school of mountaineering. He did have a bone to pick with the prophet.

"I'd like to send Moses back up the mountain," he said. "He brought back the tablets with the Ten Commandments telling us how to treat one another. But he never brought back down a thing that tells us what to do about the Earth."

This mission, Moses having screwed it up, my father undertook himself.

David Brower found his voice outdoors. As a boy in the Berkeley hills, describing for his mother, who was blind, all the natural sights she was missing, he began working on the clarity of his sentences. Grown up, speaking at the campfires of Sierra Club trips he was leading, he refined his language, overcame his essential shyness, and discovered his theme.

It was at altitude, I am convinced, that he stumbled across his true calling. At those campfires in the wilderness, talking to the circle of the tribe, he was tapping into the Paleolithic and the very beginnings of narrative. There is no more powerful form of exposition, because it goes back so far. Nothing triggers racial memory like staring into flame while listening to the rise and fall of the human voice.

Today this kind of storytelling has gone missing. Plato was apprehensive about the written word, fearing that it would diminish human capacity for memory; he should have lived to see this third millennium and the written word gone digital. One of the delusions of the Information Age is that it's all just information. Another is that texting and tweeting bring us together in some real way. In our present media richness, we are also poor. Except in the wildest outbacks and remotest villages, nothing remains of the Homeric. David Brower, who was a quick study, curious and retentive, with a very high IQ, could have easily ended up teaching at a university blackboard, but instead found himself addressing the fire.

Customarily at campfires, a Sierra Club trip leader would tell his little band what country they would travel tomorrow and how far to the next camp—eight or ten miles usually, on a big day fifteen. My father's tendency was to minimize the distance. There was a Sierra Club unit of measure called the "Brower Mile," always invoked ironically and reckoned at somewhere between 1.5 and 2 miles, depending on the degree of weariness in the hiker forced to walk it. The Brower Mile may have been a white lie to keep up the spirits of his flock, or it may simply have been cardiovascular. My father, accustomed to climbing multiple peaks in a single day, was very fast on the trail, with a stride that ate up country and could have distorted his judgment.

At campfires, then, he would conclude his routine advisories by quoting some fictional distance. After that he would preach: This wild Yosemite country around us, he would say, or this wild Sequoia or Kings Canyon country, is wilderness only through the efforts of people like John Muir. The price of keeping it wild is eternal vigilance by people like~us. The extractive interests—the miners and loggers and dam builders—only have to win once. *We* have to win every time. We can prevail in this battle, or in that one, but the ore is still there in the ground. The timber is still on the slope. We may have defeated the dam, for now, but the dam *site* is there forever, waiting down in the narrows of the canyon. For our part, we are taking nothing from this country and leaving nothing but our footprints. This Sierra wilderness is enlarging us, purifying our lungs, raising our spirits, as we pass through. We have a reciprocal obligation. It is our duty now, having enjoyed it, to protect it.

Even as a small child, I could see that my father's words were working. His audience was rapt; he was carrying the circle of fire-reddened faces along with him. This seemed normal to me. If my father was engaged at the time in some distant campaign—the fight against Echo Park Dam in the Southwest, for example—he would fill his audience in on the issues and enlist them in that cause, too.

One morning after one of these talks, a woman stopped me on my way to the breakfast line. I was about eight. "You do realize, don't you, that your father is a great man," she said in exasperation.

No, in fact, I did not realize that. I had not been thinking in those terms. Children tend to take their parents for granted. What I could have said or done to deserve this woman's irritation—how I had manifested my ignorance of my father's greatness—is hard for me now to imagine.

These campfire talks were the beginnings of what my father would later call "the Sermon." This ever-changing palimpsest of a speech, in one form or another, is what he would deliver in lecture halls and university auditoriums for the rest of his career. Elements of it appeared, too, in his testimony before Congress and governmental commissions, in his commencement addresses, in articles and books he wrote, in the dozens of forewords he did for the books he published. The Sermon was never static: he would work in local angles and news from the morning paper, and sometimes at the podium he would extemporaneously invent whole new passages and sections.

"Sermon" was apt, because for my father environmentalism was religion. He had that kind of fervor for it. "She has the religion," was his highest compliment. It meant that she really got it. She, or he, was not just paying lip service. She had the environmental ethic in her bones, a true believer. The Sermon was a celebration and defense of Creation. Anyone who doubts that environmentalism can make a complete and perfectly satisfactory religion should have grown up in our house.

My father threw every ounce of himself into his work. He never failed to bring it home with him. No group was too small for him to evangelize, including his family at the dinner table. Within a minute or two he would turn any dinner conversation into a discussion of the beauty of the natural world, or the cleverness of evolution, or the obtuseness of humanity, or the task ahead in salvation of the planet. He would seize on things he learned from any one of us. Once I brought home from junior high a few memorized verses from Pope's "Essay on Man." Pope's phrase "whatever is, is right" electrified my father. He asked me to repeat it. " *'Whatever is, is right!'*" he said. He loved the idea, which he interpreted as an endorsement of the wisdom of Nature, and this bit of Pope often found its way into the Sermon.

My father's commandeering of every conversation sounds like an immensely irritating habit, and sometimes it truly was. But most of the time it was exciting. His enthusiasm could be annoying, but it was almost always irresistible. In my teens I sometimes called him "the Gee Whiz Kid," which was James Thurber's epithet for his editor Harold Ross. My father understood that neither Thurber nor I intended this in an entirely nice way, but he liked it. He often used it on himself.

His insistence on viewing all subjects through the prism of the environmental ethic would seem, on the face of it, a lamentable narrowing of scope. In fact it was the opposite. Because the prism admitted all wavelengths of light from everyplace. My father had a Theory of Everything. Nothing, to his way of thinking, is without some bearing on the problem of safeguarding the wholeness and diversity of the ecosphere. If he had a favorite John Muir line, it was "When we try to pick anything out by itself, we find it hitched to everything else in the universe." Our dinner talk was never dull; it was always about ideas.

On the public stage he was fearless. He had a joy in combat with his corporate enemies and their lackeys in government. He was not shy about mixing it up with the opposition, but it was never personal. His argument was never ad hominem. He did not trust the experts. In a democracy, he thought, our job is to question conventional thinking and expert wisdom. He did not believe in compromise, having been burned by it several times. The environmentalist's job, as he saw it, is to fight as hard as possible on behalf of the Earth. When the time comes for compromise, leave it to the politicians. "That," he said, "is what we pay them for."

My father's life was a demonstration of the energy released in total commitment to a cause larger than oneself. There was almost too much of it. In casting about for analogy, I can think only of the heat generated by the fusion reaction in a thermonuclear bomb or the core of the sun—an exaggeration, no doubt, but sometimes it felt that way. No one ever pulled more all-nighters than my father. "Rest in motion" is a phrase I first heard from him, and this was his default mode. He had enormous physical energy. It was a conundrum for me, in observing him throughout his life, even in old age: did the physical energy come first and fire the passion, or was it the other way around?

David Brower led the transformation of the Sierra Club into the most powerful conservation organization in the United States. The 7000 members he began with, in 1952, grew to 77,000 by 1969, when the Club's board of directors kicked him out. He went on to found the John Muir Institute for Environmental Studies, the League of Conservation Voters, Friends of the Earth in the United States, Friends of the Earth International—a federation of sister organizations now in seventy nations—and finally Earth Island Institute, an incubator organization that has supported more than one hundred environmental projects worldwide. He was instrumental in the establishment of Kings Canyon, Redwood, North Cascades, and Great Basin National Parks, and Point Reyes, Cape Cod, and Fire Island National Seashores. He led the successful campaigns against dams in Dinosaur National Monument and Grand Canyon National Park. His Exhibit Format Series of large-format photographic books won the Carey-Thomas Award for Creative Publishing. He won the Blue Planet Prize, the Windstar Award, and a garage full of others. He was nominated three times for the Nobel Peace Prize.

But his influence and legacy, I have come to believe, are much less institutional than personal.

My father always led an organization, but he was never really an organization man. His impulse was for action; he inevitably grew impatient with institutional inertia that developed in the various outfits he built. He had no deep interest in operating in the black, a fatal trait in an executive who reports to a board of directors. His lifecycle mimicked that of an insect that he, as it happens, was the first to tell me about, as we listened to its buzz in the High Sierra: the North American cicada, genus *Magicicada*, which hatches out every seventeen years. After seventeen years as executive director of the Sierra Club, he was forced by the board to resign. After sixteen years at Friends of the Earth, the same thing happened. He would swell, split the exoskeleton of the constraining organization, emerge, spread wings, and fly off to start a new one.

His lasting effect, I think, was not in his organizations or books or films, but in the flesh, one-on-one, or one-on-five, or one-on-auditorium, or one-on-saloon, or wherever it was he delivered the Sermon. The Sermon worked best when he was winging it, taking a chance, stretching for some idea just out of reach. The audience sensed this and began pulling for him. *Is he going to make it? Where are we going?* John McPhee, in his fine book on my father, *Encounters with the Archdruid,* observes that at the podium he would bend his knees with the effort, like a skier. The Sermon could bomb horribly. If he got no feedback from the faces in front of him, his engine would cough and sputter and stall and he would go down in flames. He needed the crowd behind him. When the Sermon succeeded, the effect was electric. At the conclusion, young people would stream down the aisles and ask how to sign up in his movement. It was the campfire all over again.

The organizations David Brower built have all grown and changed, and none, save the last, really bears his stamp any longer. But many of the people compelled by the Sermon, those young people who lined up afterward at the podium to offer their services, do retain his stamp. Many are now leaders of the environmental movement.

A small sampling of this group testifies in the pages that follow. For me, the interviewer, the sessions that produced these recollections were a very fine thing, almost a kind of séance, a chance to spend many weeks again in my father's company.

Paul Ehrlich

PAUL EHRLICH

T HE CABIN AT Rocky Mountain Biological Laboratory was a one-room shack with a sleeping loft when Paul and Anne Ehrlich began summering there a half century ago. Since then, additions have allowed room enough for computers and a bed downstairs. Outside the windows, aspens stretch away in all directions and, in most directions, mountains. To the west stands Mount Gothic, 12,200 feet tall and buttressed like a Gothic cathedral. The big Notre Dame of the mountain "subtends 60 percent of the view," Professor Ehrlich told me, slipping uncharacteristically into monograph lingo.

The Rocky Mountain Lab sits at 9,500 feet in the West Elk Range. It was once the mining town of Gothic, Colorado, but in the 1880s the ore played out, and in 1928 scientists bought the ghost town for $200 and began its conversion to a high-altitude research station. Outside the Ehrlich cabin window, on the day of the interview, lay more summertime snow than the couple could remember in all their fifty-odd years of working there. Lately the Rocky Mountain Lab has been emphasizing studies of climate change, and there beyond the window, in white drifts under the aspens and on the shoulders of Mount Gothic, was the evidence that change is indeed upon us.

It was afternoon when we talked. Over the summits of the Elk Range, thunderheads were building.

Paul Ehrlich is Bing Professor of Population Studies at Stanford and president of the Center for Conservation Studies at the university. He is cofounder, with Peter Raven, of the field of coevolution. He is a member of the National Academy of Sciences and a fellow of the American Association for the Advancement of Science, the American Academy of Arts and Sciences, and the American Philosophical Society. He has won the John Muir Award of the Sierra Club, the Gold Medal of the World Wildlife Fund International, a MacArthur Prize Fellowship, and the Sasakawa Environment Prize of the United Nations. In 1999, the year after David Brower won the Blue Planet Prize, Ehrlich won it himself, bringing home from Japan the heavy glass globe on its silvery pedestal and the fifty million yen that accompanies the prize.

This summer Professor Ehrlich was working, as he often is in Colorado, on the biology and ecology of checkerspot butterflies. One season, for example, the professor and his team conducted a large-scale study of the population structure, movement, and mating habits of Rocky Mountain checkerspots. They captured, numbered, and released hundreds of butterflies. The males caught along a ridgetop had their sex organs dipped in a red fluorescent pigment; the males caught on the slopes below had theirs dipped in green. In copulation, some of the dye would rub off on the females. In follow-up, with what amounted to little butterfly rape kits, the team investigated who, from where, was mating with whom. This year's experiment involved the continued study of a population of checkerspots that Ehrlich and a colleague, Cheri Holdren, had transplanted from Yellowstone decades ago.

On the cabin shelves were books: *The Butterflies of North America,* by James Scott. *Doc,* the new Maria Doria Russell novel, a reconsideration of Doc Holliday. *The Human Career,* by Richard Klein ("the best of the paleontological anthropologists," in Paul Ehrlich's opinion.) *Mammals of the World,* by Walker, in two volumes, kept handy because the Ehrlichs were at work on a book on mammal extinctions. *Maximum Entropy and Ecology,* by John Harte, a new book on ecological theory—a very good one, Professor Ehrlich thinks. There were many Ehrlich books, some by Paul, others by the wife-and-husband team of both Ehrlichs. Among these was Paul's *The Population Bomb,* the original 1968 paperback, with a foreword by David Brower.

Ehrlich begins:

I have understood the population explosion intellectually for a long
time. I came to understand it emotionally one stinking hot night
in Delhi a few years ago. My wife and daughter and I were return-
ing to our hotel in an ancient taxi. The seats were hopping with
fleas. The only functional gear was third. As we crawled through
the city, we entered a crowded slum area. The temperature was
well over 100°F; the air was a haze of dust and smoke. The streets
seemed alive with people. People eating, people washing, people
sleeping. People visiting, arguing, and screaming. People thrusting
their hands through the taxi window, begging. People defecating
and urinating. People clinging to buses. People herding animals.
People, people, people, people. As we moved slowly through the
mob, hand horn squawking, the dust, noise, heat, and cooking fires
gave the scene a hellish aspect. Would we ever get to our hotel?
All three of us were, frankly, frightened. It seemed that anything
could happen—but, of course, nothing did. Old India hands will
laugh at our reaction. We were just some overprivileged tourists,
unaccustomed to the sights and sounds of India. Perhaps, but since
that night I've known the feel of overpopulation.

The Population Bomb, thrown together in weeks by Paul and Anne
Ehrlich when they were young, will be forever associated with Paul's name,
almost a kind of epithet. Ehrlich has written countless scientific papers and
many notable books since, but on the covers of those books—as in his
Wikipedia entry and his mugging in Dossier, a right-wing website dedicated
to exposing left-wing lunatics like himself—he is almost invariably identified
as "Author of *The Population Bomb.*"

That pivotal book, which begins in the throngs and heat and smoky
haze and babble of the Delhi slum, ends with the acknowledgments and
these last words:

My wife, Anne, has been my constant collaborator in my work on
the population problem and is virtually a co-author of this book.

My mother, Mrs. William Ehrlich, is an English teacher. She also read and criticized the manuscript. She wishes it publicly stated that she is not responsible for my abuse of the English language. She agrees heartily with what I say in the book. Recently she told me, in the middle of an argument about why I had not taken Latin in high school, that her only regret is that she found out about birth control too late (the meaning of that statement is obscure to me, but she insisted that I include it).

This playful send-off is an unusual coda for a treatise warning of catastrophe. Our Cassandras are usually grimmer. The book's instigator, David Brower, often complained that "The trouble with environmentalists and feminists is that they have no sense of humor." Humor, to his way of thinking, is as important to an environmentalist as to any stand-up comedian. Without some laughs, environmentalism gets just too bleak. In Ehrlich my father found the balance he liked in an author: Paul Ehrlich can doomsay with the best of them, but he can also tell a joke.

THE DETAILS, of course, are lost in the haze of history. But Dave heard me talking about population on the radio. I can't remember whether he came to me individually, or with Ian Ballantine. Dave had made some kind of a deal with Ian, who was the founder of Bantam Books and Ballantine Books. Dave asked if Anne and I could get together a short book saying what I'd been saying on the radio shows. And I'd done a series of them by then. Dave and Ian wanted to try and get it out right away, in hopes of having some influence on the election, which was Nixon versus Humphrey in 1968. It just shows you how naïve Dave and Ian and I were in those days. So *The Population Bomb* became a Sierra Club–Ballantine Book. Dave wrote the foreword.

The book fell together quickly because Anne and I had been working on this subject, and I'd been talking a lot about it. It was basically part of my lecture in a class on evolution that I was teaching then at Stanford. It took Anne and me about two weeks, working nights. Then Ian said that it should have only a single author, and I let him take Anne off the cover. Ballantine Books claimed they could do a better job of marketing it with just a single author. I was very young and naïve in those days, and Anne did not get her name on the book, which I consider somewhat of a disgrace of mine, to this very day. It was a different world back then, you've got to remember. Women didn't count.

The course was very popular. It was a ten-week quarter, and I used the first nine weeks of the course to talk about evolution. In the last week I talked about the stuff in *The Population Bomb*. People particularly liked that last week. Students started telling their parents, and the alumni started requesting that I talk, and someone made contact with the Commonwealth Club. I didn't even know that talks at the Commonwealth Club were normally broadcast. But they did broadcast my talk, and then I started getting asked to go on all kinds of radio and TV shows in the Bay Area. My view was that instead of just lecturing to sixty or seventy students in a class about this problem, if I could lecture to six or seven thousand on a Bay Area radio station, all the better. I'm a born loudmouth. So I started doing that, and after *The Bomb* came out, I continued to do it.

I had never had a popular success like *The Bomb*. None at all. I was naïve about that. The big breakthrough was probably when Arthur Godfrey gave a copy to Johnny Carson, and I got invited on the Tonight Show.

Somewhere in that same period, late '68, early '69, we founded Zero Population Growth. It was the idea of an East Coast attorney, Richard Bowers. I ended up meeting him at Yale, because I was visiting a colleague, somebody from right here at Rocky Mountain Biology Lab, actually, an entomologist I had known from my work with butterflies for several years already, a guy named Charlie Remington. The three of us met in a garret at Yale and founded ZPG. By the time *The Bomb* came out, Zero Population Growth had a headquarters in Los Altos. In the back of *The Bomb* was a little ad that said, "Write to Zero Population Growth." The first time I went on the Tonight Show, Johnny let me give the address. It resulted in the single biggest mail delivery in the history of Los Altos.

John Carson was, first of all, on top of the issue. Second of all, he was, of all that kind of TV celebrity, the best one at interviewing. We had a great time. I did the show twenty or twenty-five times. I always enjoyed working with him. ZPG gave him an award for his contributions, but he wanted it kept private. He had a wonderful sense of humor. The first time I went on, we met beforehand and talked about what we would do. But after that, all I would do was to send him a list of questions and possible answers, which he never paid any attention to. We always just went out there and had a good time.

But I did have reservations. I was extremely worried about whether this would cash in my chips with the scientific community. I needn't have worried. My closest colleagues were all totally on board. In fact, if you look here in the book, at the acknowledgments, the people who read the manuscript and so on, it contains many of my closest colleagues. Dick Holm, probably my closest colleague. There's a guy in here named Peter H. Raven, a name you might remember. John Thomas. Holm, Raven, and Thomas were all faculty members in our department at the time. The head of the department is also acknowledged for reading it, a professor named Donald Kennedy. Does that ring a bell? Don Kennedy and I are still working together. Ernst Mayr, too, who was probably the top person in evolutionary biology at that time, every year I would get a letter from him saying, "You're absolutely right. Go for it." I never had any serious problem with anybody in biology, or with anybody at Stanford. Nobody ever told me to shut up, or to stop making waves. All of my colleagues in the business, there's just no disagreement. I was very concerned, but I needn't have been.

A lot of vitriol got heaped on the book, of course. The attack still goes on today, particularly because of my connection with John Holdren. Holdren is President Obama's science and technology advisor and he draws a lot of fire. Holdren and I wrote a huge amount of stuff on this population topic, several books, and so on. So when, what's his name, Rush Limbaugh, spouts off, who cares? Or, what's her name, the lady—that woman—Michele Bachmann? To use the technical language, I don't give a flying fuck.

I live, like every scientist, on the opinions of my colleagues. And since my colleagues have essentially been 100 percent on my side—certainly all the important people in my field—the chattering hasn't bothered me. So much of the response is idiotic. When John Holdren and Peter Raven and Don Kennedy all say, "You're doing the right thing," then the opinion of Russ Limbaugh sort of rolls off your back.

My career would have been different politically, I'm sure, without *The Population Bomb*. But I think the books that followed it would still have come out, in one form or another. Because my colleagues and I were getting more and more concerned. The *Race Bomb* and *Ark II* and *The Machinery of Nature* would have been written. The books Anne and I did, *Extinction* and *The End of Affluence*, would have come out. You know, the original title of *The Population Bomb* was supposed to have been *Population, Resources, and Environment*, and Anne and I later wrote a book under that title. Anne, John Holdren, and I wrote a third edition of that book, which is called *Ecoscience*, and on which John is still attacked almost daily on the blogs, along with me. I think all these efforts would have happened without *The Bomb*, one way or another. I was a biologist watching the biology that I worked on gradually disappear, and all my colleagues were having the same kind of problem.

Obviously, the career would not have been identical. *The Bomb* actually probably got me into more research in biology than I ever would have gotten into otherwise, because it got me invited all over the world. At least it was the *start* of what got me invited all over the world. I was able to do fieldwork in places that I normally couldn't have.

I don't remember how the original plan for *The Population Bomb* was generated, among David Brower and Anne and me and Ian Ballantine. But one point I was making on the radio at the time was that Rachel Carson had started something really important. You'll notice that in *The Population Bomb* there's a fair amount on pesticides, because they were a huge issue in those days. But I thought that the population dimension of that problem was being ignored. Trying to bring that dimension into the picture led to very high levels of abuse from the right wing, but also very high levels of interest and support from the scientific community.

The population discussion was lively for a while. The movement had some steam, but then it was knocked off by a number of factors. One was that attaining replacement reproduction in this country was misinterpreted as an end to the growth of the population in the United States. There was also a huge push for reproductive rights for women, which I think is very important, but a lot of the people pushing it, to this very day, don't seem to understand that if we don't solve the overall problem of population, then the issue of reproductive rights will become moot.

And then there was Ronald Reagan, who in my personal opinion did more than anyone to reverse progress in this area, and in any number of other areas. I think he's the worst president in the history of the United States. Not that there might not have been some nineteenth-century president who was equally stupid, but that president, whoever he was, didn't have the power that Reagan had. If, say, Fillmore was no good, still he couldn't have destroyed the world. Whereas Reagan could have. And went a good ways towards doing it. He shredded the Global 2000 Report. He took the solar panels off the top of the White House. What was the name of the jerk who was his secretary of the interior? James Watt. Reagan just turned everything backwards.

And now there's the rise of the Tea Party mentality, people who name themselves after an historic event they clearly don't understand. The original Boston Tea Party was not a protest against *taxes*, it was a protest against taxation without representation—a very different sort of thing.

I don't know, but I think interest in the population issue is coming back slightly today, and interest in some other environmental issues, too. But I must say the whole political situation now horrifies me. And in general the environmental crisis is much, much, much worse than it was forty years ago, when *The Population Bomb* came out. We have made a little progress on the population front. Birthrates are down in much of the world, and that's helpful. The trouble is they're not down so far that we're not still heading towards ten billion on the planet, when we ought to be about one and a half or two billion.

So many people don't understand the problem. So many people, building on a perception that's *partly* right, have come to consider concern about population control as a sort of a racist movement. And of course there have been a lot of racists in the population movement. I run into a lot of them myself. My big argument is that, well, if it's racist, you can't count me in, because I have only one kid, I'm not trying to outbreed anybody. But I know Jewish people who are trying to outbreed the Arabs. And a huge amount of the immigration issue in this country has to do with skin color. It's not a pretty picture.

Dave Brower and I were almost always on the same side of things. But I did not get much involved in his organizations, or in any other environmental organizations. Anne actually did more of that. She sort of took on the job of trying to bring science to NGOs. I had very few interactions of that sort. I served on the board of Audubon for a while. They were crazy for recycling, and I tried to persuade them, on every piece of recycling literature, to put something about, "Recycling can be very helpful, but if we don't solve the population/consumption problem, it won't make any difference." But I could never get anywhere on it.

Dave was always stirring up trouble, and I was always happy to pitch in. But we were in different fields. We were optimally foraging. He was doing the things that he was best at, and I was doing the things that I was best at. When we got together, we talked butterflies and we talked natural history. But mostly we talked how distressed we were about what the hell was going on on this planet. I consider my life a life of failure, and, I hate to say it, I consider your old man's life a life of failure, too. If you look around the world today, it isn't what we would have wanted. It isn't what we worked for.

Dave, first of all, had the quality of being able to see into the problem. To realize what was going on. And then he had the guts to say something about it: "We shouldn't make an amusement park out of Yosemite," or whatever the latest crazy plan was. He instantly latched on to the population issue. I can't ever remember him *not* being concerned with it. His coming immediately to me after that radio broadcast and saying, "You know, this is a thing we've really got to push."

How many people in the world grasp it, even now? Today we have not three and a half billion people, as we did forty-something years ago, when Dave and I were talking about doing *The Population Bomb*. We have *seven billion people.* Yet 99 percent of my colleagues are not desperately concerned. You know, at Stanford, talk to the average professor, ask him to name the ten most important problems in the world, and I don't think population, or even environment, will make the list. They'll say global warming, because they've all heard about that. But that's about it. And they won't know the connection there. Where have you seen, even in the media, the point made that the more of us there are, generally the more greenhouse gases there are going to be?

So Dave had insight already. And I have no idea—you probably have a better idea than I do—where he got it. Maybe his wilderness experience had something to do with it. I can believe that. Because I see a huge difference between my colleagues who do fieldwork and those who don't. If you've seen the plants and animals you're working on being plowed under in front of your eyes, it brings the problem to your attention.

I think Dave and I probably shared many of the same flaws, but I was probably in an easier position to avoid getting caught up in *administration.* I would occasionally be asked whether I wanted to be a dean or something like that. I would always say that if I took on that job, and did it right, it would kill me, and if I did it the way I wanted to do it, it would kill all my colleagues. I tended to be on Dave's side in the big bean-counting battles at the Sierra Club and Friends of the Earth. I left the board of Audubon over a bean-counting issue.

When Audubon was financially going into the ground, they hired a really good guy, Peter Berle, to run it. He brought Audubon back from a big deficit way into the black. Then he made a big hiring mistake and it cost him a million dollars. For one year they ran a deficit. The board basically said that we should stop all activities until we've cleared the deficit. A number of us said, "That's nuts! You're not going to raise any money if you're not doing anything!" There was a huge fuss over it, and I actually left in the middle of a board meeting and resigned, I was so annoyed at the way the bean counters wanted to run it. I've sort of always had the feeling that's where your old man ended up in the Sierra Club and a couple of other places. At odds with the bean counters.

That's the one administrative issue I ever got involved in that he was also involved in—the original Sierra Club troubles, where I thought it was so incredibly stupid to be arguing against him on the grounds that the books were costing the Sierra Club some money, rather than making some money. The books did so much to build the whole Sierra Club program!

These organizations, it's hard to live with them. I mean, after all, Zero Population Growth changed its name and disappeared. Do you even know its current name? If it still exists? I think it's called the Population Connection, but it shows you what a brilliant move it was to change the name.

I always see Dave standing for the right thing against gigantic forces, either of evil or stupidity. I suppose that's my own history, too. Dave and I never had, as far as I can remember, any difference on any real issue. Almost everything he was in favor of, I was in favor of, too. Not because *Dave* was in favor of it, but because it was so goddamned obvious.

David Brower leading the first ascent of Shiprock, New Mexico
Photograph by John Dyer

STEVE ROPER

THE IMPULSE IN all climbers is to get to the top, and Steve Roper's house perches, as one might expect, high in the Oakland hills. His deck and living room windows look down past the crowns of trees toward the southern end of San Francisco Bay. On the summer day of the interview, the bay waters in that direction were bright and slightly hazy.

Roper's interviewer, as it happens, attended the same elementary school that the climber did, Hillside, in Berkeley, passing through four years after Roper. He, the interviewer—me—knew the climber's ridgetop home from previous visits. I had come with my tape recorder several years before to interview Roper about a Hillside School classmate of his, the great mountaineering photographer Galen Rowell. I had learned, among other things, that Rowell led Roper on climbs up the big redwoods of our alma mater in order to pee on people below. I escaped this bombardment myself. I cannot remember either Roper or Rowell from grammar school. I was entering second grade as they were entering sixth. They might as well have been college men. We inhabited different universes.

Today I brought Roper a gift, a yellow box of Hasselblad color transparencies, two and a quarter inches square. I had found the box in one of the many crates of photographs David Brower shot over his lifetime. The yellow box contained about a dozen portraits of Roper that my father had taken forty-seven years before. "Roper," the box was labeled, in my father's handwriting. "Jan 3, 1964."

Roper held the box for a moment before opening it. "January 3, 1964," he mused. "That's weird, because I was in Georgia on that day. I was drafted. Two years in the Army, Georgia and Vietnam." He calculated for a moment. "God, did I come back on leave? No! No, I know what it is. I was drafted five days after Kennedy's assassination. In early January, I was in basic training at Fort Ord. I wasn't in Georgia on that date. I was down at Fort Ord, so I came back on leave."

He opened the box and shuffled through the first few photographs of himself at twenty-three. "Christ Almighty!" he said.

The young man in the photos wears glasses with the thick plastic rims of the era. His hair is in a buzz cut, a term that had not been invented yet. "Crew cut," we called it then. His face seems poised between uncertainty and confidence. Clearly now Roper was having trouble connecting the young man in the photos with his present self. In some humans, metamorphosis is total, as in tadpole to frog. Roper paused to stare at himself in one image. "I had my hair so short because I'd been in the Army about six weeks," he said. He shuffled through the rest of the photos. "God Almighty. Great, thank you."

On Roper's shelves were the books he had written, or cowritten: *A Climber's Guide to Yosemite Valley. A Climber's Guide to the High Sierra. Camp 4: Recollections of a Yosemite Rockclimber. Fifty Classic Climbs of North America.* And a number of others. On Roper's coffee table were several mountaineering journals and a collection of rocks. Among the rocks I spotted an artifact, a tin cup tarnished nearly black. The cup was deeper than normal in cups of this brand. Looking inside, I could just make out, through the oxidation on the bottom, the embossed words *Sierra Club of California*. We grinned, Roper and I, as happy as a couple of philatelists admiring the two-pence "Blue Mauritius," issued in 1847, or the Swedish "Three-Skilling Yellow" of 1885. The cup was a rarity. From 1905 through the 1940s, the Sierra Club cup was tin and made its "of California" reference. From the 1950s onward, Sierra Club cups were of stainless steel and stamped simply *Sierra Club.*

The shiny new cup was introduced, coincidence or not, about when the Sierra Club hired its first executive director. David Brower, at the time of his appointment, was in the process of transforming Muir's hiking club into the most powerful conservation organization in the United States, and the *of California* soon became vestigial.

"You see the 'Sierra Club of California?'" Roper asked. "I could probably sell it on eBay for two or three dollars. Prewar. I found that in Milestone Basin, I believe. I was wandering around, and saw it sticking out of sandy soil. I thought, That's a Sierra Club cup. It's much deeper, a quarter inch deeper, than the later cup. I dug it out, and I thought, Holy Shit! Of course, I could take all the rust off with chemicals, but I don't want to. No! No."

On the coffee table near the cup was a strange, irregular, dull-metallic plate. It was roughly the shape of a cartoon lightning bolt. I picked it up. The bottom was perfectly flat, but the top was bumpy and fluid-form, like pahoehoe lava. It was heavier than stone.

"It looks like lava," I said.

"No. It's aluminum. From the Oakland Hills Fire. Three days after the fire, I was wandering around and I came across a Porsche. A burned-out Porsche. Underneath was the Porsche engine. Talk about 2000 degrees! Only about five minutes of that, maybe, but it melted a Porsche engine. Or part of an engine."

Here the interview on David Brower, not yet begun, wandered off subject.

We spoke first of the terrible 1991 firestorm in the Oakland and Berkeley hills. The fire killed twenty-five people, destroyed thirty-eight hundred dwellings, and melted that Porsche engine. It badly burned an old climbing partner of my father's, Al Baxter, as Al tried to escape by car. Gail Baxter, his wife, a woman I liked very much as a boy on Sierra Club High Trips, was burned to death.

I told Roper that I had once co-owned a house in what would become the fire zone. One day in the early 1980s, half-finished reading a John McPhee story on the dynamics of convective firestorms in the ravines of Southern California, I was driving homeward, uphill through a ravine of thick groves of eucalyptus—young trees shedding their strips of oily, combustive bark—when I realized that all the requisite conditions for a firestorm existed right here. Someday, if I stayed long enough, my house would burn. I sold my half to my friend, and ten years later the house burned indeed, along with those thousands of others.

We reminisced about Al Baxter, gravely burned in the fire.

On Sierra Club High Trips in the fifties, I remembered, Baxter would start hiking early, moving fairly well, but we would always catch him by afternoon, moving slowly. One day as we overtook Al, laboring up the next switchback of the trail—a pained hobble, with an occasional grimace—I said something to my father about Al's pace. Quietly, so that Baxter would not hear, my father explained that Al had fallen on a climb. His belayer had arrested his fall too abruptly, causing Al to swing back hard into the face, telescoping his legs as he tried to fend off the cliff.

My father intended the story in two ways, I believe. First was as an object lesson on the correct way to arrest a fall. Second was to nip any unwarranted pride I might feel as a ten-year-old in outwalking a grown man. As always on the trail, as we greeted Baxter and passed him, we slackened pace, so as not to make him feel any slower than he already was.

A couple of switchbacks ahead, with Baxter out of sight behind us, my father elaborated on the accident.

Al and two companions had been climbing Upper Cathedral Spire in Yosemite Valley. It was Al's turn to lead. Leaving a slight ledge and his belayer below him, he climbed twenty feet up to an old Army piton. He tested it, and it seemed secure. He clipped in and continued upward, where he saw a second old piton, a ring piton, protruding from the rock a few feet above him. He climbed to this one, without direct aid. He had inserted his fingers through the ring when his foothold failed, or the piton came out—in retrospect he was never sure which. He fell. The Army piton below him held long enough to swing him against the cliff, a glancing strike with both feet, and then the piton popped out. He somersaulted back over the ledge from which he had started, and a good distance below struck the wall again, hard, shattering both legs. Here the fall came to a stop. He dangled four feet off the rock face, about thirty feet below his belayer and seven hundred feet above the talus at the base of Upper Cathedral Spire. He had free-fallen sixty feet.

With tension on the ropes from his companions above, Baxter managed to climb five feet to a slight ledge and take the strain off his friends. The five feet took him five minutes, for his legs were useless. In three rappels his companions got him down to the talus at the base of the spire, where he was met with a Park Service rescue party and a stretcher. They splinted his legs and began a difficult carry down through the talus. Al got a shot of morphine, for which he was very grateful.

At the conclusion of Baxter's account of his fall in the "Accidents" section of the Mountaineering Notes for the *Sierra Club Bulletin* of March 1948, my father, the editor, had appended an analytical note. The lessons of the accident were still very clear in his mind when he passed them on to me.

Baxter had outweighed his belayer by seventy pounds—not a good idea. Whenever possible the belayer should have the weight advantage. The belayer was not anchored, nor was the third climber, who also had a rope to Baxter. Anchored, the belayer could have begun the rescue sooner, having freed himself of Baxter's weight by tying Al's rope into the anchor. The belayer had not allowed the rope to run on either the first or second impacts. He should have eased the fall to a stop, a technique stressed since the early thirties by the Sierra Club Rock Climbing Section.

Al, for his part, had erred in trusting the old pitons. The leader himself should always drive in any piton that might be critical in a fall. There is no other way to be sure of it. He must listen to the timbre of the ding the piton makes when struck by the piton hammer. Is the sound first clear and bell-like and then muted, as the iron blade, driven in tight, takes on the resonant frequency of the rock? Or is it in any way polyphonic and equivocal? The climber must feel, through the hammer handle, the piton's wedgedness or looseness in its crack. He must watch the reaction of the rock. His life could depend on it. As hard as a piton is to drive in, that is, more or less, how hard it will be to yank out. On practice climbs in the past, my father, driving in good pitons and bad ones, had asked me to listen to the difference. Handing over the hammer, he had instructed me to drive in pitons of my own, to see how a solid one sounded, looked, and felt.

When he finished with the particulars of the Al Baxter case, my father gave a quick summary of an overarching philosophy that I had heard several times before. It was a climbing credo honored today, I think, mostly in the breach: A climber should always work within his margin of safety. The thrill should not be in the danger. The thrill should be in technical proficiency, and effort, and camaraderie, and the views from the summit, and the thin air and blue-black sky at 14,000 feet, and the pure pleasure of good Sierra granite under your hands.

Al Baxter had let his margin grow too thin.

We continued up the trail. I could not stop thinking about Baxter and what had happened to him. He was a big, handsome, affable man with a dry wit and a resonant voice that I liked, and now he was all busted up in the legs. Yet he would not give up hiking. Those grimaces he made toward the end of the day, and the sudden beads of sweat that would jump out on his forehead when his foot hit the ground wrong, were a measure of how much he still loved the Sierra Nevada, and it made me want to cry.

We came into a stand of whitebark pines by a stream where Ethyl Rose and Bill Horsfall had started a fire under their billycan. They were brewing tea, as usual. It was a tradition with this old couple to stop a mile, or half mile, before camp and make tea: a reinvigoration service they provided for fellow Sierra Club hikers on the final stretch into camp.

My mother did not approve of the Horsfall marriage. Anne Brower was a great democrat, but on occasion she could be a little snooty. It seemed to her that Ethyl Rose Taylor, now Mrs. Horsfall, was too much a lady for an uncouth character like Bill. Bill Horsfall was a rough type for sure, a weather-beaten reprobate who had blown the tips off several fingers fooling with blasting caps as a boy. I liked Ethyl Rose a lot. I did not like Bill Horsfall as much, but he was a more interesting figure. When I was younger, he would show me his stumps if I asked.

At the Horsfall fire my father stopped, out of good manners, and we had tea. Al Baxter had yet to appear on the trail behind us, but I felt better about him. He was close to home. This evening Horsfall tea would power his bad legs for the last mile through the dusk into camp.

"Do you realize who the belayer of Al Baxter was, the guy who held that fall?" Roper asked, when I had finished a very abbreviated version of this story. I confessed that I did not. He filled me in. "Al Baxter was a big guy, about two hundred and ten. The belayer was a hundred-and-twenty-pounder—almost a hundred pounds less—a guy named Ulf Ramm Ericson. He was killed on 9/11 at the World Trade Center. I describe that in my book *Ordeal by Piton*."

No one else in the world, I think, would have known this detail. No one but Roper would have been able to connect, by thirty feet of manila climbing rope, those two old climbers and those two conflagrations.

Steve Roper was a very good climber himself. He made the third ascent of the Salathe Wall on El Capitan, and the first one-day ascent of the Northwest Face of Half Dome, and the third ascent of the Nose of El Capitan, and the first solo ascents of the Royal Arches and the Lost Arrow Spire, among other hard Yosemite climbs. But Roper is not, by his own admission, one of the superstars of his generation. Where he is unsurpassed is not on the granite itself, but in chronicling what goes on up there. He is the preeminent historian of Sierra Nevada rock climbing. No historian in any field has a more apt surname. Roper is the Herodotus of mountaineering in what Muir called "the Range of Light."

YOU WERE YOUNG, not even born, when your pop was doing most of his climbing. Well, his climbing was utterly brilliant, back in the thirties. As I said in one of my books, he was an incredibly delicate climber on friction, specially. We didn't do too many cracks back then. I say "we," but I was not there, of course. *People* didn't do too many cracks back then. If somebody did cracks, they were very low-angle. Now kids are doing overhanging cracks.

In 1939, you know, Dave Brower, Bestor Robinson, Johnny Dyer, and Raffi Bedayn made the first ascent of Shiprock, in New Mexico, "the last great American climbing problem," according to the media at the time. Your pop wrote an article on the climb for *The Saturday Evening Post*. Bestor Robinson wrote an account, too. In his article, Bestor talks about "David Brower's fine balance and long orangutan arms." Dave was tall, with long arms to boot. So he could do reaches that little Johnny Dyer, who was only about five foot five, could not possibly do. "Brower seemed somehow to be able to move on slight discolorations of the rock," Bestor wrote.

So Dave Brower was well known even in the thirties for being a brilliant friction climber. Friction climbing requires great balance. Footwork. There's the old rule about standing upright over your holds and not leaning into the rock. Dave was a master at it.

In researching my book *Camp 4*, I found somewhere, in the Bancroft Library or someplace, that everybody in those days was rated. There were very few climbers in the Sierra Club Rock Climbing Section, but in 1935 they were rated by Dick Leonard, who was sort of the boss of the Cragmont Rock climbers in Berkeley.

So here's how I wrote it up:

> The most active person during this period was Dave Brower, a graceful, lanky climber who began climbing on the Berkeley rocks in 1934, at age twenty-two. A few months after he first touched rock, a confidential report prepared by the Rock Climbing Section's Technical Climbing Committee rated Brower's 'climbing technique' a fourteen on a scale of fifteen. The only ones to get the top rating were Leonard and Eichorn. No one else was close. On the same chart, neophyte Brower scored two out of a possible ten for 'experience' and sixteen out of thirty for 'judgment.'

Well. He was probably a little bit reckless. Climbing ability rated way up there high; judgment, not too high. He was twenty-three years old, just starting climbing, and probably showing off a bit. Doing little solo stuff. Soloing on Indian Rock, or something. "Oh, you need a rope there, David!" That kind of judgment question.

It's interesting, in light of would happen at the Sierra Club thirty-five years later. In 1969, Dick Leonard would be one of the leaders of the faction that kicked Dave out as executive director. For Leonard it was a question of your pop's judgment, again. Here's Dick Leonard, who in the thirties gave only himself and Eichorn the highest climbing rating—nobody else close—and he decides again that Dave's judgment is poor and that Dave is soloing too much.

I never actually climbed with Dave. But between, say, 1954 and '56, he would come out to the local rocks occasionally. He came out to Hunter's Hill, that wonderful cliff up by Vallejo. As you're driving eastward through Vallejo on Highway 80, and start up the grade, off to the right there's a whole bunch of rocks, and one of them is this enormous thing, 170 feet high, I think, and 85 degrees. Not very good rock. But we went there all the time. And I remember Dave out there teaching me about rappelling.

Here I am facing this 170-foot drop, down about 100 feet to a ledge you can walk off. And we have manila rope, five-sixteenth-inch manila rope. Oh, God. And all these weird leather patches to protect our genitalia. This was in the days of body rappels. You wrapped the rope around your genitalia *and* your shoulder and neck. It was horrible. It's a lot easier now on the genitalia.

So, anyway, I remember him being on top of the rock, helping me get into the rappel. I was quite scared. He was also belaying people in the rappel. It was much safer that way. We don't do it anymore, of course. So I tied in the bowline with regular old nylon rope. Dave was standing there, making sure the rope went around my body in the correct way. It's easy to screw up. You might do it backwards and tear out your genitalia for sure. And he was belaying me, and off I go over the edge. I was thirteen or fourteen, going right off the edge.

"Is this rope tied?" I asked.

"We got you on belay, anyway, even if the rope breaks," Dave said. So he was teasing me a bit about being scared. I wasn't too scared. I was scared, but I wasn't screaming, or anything. I was just, "Are you sure you got me here? How's the anchor?" He said, "Go on, just go over the edge. Just keep your feet into the wall. Don't get vertical. Get a forty-five degree angle." And of course I was thrilled. I didn't know that he was famous. Though he wasn't quite famous yet, actually. I was thrilled to have an older man say, "Hey, you're doing a good job." Somebody teaching me and saying I did well.

In those days they had to sign off on you. People who were either members of the Sierra Club Rock Climbing Section or qualified leaders had to approve you. You had to do proficiency tests. Rappelling, belaying, and stuff.

Here, you probably haven't seen this yet, but I got the lead article in this magazine. It's the newest *Ascent* done by *Rock and Ice* magazine. It has nothing to do with the *Ascent* magazine that Allen Steck and I did for the Sierra Club. *Rock and Ice* asked us if they could use the title, and we told them, yes, of course. It's been twelve years since Al and I did the last issue of the original *Ascent*. Anyway, in the article I have a sort of mini-biography about how I became a climber and a writer. And I talk about your pop here. Here's the passage:

> I was thirteen when I learned to climb in Berkeley, a perfect age to learn the ropes. Old enough to belay properly, old enough to be limber and fairly strong, yet young enough to absorb wisdom from my elders without seeming to be a rebellious pain in the ass. Absorb wisdom I did, for what now seems like a ludicrously long time. Two full years went by as my taskmasters trained me. Belay, rappel, belay, rappel. Tie a bowline behind my back. Do it again. Tie a reef knot blindfolded. Reason: you might be doing all this in the dark. Use the correct signals. Reason: you could be misinterpreted if they are not standardized. Repeat everything again. Had I been a few years older, I would have told these gentlemen, including the soon-to-be-famous conservationist David Brower, to fuck off. As it was, it became a game, far more attractive than junior-high sports.

That was the truth. It was an apprenticeship, two years of just training at Indian Rock, before they trusted me to go to Yosemite with them.

The climbers of your pop's generation, the cast of characters, I did get to know some of them. Never met Bestor Robinson. He was old and got senile quite early. I did know Dick Leonard moderately well, because all the Sierra Club ropes were stored in Dick Leonard's garage on Keeler Avenue. In the back of the garage there was a whole pile of ropes. Not much else. They were Sierra Club ropes. Very frayed. I was a little scared of them. They were well used.

Two or three of us went out every Sunday when the climbs were on the three local rocks. Somebody would go up to Leonard's garage at, say, eight o'clock, or nine. A little bit before the climb started. And he'd pick up six ropes, or however many were needed that day, and take them down to the local rock. Leonard would come out with his bathrobe. This was always on Sunday, so he'd come out in his bathrobe. He'd say, "How are you guys doing?" And then, "Good luck." I wrote an article for *Summit* once called "Mr. Careful." It was Leonard's obituary. He'd come out in his bathrobe and wish us luck. He'd always say, "Tie the knots carefully," and stuff like that. He was very safety conscious. Leonard was the famous guy who wrote, in the thirties, "My first thought, if I fell, would be, 'What would Robert Underhill say?' " Underhill was the guy who taught all the young guys from the Sierra Club in the early thirties.

"What would Underhill think. If I fell." Leonard would tell us that story all the time. I must have gone to that garage twenty, twenty-five times, because I was always volunteering to do it. I was so excited to be climbing. I never saw Leonard climbing. And I never saw Jules Eichorn climbing. I met Eichorn three or four times. Apparently, he was a very good climber. Very nice fellow, a pianist, who studied with Ansel Adams. So I didn't know many of the old guys well at all.

There was a famous thirties climber named Bill Horsfall, who your father climbed with a bit. He died tragically in a fire in San Francisco in the sixties, when he was about eighty. He'd been divorced for years. He lived alone. He became a hermit by the late fifties, I'd say. He would come out to the Berkeley climbing rocks, but never climb. Just kibitzing. Then maybe in the midsixties I heard that he died in a fire. There was an article in the *Chronicle* about it, a little tiny blurb. It said, "Many ropes were found in his burned-out apartment." So, apparently, he had been hoarding. He had been taking ropes. Maybe because he thought these were old ropes and should be retired. Some people collect newspapers and magazines. Horsfall had a mountain of rope.

I met Morgan Harris a few times. He and Dave climbed a lot together in Yosemite, and at your parents' wedding Morgan was the best man. Morgan Harris and Dave were camped at Lake Ediza with Ansel Adams and Virginia Adams and Edward Weston on the trip where Ansel took that famous photograph of Dave and Morgan climbing in the Minarets. The two of them silhouetted against a summit and clouds, with a rope between them. It's the first image in Ansel's book *Sierra Nevada: The John Muir Trail*. I wrote the obituary for Morgan in *The American Alpine Journal*. In fact, I wrote the obit for your old man in *The American Alpine Journal*.

One reason I took to climbing myself is that, obviously, it's more or less a solitary sport. It's not a team sport. You're alone with your thoughts. And also, of course, there's the beauty of the mountains and seashores. I never liked crowds. Cities are okay, but crowds I don't like. I hated school. I could hardly wait to get home. I got home and played basket-ball with myself.

In climbing, yes, somebody's belaying you. But they're a hundred feet away. When you climb with a good friend, it's wonderful. Climb-ing with one friend is wonderful. Climbing with maybe five people is not so wonderful. Because the various interactions get complicated. Being shy, as I was, you don't want to be around crowds. Or dances. You're shy around women. So what else are you going to do with your goddammed life? Just read books all the time? I read much of the time. So I looked forward to the climbing. I didn't mind the crowds at Indian Rock, crowds of twenty, because they're all like-minded souls. There was no bullshit. I was probably a pretty good conversationalist around *those* people. Unlike around my teachers, or my high school friends, or my grammar school friends. I didn't have much to say to them.

I remember when I was in third grade at Hillside, we could go up behind the school and get up into Codornices Creek, maybe, or one of the other creeks that went uphill. Creeksides covered with poison oak. The stream was maybe four feet wide and five inches deep in the winter, and we would explore it, a guy named Alan Singer and myself. We'd go up about a hundred yards, get a little scared, and come back. The next time we'd go up five yards farther. Just the two of us. It was so much better than school. Better than civics class and stuff like that. The sense of exploration. What's on the other side of the ridge?

That always attracted me. And the idea up on the rock, of course, is that everything is new. You're not just walking down the steps like you've done a million times. It's going out and finding something new, and you don't know what's going to happen. Rock climbing is certainly like that. You'd think that rock climbing would be repetitious, but no. It's not just hand-over-hand. Every single move is different. Every single move on every climb I ever did was basically different. Well, nowadays people do cracks, two-inch cracks for a hundred feet, and you're doing the same movement over and over. But in the old days, every single move on every single climb was thought provoking. Your father must have felt the same way. Curiosity. And of course, obviously, being out of doors, which he loved all the way from the time his family took him to Tahoe.

Take poor inner-city kids, it's just horrible. The inner-city kid, never going to the redwoods, not even going to *Muir Woods*, or maybe going once, and hating it because you don't do it enough. And because you're doing it with thirty screaming children and teachers. Imagine your pop being at Tahoe. Your pop in 1920, seeing the pristine water, going swimming when he wants, and no crowds. He grew to love it. He probably loved solitude also. When he was a kid, he must have loved being more or less alone.

When I decided to write my climbing guide to Yosemite Valley, Dave was very encouraging. He took the time to sit down with me on several occasions at the Sierra Club office and help with it. He pointed out gently that I might have command of the climbing stuff, but I wasn't a writer yet. He aimed me in the direction of becoming a better one. He personally designed the 1964 version of the Yosemite guide, which is a collector's item now.

With *Ascent*, Allen Steck and I have differing views of your old man's role. But basically the story was that the *Sierra Club Bulletin* was no longer doing "Mountaineering Notes." The Club had stopped "Notes" because conservation had become more important to them, obviously. So Steck's brilliant idea was to make a new mountaineering magazine. Unbelievable. In that he's not known for being that decisive. He came up with this idea by himself. Well, we sneered at him. We sneered at the possibility of doing a magazine devoted entirely to climbing. But then Allen Steck said, "Come over for dinner." Eight of us came over to his house. Your pop was there, invited specially. We were talking about a potential new magazine. That was the purpose of the meeting. But we were afraid that the Sierra Club board of directors would veto it—this idea of a whole magazine devoted to climbing. And earlier Dave Brower had argued against it, because he didn't want another magazine to steal stuff from the *Bulletin*. Dave was noncommittal all evening. So Allen was showing all his slides from Hummingbird Ridge, this snowy ridge on Mount Logan. Your old man shouted out, "Stop! Stop that one. Look at that. Look at that one. That's a fabulous photograph. That's the cover."

Later, putting on his jacket to leave that night, he said, "Money's no object. We'll use duotone for the black-and-whites and do a color cover." So *Ascent* was born. Did the Sierra Club ever pay Allen Steck and me, the editors? Nope. A token amount, maybe a hundred bucks an issue. Did we ever pay our contributors? We did not. Just a token honorarium, twenty-five bucks in the beginning. I think toward the end we paid David Roberts $900 or something. He couldn't believe it. Did our contributors care that we didn't pay? They did not. Writers loved appearing in *Ascent*. Did it matter to Dave Brower that the magazine never made a cent for the Sierra Club over many years? It did not. In his mind it was just the right thing to do.

David Brower, far right, looks on as President Kennedy signs the bill establishing Point Reyes National Seashore

HAROLD GILLIAM

T HE ENVIRONMENTAL reporter Hal Gilliam, who joined the
staff of the *San Francisco Chronicle* in 1948, continues to produce
the occasional story for the paper today, a journalistic career of
sixty-three years and counting. Gilliam's beat, the San Francisco Bay Area,
is the epicenter, or one of the epicenters, of the modern environmental
movement. The larger sphere of influence of his newspaper includes most
of Northern California, the most fertile soil in the nation for germination of
environmentalist passions, principles, and creed. For most of the second
half of the twentieth century, Harold Gilliam was the preeminent morning-
coffee chronicler of the new environmental cause to the populace largely
responsible for inventing it.

Gilliam has long lived in the Sunset District of San Francisco, on Tenth
Avenue, halfway up the long slope to Sunset Heights, in a block of post-
Victorian houses, each built flush with the wall of its neighbor. Inside, the
Gilliam place feels very lived-in, as one might expect in the dwelling of a
ninety-two-year-old. Nothing looks new. On the evidence, Gilliam, a widower,
no longer has the energy or inclination to keep everything in perfect order.
Books are everywhere. He makes frequent reference to them, apparently,
for no volume on any of the shelves is neatly aligned with its neighbor.
This interior arrangement is exactly opposite of that which prevails outside,

where the sides of the houses are flush and the façades line up evenly all along the block.

It was a cool March afternoon on the day of the interview, and Gilliam was cheating Pacific Gas and Electric by wearing a parka inside the house. The parka was not immaculate. It had the outdoorsy look that a parka assumes after two or three days on a Sierra trail. Among the books in Gilliam's library was his first, *San Francisco Bay,* published by Doubleday in 1957. This debut seems to have established the pattern, for Gilliam's subsequent titles are: *San Francisco: City at The Golden Gate* (1959), coauthored with his wife, Ann Gilliam. *The Face of San Francisco* (1960). *The Natural World of San Francisco* (1967). *Between the Devil and the Deep Blue Bay: The Struggle to Save San Francisco Bay* (1969). *For Better or for Worse: The Ecology of an Urban Area* (1972).

Salted away on the shelves—Gilliam was not sure exactly where—were several copies of his *Island in Time: The Point Reyes Peninsula,* published by Sierra Club Books and Charles Scribner's Sons in 1962, with photographs by Philip Hyde, a foreword by Secretary of the Interior Stewart Udall, and a publisher's note by David Brower. For this book, Gilliam managed to get out of town, but only by about thirty miles.

The Gilliam fireplace was of white brick. Atop the mantelpiece were half a dozen books stacked on their sides, spines to the wall, so that the titles were impossible to read. Only the uppermost was turned the right way: *Emerson: The Mind on Fire.*

Above the mantel was a watercolor of a Yosemite Valley meadow in autumn. In the middle distance of the painting stood a black oak, golden leafed, with the monolith of Half Dome rising behind. This Yosemite meadow was special to Hal and Ann Gilliam. The black oak at the meadow's far edge was their favorite tree in the world. To the left of the watercolor hung a black-and-white photograph of Ann standing on a beach, in a Norwegian sweater, with the south tower of the Golden Gate Bridge rising behind. Ann died in 2002.

In front of the fireplace, propped against the legs of a chair, was an oversized art book, *Venice: Art and Architecture.* On an adjacent chair, resting on the seat, was a second big art book, *Donatello.* Both books had belonged to Ann Gilliam. She loved Norway, where she once taught, and Florence, where she once lived, and Venice, and art. Why Hal Gilliam had taken these books off the shelves for perusal now, I did not ask. Perhaps it was a form of communion.

We succeeded in finding a copy of *Island in Time: The Point Reyes Peninsula,* the collaboration between Gilliam and the photographer Philip Hyde. David Brower commissioned the book, along with a Sierra Club film by the same name, as weapons in the successful campaign he led, along with George Collins of Conservation Associates, Congressman Clem Miller of Marin County, and Secretary Udall, to establish Point Reyes National Seashore. This multifaceted approach was characteristic of my father's campaigning, beginning in the 1950s with the successful effort to keep dams out of Dinosaur National Monument in Utah: a book, a film, slideshows, grassroots organizing, state and federal lobbying, and Sierra Club outings to the river or wilderness in question, so as to build a constituency of people who actually knew and loved that place.

The text of *Island in Time* is set in OldStyle. The display faces are Weiss and Centaur. Secretary Udall's foreword comes first. He concludes:

"A hundred years ago the heroes of the West were Kit Carson and John Fremont. Today's heroes, honored by tomorrow, will be those who espoused the rare land treasures of the country, and preserved them. Among the names, I am confident, will be Harold Gilliam and Philip Hyde."

Gilliam's preface comes next. He begins:

Outside of the New York area, there is no more densely populated city in the United States than San Francisco. This density has not yet become oppressive, for it has always been easy to get out into the countryside—to enjoy a great range of superb natural scenery without traveling for hours through monotonous suburbs. This kind of egressibility, which has contributed in large measure to San Francisco's uniqueness and charm as a place to live, is steadily disappearing as the population explosion turns countryside into city and hillsides into subdivisions. As a result, the few near-by natural areas have acquired a special value for those who live here and for those all over the world who love San Francisco.

The great coinage of this paragraph, "egressibility," at first seems unfortunate, a concoction as suspect as the "drinkability" of Budweiser, but in fact the word is perfect and it crystallizes the whole passage. Ease of egress is what distinguishes San Francisco, as surely as do its famous hills and bridge. You can get away! It is simple here to slip the surly bonds of civilization. Parks and open space bound the urban Bay Area on all sides.

Gilliam's preface ends:

"This book would not have been written at all if I had not been relentlessly needled into action by David R. Brower of the Sierra Club, whose mighty efforts on behalf of conservation deserve the gratitude of everyone concerned with saving the natural beauty of the American landscape."

Last comes the publisher's note by Gilliam's relentless needler. Brower concludes:

> I think the author, the photographer, the cinematographers, the Secretary, the National Park Service, and the conservationists would sum up the Point Reyes opportunity about like this: The peninsula is what we have and there is no more where it came from. It is part of a shore that must serve uncountable millions in the more crowded time to come. We need to have what it takes to act boldly in their behalf—to save enough in the first place, and to remember, ever after, that the important things are not those we put on that shore, but those we find have always belonged there.

I FIRST CONTACTED Dave when I had backpacked out of Tuolumne Meadows into the Cathedral Lake area. There seemed to be a lot of dead or dying trees. I found out that the cause was the lodgepole needle miner, this little gray moth that spends its larval stage inside the needles of lodgepole pines. I was at the *Chronicle* at that time. I thought I would write a story on what was going on up there. I found out that the Park Service was proposing to spray in order to get rid of the needle miner. I can't remember whether it was DDT, or what.

Well, I knew about Dave Brower, of course. I'd been a member of the Sierra Club for some years. I called up to get his opinion on the spraying. Of course he was against it. That was his deal: let Nature take care of herself. I said, "Well, can I get a sentence or so from you, saying that?" He said yes, but then he was interrupted, or I was interrupted. I called back later, and he gave me not a sentence, but a whole essay on the thing. He had just dashed it off, with a purpose. He was very generous with his advice. That was first time I ever talked to him.

Before the war I was an undergraduate at UCLA, and then came up and got a master's in economics at Cal. Then in '41 came Pearl Harbor. I signed up in '42 and was in the Army for five years. I was in Europe with the Eleventh Armored Division. We started in France and went on through—the Battle of the Bulge and all that. I had an injury after the war was over. A jeep turned over on the road, skidded on the ice. I was a passenger, got thrown out, and had a bad injury to my arm. I was mending from that for another year or so. After I came back, I was at the Presidio here in San Francisco for some more surgery on my arm. That was great, because I was ambulatory. I didn't have to be at the Presidio all the time, so I wandered all over the city, all over the Bay Area, Tamalpais, Point Reyes.

I started graduate work at Stanford, working with Wallace Stegner. This was Stegner's famous Creative Writing Program. I was really not in my element—the class was primarily fiction writers—but it was very educational for me. I spent a year there. It was '48 when I first went in to the *Chronicle*.

By the late fifties, my *Chronicle* reporting was focused on conservation and the environment. I had been writing about places, natural places, about Bay Area parks as part of the total landscape. But this was the postwar period, when all the development that had *not* been taking place here during the war was going ahead full blast, with bulldozers going everyplace. All these natural places were threatened. So just writing about the natural places was not enough. I wanted to note that they were threatened. In many ways the conservation movement began in San Francisco and then expanded beyond the immediate Bay Area, to the whole region and beyond. This was the time the big controversies came up, the Grand Canyon, the redwoods. I was lucky to have a free rein at the *Chronicle* to do whatever I wanted to do.

Work on the book *Island in Time* began about 1960. George Collins had made his National Park survey recommending that Point Reyes be made a national something or other—a national park or a national seashore. Clem Miller, the congressman from Marin, was thinking about introducing his Point Reyes bill. Dave had become acquainted with my articles in the *Chronicle,* and he asked me to do an article on Point Reyes for the *Sierra Club Bulletin.* Which I did. On that story I coined the phrase "Island in Time." Because geologically and botanically, and in other ways, the Point Reyes Peninsula is just different from the mainland, having drifted up from the south. It slid up the coast along the San Andreas Fault.

Dave asked Laurel Reynolds to do the film on Point Reyes, for which they borrowed the title *Island in Time,* and he asked me to do a book on the subject. The book would be an extension of the article. Dave got Phil Hyde to do the pictures. I had been to Point Reyes before, as an occasional visitor, so I knew something about it. In order to do the book, I had to cover a lot of new territory there. It's quite fascinating from the geological standpoint, and from the botanical standpoint—redwoods to the east of the fault, Douglas firs to the west of the fault, and so on.

There was some sense of urgency. Things were boiling at the time. George Collins, who had spent thirty years in the Park Service, had started Conservation Associates on retiring, and he was conducting conferences in Marin County on the future of Point Reyes. Word came out in the *Chronicle* at some point that the Park Service was considering park status for the peninsula. There was just a lot of commotion going on. In a sense the prospect of a bill being introduced in Congress hurried the book along. I don't remember that I had a firm date for a deadline, but I was very much aware that it needed to be done in a hurry.

When the book finally came out—the original edition—the Clem Miller bill for the Point Reyes National Seashore was coming up before Congress, and Dave sent a copy to every congressman.

I forgot to say that Dave had asked Stewart Udall to do the introduction to the book. Secretary Udall's involvement sort of opened up a whole series of events for me. My life took a turn, as a result of this book.

At that time, Wallace Stegner, whom I had studied under at Stanford, was in communication with Udall. Udall had been an admirer of Stegner's writing. He asked Stegner if he could be a consultant, come back to Washington temporarily and help him set up his program at the Department of the Interior. Stegner was impressed by Udall, and vice versa. Stegner thought that Udall had a good sense of what the West was about. He suggested to Udall that he should do a book on it. Udall took his advice. Stegner gave him an outline of the history of conservation. And I think Stegner might have written a chapter or two, I can't quite remember. But Stegner had to return to Stanford after three months, to take up his duties there. So Udall was looking around for another writer. Having written the introduction to *Island in Time*, Udall had read my text, of course, and he was impressed by it, apparently. He needed a writer, so he asked Dave, and Dave endorsed me, so I got the job.

Udall asked me if I'd like to come down and meet him personally. Trouble was, he was in the Soviet Union at that time, visiting with Robert Frost. They had gone over there on a cultural mission. At any rate, I had this phone call asking if I could come back and see the assistant to Secretary Udall. It was supposed to be a temporary assignment of about three months. Of course I got excited about that, even though I had two babies. One was actually two years old, and one was three months old. So we bundled up everything and got a car that would get across the continent—which I hadn't had before. My main job was to help Udall with that book, *The Quiet Crisis*.

Dave asked me at one point if I had ghosted the book. I did not, of course. Well, I shouldn't say "of course," because a lot of people do ghost books. But I and other members of Udall's staff mainly did research for him. There were three or four other staff involved. They weren't editing so much as doing research. I remember one draft on John Muir that I did for him; I don't think he changed anything in that. But that's the only instance. I read over chapters that Udall had written himself and researched himself. We had many a midnight conference after everybody had gone home. We remained there, in Harold Ickes's old office, way into the morning. I remember one night, we went over it almost sentence by sentence. Stewart would say, "Do you think Wally Stegner would approve of this?" And I'd say, "Yes, he'd approve of it." One time we got laughing about something—I can't remember what it was—and it was one of those situations where you're doing some hard work, and you don't want to be distracted from it, and you try to suppress the laugh, but you can't do it. You sober up enough to go over a few more words, but it starts again, and you just get hysterical. Very late at night. Both of us had been working all day.

That was Udall's first book. He was a good writer. He had a talent for it, but he had never done a book, and he just wasn't quite sure how to go about it. In subsequent books he did pretty much all of it, without any editorial assistance.

I spent about a year in Washington working for Udall. I did other work besides the book. The National Parks Advisory Board was giving advice to the secretary of the interior on national parks. They'd meet four times a year. Udall couldn't attend them all, so part of my job was to attend those meetings. I was also on the advisory board for the Bureau of Outdoor Recreation at one time, and worked for them. And I was on the environmental council for the Army Corps of Engineers.

My career in government! And it was Dave who steered me into it. It was the Point Reyes book.

One day when I was in Udall's office at Interior, working there, there was just some general conversation between Stewart and a couple of his assistants. Stewart said, "I got a wire from Dave Brower today." Somebody asked what the wire was about. Udall said, "Well, he clobbered me, like he always does."

When I got back to California, I told Dave about that episode. He thanked me profusely for passing that information along. I think he was not aware that this was his dominant theme with Udall, always clobbering the guy, featuring what he was doing wrong. I was a little reluctant to tell Dave the story at first. One, it might have been violating a confidence, in that I had picked it up in the secretary's office, and two, because I don't like to pass on negatives. But I knew Dave well enough to know he would listen to what I was saying. And I knew he would think about it.

When Udall came out here a year or so later, he asked if I could set up a meeting between him and Dave at some natural spot—on the bay, or something like that. So I picked up both of them and drove them down to Coyote Point. We walked along the shore of the bay down there. Had a chat, and it was very amiable. Dave, I could see, had taken to heart the story I had given him about clobbering Udall. He was more balanced in what he was saying, in terms of expressing some approval of things Stewart Udall was doing, without always hammering on the opposite side. Earlier Dave had told me, when I first related the story to him, that he realized he had been doing that—just hammering—and now he was trying to make amends. They admired each other, in spite of differences. Udall had a lot of conflicting impulses on the Grand Canyon dams. He backed off from being in favor of the dams in the latter part of his administration. Dave surely had a lot to do with that.

That was such a dramatic time for conservation, the early sixties. The Save the Bay effort began back then. We forget nowadays how fast they were filling in San Francisco Bay. I remember as a student at International House, looking out my window down at the bay and seeing the garbage dump, which was growing out into the bay, and watching the fires in the garbage at night. By the sixties I had become a student of the bay. In the late fifties, I had seen an article in *The New Yorker* on New York Harbor. A sensible article. I thought, Why not do one on San Francisco Bay? So I did an article on the bay for the *Chronicle Sunday Magazine*, and the Doubleday people called me and asked if I'd like to do a book on it. And of course I did.

Then in 1961 I had a call from somebody who said she was Kay Kerr. I wondered who Kay Kerr was, and she quickly added "Mrs. Clark Kerr." So then I knew immediately who it was. Clark Kerr was the first chancellor of the University of California and later the president. Kay Kerr said that she and her two friends, Sylvia McLaughlin and Esther Gulick, were very worried about what was happening in the bay, and they were having a meeting in the Gulick house up on Grizzly Peak Boulevard. Would I come to the meeting? Since I had done a book on the bay? Well, sure I would. I think Mrs. Kerr used this tactic in contacting other people. "Mrs. Clark Kerr" attracted attention, especially among faculty members.

At any rate, a meeting took place. Dave was there, of course, so the Sierra Club was represented. And Audubon, too. Newton Drury was there, and several other people. The discussion didn't go the way the three women hoped. Kay and her two friends were rather disappointed that they couldn't persuade the Sierra Club or somebody to take this ball up and run with it. Dave explained it. "Newton Drury is busy saving redwoods," he said. "The Sierra Club is busy saving Grand Canyon and North Cascades and a few other places." And so it went, all around the circle—everyone was overextended. Dave finally said, "You know, we're all too busy to do this, so it looks like we need a new organization." That was the beginning of the Save the Bay Association. Dave said, "We'll give you our mailing lists, and we'll help you all we can, and give you information, and work with you on the campaign, but you're going to have to do it yourselves. It's up to you to save the bay." After everybody left, just the three women were there, and they decided that they would have to do it themselves. And they did.

In his field, Dave was a genius. His ability to inspire people and stimulate people and get the voters following what he was doing, both by the written word and the spoken word and in individual contacts, that was extraordinary. It was genius. It got expressed in individual contacts with people, including myself, and at public meetings where he would speak very eloquently on what he was doing and what needed to be done.

"The Religion," he called it. Conservation was a religion for him. I'm sure that his experiences of the Sierra contributed to his total philosophy. Love of Nature. Allowing Nature to take its course. Trying to preserve the natural world. It was, again, a statement of *religious* belief that came through so well. A lot of people have religion of various kinds, but they don't have the ability to communicate it the way he did.

I had a thrill one time in climbing a peak in—where was it? I think we were in the Middle Fork of the San Joaquin, looking over into Humphreys Basin and the Sierra Crest. There was one peak over in that direction, I can't remember the name. Was it the Hermit? No, the Hermit is over in Evolution. In any case, we climbed it and on the summit I found a cairn and a register. It was from the 1920s or 1930s. There was Dave's name in the register. Along with some notation about what he had been doing up there. Bagging peaks somewhere up north. I guess he'd been on the North Palisade, places like that. I can't remember just what he said. But I showed it around to my fellow climbers, and it was quite a thrill. To see the fact that he really did climb all these peaks.

Dave didn't talk much about his climbing, about all the first ascents he'd done. I do remember him saying that old Norman Clyde, in going up North Palisade, I think it was, taught him about three-point contact. Dave did tell me that. I got Norman Clyde and the three-point-contact method directly from David.

Like all geniuses, Dave had his shortcomings. We all do. That's part of the picture. He was very knowledgeable in his field, with a lot of experience there. He was very single-minded about what he was doing. Sometimes, as a result, he was insubordinate to the Sierra Club board. I was slow to understand the controversy going on inside the organization. The Sierra Club was pretty much Dave Brower at that time, from my standpoint. I didn't know at that point about all the inner goings-on.

When Dave saw something that needed to be done, he'd say it's urgent to do it, and if we do it right, we'll find the money to spend on it. Not everyone on his board was comfortable with that approach, to say the least.

I remember an incident during a Sierra Club wilderness conference. The pro- and anti-Brower factions had formed, so it would have been in '68 or '69. I think it was held at the Hilton. After one of these meetings, there was a small reception at one of the upstairs rooms. And I happened to be in the elevator with Dave. Or he was in the elevator with me, however you like it. And he was affable, as always. We went upstairs to the room where the reception was. People were talking, of course. The pro-Brower people were talking to the pro-Brower people, and the anti-Brower people talking to the anti-Brower people. There was no recognition between the two groups. They were all affable with each other, but not with the other group.

I asked Dave one time, during all the commotion, what he thought the basic problem was. He said, "Well, I guess I went on ahead and didn't pay enough attention to the rest of the team. Left them behind me. Should have turned around and said, 'Come on, let's get with it!'" I can't quote his exact words. But what he said was he should have brought the team along with him.

I've had a feeling, over the years, that there's a role for the crusaders, and there's a role for the negotiators. I think both are important. You don't see the word *"crusaders"* anymore, do you? But we need crusaders. Dave was a crusader. We don't see many of them around these days.

Part of his whole charisma was moving ahead. He was not listening to all those people who always find reasons why we can't do this, we can't do that, why we have to compromise with this other thing. Dave was always just moving on ahead. This had a tremendous impact on young people. Remember, we're talking about the sixties, when the young people were coming to the fore, asserting themselves in many different ways. They clustered around him. I wonder if he had made various compromises, it wouldn't have detracted from his whole charisma. He was moving forward. He was carrying the torch. Other people were following him. He didn't want to dim the torch.

Dave Pesonen and Hazel Bonneke at PG&E's "Atomic Park" at Bodega Bay

DAVID PESONEN

THE PESONEN HOUSE is out on Sixes River Road, in Sixes, Oregon, on the bank of the Sixes River. The nearest neighbor is a quarter mile away. Dave Pesonen, who spent most of his career in the law, is now a semiretired solo arbitrator. His workspace at home is a corner about ten feet by ten. None of the books in his corner are the kind with alluring covers—nothing but legal tomes and technical books on arbitration. Outside the window is an orchard of about forty fruit trees and twenty acres of grass. On the day of the interview, looking out, Pesonen conceded that his grass needed cutting.

"I got about seventy-five acres. Most of it is timber, and it's on the other side of the river. It rains a lot up here, that's why it's all green. When the weather's nice, I do as much as I can outside.

"It's an old orchard. It was planted by somebody a long time ago. It's very well thought out. There are three or four different varieties of apples, which come in at different times. Four different types of plums. And some pears. And walnuts. And filberts. The filberts don't produce very well. One of the walnut trees; it produces real well.

"This house was built by a doctor. I had a friend, a fishing pal, who had moved up here, and one day the doctor told him he wanted to sell. It was the very day I'd been looking up here for a full year for the kind of place we wanted. I had seen this spot, because I'd floated this river, fishing. And I admired it. There's a big swimming hole right off the deck. So I got up here the next day. We sat out on the porch with a jug of wine and made the whole deal that afternoon."

A potential client searching online for an arbitrator learns, from Pesonen's résumé on the website of the National Arbitration Center, that David Pesonen got his B.S. from the School of Forestry at the University of California in 1960, with a minor in English literature. In 1968 he graduated from Boalt Hall School of Law at Berkeley and was class valedictorian. Then, starting in 1969, came a private law practice in San Francisco, and then a stint as director of the California Department of Forestry, and then as superior court judge, and then as general manager of the East Bay Regional Park District, in Alameda and Contra Costa counties of California, and then as an employment class-action attorney, and finally his present part-time practice as an arbitrator in Oregon.

This curriculum vitae leaves a big hole near the start. It provides no account of what Pesonen was doing between 1960, when he graduated from the School of Forestry, and his graduation from law school eight years later. Most of that turbulent decade, the sixties, has gone missing. The résumé says nothing about Pesonen's triumph, fresh out of forestry school, in a David-and-Goliath battle against a gigantic and arrogant public utility. The field of combat—Pesonen's Valley of Elah—was the long crack of the San Andreas Fault. He became, in his twenties, the leader of the first important citizen campaign against nuclear power. But personal history of this sort is no great selling point to seekers of arbitration, apparently.

The résumé says nothing, either, about the career-changing letter, elicited by Pesonen from a great Western writer, a 2500-word note which in a roundabout way triggered the chain of events that sent Pesonen out against Goliath. The letter ended with the now-famous phrase, "the geography of hope." Evidently, that phrase, and the letter it concluded, are of more interest to historians of environmentalism than to folks simply searching the web for an arbitrator.

The letter reads, in its entirety:

Los Altos, California,
December 3, 1960

David E. Pesonen
Wildland Research Center
Agricultural Experiment Station
243 Mulford Hall, University of California
Berkeley 4, Calif.

Dear Mr. Pesonen:

I believe that you are working on the wilderness portion of the Outdoor Recreation Resources Review Commission's report. If I may, I should like to urge some arguments for wilderness preservation that involve recreation, as it is ordinarily conceived, hardly at all. Hunting, fishing, hiking, mountain-climbing, camping, photography, and the enjoyment of natural scenery will all, surely, figure in your report. So will the wilderness as a genetic reserve, a scientific yardstick by which we may measure the world in its natural balance against the world in its man-made imbalance. What I want to speak for is not so much the wilderness uses, valuable as those are, but the wilderness idea, which is a resource in itself. Being an intangible and spiritual resource, it will seem mystical to the practical minded—but then anything that cannot be moved by a bulldozer is likely to seem mystical to them.

I want to speak for the wilderness idea as something that has helped form our character and that has certainly shaped our history as a people. It has no more to do with recreation than churches have to do with recreation, or than the strenuousness and optimism and expansiveness of what the historians call the "American Dream" have to do with recreation. Nevertheless, since it is only in this recreation survey that the values of wilderness are being compiled, I hope you will permit me to insert this idea between the leaves, as it were, of the recreation report.

Something will have gone out of us as a people if we ever let the remaining wilderness be destroyed; if we permit the last virgin forests to be turned into comic books and plastic cigarette cases; if we drive the few remaining members of the wild species into zoos or to extinction; if we pollute the last clear air and dirty the last clean streams and push our paved roads through the last of the silence, so that never again will Americans be free in their own country from the noise, the exhausts, the stinks of human and automotive waste. And so that never again can we have the chance to see ourselves single, separate, vertical and individual in the world, part of the environment of trees and rocks and soil, brother to the other animals, part of the natural world and competent to belong in it. Without any remaining wilderness we are committed wholly, without chance for even momentary reflection and rest, to a head-long drive into our technological termite-life, the Brave New World of a completely man-controlled environment. We need wilderness preserved—as much of it as is still left, and as many kinds—because it was the challenge against which our character as a people was formed. The reminder and the reassurance that it is still there is good for our spiritual health even if we never once in ten years set foot in it. It is good for us when we are young, because of the incomparable sanity it can bring briefly, as vacation and rest, into our insane lives. It is important to us when we are old simply because it is there—important, that is, simply as an idea.

We are a wild species, as Darwin pointed out. Nobody ever tamed or domesticated or scientifically bred us. But for at least three millennia we have been engaged in a cumulative and ambitious race to modify and gain control of our environment, and in the process we have come close to domesticating ourselves. Not many people are likely, any more, to look upon what we call "progress" as an unmixed blessing. Just as surely as it has brought us increased comfort and more material goods, it has brought us spiritual losses, and it threatens now to become the Frankenstein that will destroy us. One means of sanity is to retain a hold on the natural world, to remain, insofar as we can, good animals. Americans still have that chance, more than many peoples; for while we were demonstrating ourselves the most efficient and ruthless environment-busters in history, and slashing and burning and cutting our way through a wilderness continent, the wilderness was working on us. It remains in us as surely as Indian names remain on the land. If the abstract dream of human liberty and human dignity became, in America, something more than an abstract dream, mark it down at least partially to the fact that we were in subdued ways subdued by what we conquered.

The Connecticut Yankee, sending likely candidates from King Arthur's unjust kingdom to his Man Factory for rehabilitation, was over-optimistic, as he later admitted. These things cannot be forced, they have to grow. To make such a man, such a democrat, such a believer in human individual dignity, as Mark Twain himself, the frontier was necessary, Hannibal and the Mississippi and Virginia City, and reaching out from those the wilderness; the wilderness as opportunity and idea, the thing that has helped to make an American different from and, until we forget it in the roar of our industrial cities, more fortunate than other men. For an American, insofar as he is new and different at all, is a civilized man who has renewed himself in the wild. The American experience has been the confrontation by old peoples and cultures of a world as new as if it had just risen from the sea. That gave us our hope and our excitement, and the hope and excitement can be passed on to newer Americans, Americans who never saw any phase of the frontier. But only so long as we keep the remainder of our wild as a reserve and a promise—a sort of wilderness bank.

As a novelist, I may perhaps be forgiven for taking literature as a reflection, indirect but profoundly true, of our national consciousness. And our literature, as perhaps you are aware, is sick, embittered, losing its mind, losing its faith. Our novelists are the declared enemies of their society. There has hardly been a serious or important novel in this century that did not repudiate in part or in whole American technological culture for its commercialism, its vulgarity, and the way in which it has dirtied a clean continent and a clean dream. I do not expect that the preservation of our remaining wilderness is going to cure this condition. But the mere example that we can as a nation apply some other criteria than commercial and exploitative considerations would be heartening to many Americans, novelists or otherwise. We need to demonstrate our acceptance of the natural world, including ourselves; we need the spiritual refreshment that being natural can produce. And one of the best places for us to get that is in the wilderness where the fun houses, the bulldozers, and the pavement of our civilization are shut out.

Sherwood Anderson, in a letter to Waldo Frank in the 1920s, said it better than I can. "Is it not likely that when the country was new and men were often alone in the fields and the forest they got a sense of bigness outside themselves that has now in some way been lost...Mystery whispered in the grass, played in the branches of trees overhead, was caught up and blown across the American line in clouds of dust at evening on the prairies...I am old enough to remember tales that strengthen my belief in a deep semi-religious influence that was formerly at work among our people. The flavor of it hangs over the best work of Mark Twain...I can remember old fellows in my home town speaking feelingly of an evening spent on the big empty plains. It had taken the shrillness out of them. They had learned the trick of quiet..."

We could learn it too, even yet; even our children and grand-children could learn it. But only if we save, for just such absolutely non-recreational, impractical, and mystical uses as this, all the wild that still remains to us.

It seems to me significant that the distinct downturn in our literature from hope to bitterness took place almost at the precise time when the frontier officially came to an end, in 1890, and when the American way of life had begun to turn strongly urban and industrial. The more urban it has become, and the more frantic with technological change, the sicker and more embittered our literature, and I believe our people, have become. For myself, I grew up on the empty plains of Saskatchewan and Montana and in the mountains of Utah, and I put a very high valuation on what those places gave me. And if I had not been able periodically to renew myself in the mountains and deserts of western America I would be very nearly bughouse. Even when I can't get to the back country, the thought of the colored deserts of southern Utah, or the reassurance that there are still stretches of prairies where the world can be instantaneously perceived as disk and bowl, and where the little but intensely important human being is exposed to the five directions of the thirty-six winds, is a positive consolation. The idea alone can sustain me. But as the wilderness areas are progressively exploited or "improved", as the jeeps and bulldozers of uranium prospectors scar up the deserts and the roads are cut into the alpine timberlands, and as the remnants of the unspoiled and natural world are progressively eroded, every such loss is a little death in me. In us.

I am not moved by the argument that those wilderness areas which have already been exposed to grazing or mining are already deflowered, and so might as well be "harvested." For mining I cannot say much good except that its operations are generally short-lived. The extractable wealth is taken and the shafts, the tailings, and the ruins left, and in a dry country such as the American West the wounds men make in the earth do not quickly heal. Still, they are only wounds; they aren't absolutely mortal. Better a wounded wilderness than none at all. And as for grazing, if it is strictly controlled so that it does not destroy the ground cover, damage the ecology, or compete with the wildlife it is in itself nothing that need conflict with the wilderness feeling or the validity of the wilderness experience. I have known enough range cattle to recognize them as wild animals; and the people who herd them have, in the wilderness context, the dignity of rareness; they belong on the frontier, moreover, and have a look of rightness. The invasion they make on the virgin country is a sort of invasion that is as old as Neolithic man, and they can, in moderation, even emphasize a man's feeling of belonging to the natural world. Under surveillance, they can belong; under control, they need not deface or mar. I do not believe that in wilderness areas where grazing has never been permitted, it should be permitted; but I do not believe either that an otherwise untouched wilderness should be eliminated from the preservation plan because of limited existing uses such as grazing which are in consonance with the frontier condition and image.

Let me say something on the subject of the kinds of wilderness worth preserving. Most of those areas contemplated are in the national forests and in high mountain country. For all the usual recreational purposes, the alpine and the forest wildernesses are obviously the most important, both as genetic banks and as beauty spots. But for the spiritual renewal, the recognition of identity, the birth of awe, other kinds will serve every bit as well. Perhaps, because they are less friendly to life, more abstractly nonhuman, they will serve even better. On our Saskatchewan prairie, the nearest neighbor was four miles away, and at night we saw only two lights on all the dark rounding earth. The earth was full of animals—field mice, ground squirrels, weasels, ferrets, badgers, coyotes, burrowing owls, snakes. I knew them as my little brothers, as fellow creatures, and I have never been able to look upon animals in any other way since. The sky in that country came clear down to the ground on every side, and it was full of great weathers, and clouds, and winds, and hawks. I hope I learned something from looking a long way, from looking up, from being much alone. A prairie like that, one big enough to carry the eye clear to the sinking, rounding horizon, can be as lonely and grand and simple in its forms as the sea. It is as good a place as any for the wilderness experience to happen;

the vanishing prairie is as worth preserving for the wilderness idea as the alpine forest.

So are great reaches of our western deserts, scarred somewhat by prospectors but otherwise open, beautiful, waiting, close to whatever God you want to see in them. Just as a sample, let me suggest the Robbers' Roost country in Wayne County, Utah, near the Capitol Reef National Monument. In that desert climate the dozer and jeep tracks will not soon melt back into the earth, but the country has a way of making the scars insignificant. It is a lovely and terrible wilderness, such as wilderness as Christ and the prophets went out into; harshly and beautifully colored, broken and worn until its bones are exposed, its great sky without a smudge of taint from Technocracy, and in hidden corners and pockets under its cliffs the sudden poetry of springs. Save a piece of country like that intact, and it does not matter in the slightest that only a few people every year will go into it. That is precisely its value. Roads would be a desecration, crowds would ruin it. But those who haven't the strength or youth to go into it and live can simply sit and look. They can look two hundred miles, clear into Colorado: and looking down over the cliffs and canyons of the San Rafael Swell and the Robbers' Roost they can also look as deeply into themselves as anywhere I know. And if they can't even get to the places on the Aquarius Plateau where the present roads will carry them, they can simply contemplate the idea, take pleasure in the fact that such a timeless and uncontrolled part of earth is still there.

These are some of the things wilderness can do for us. That is the reason we need to put into effect, for its preservation, some other principle than the principles of exploitation or "usefulness" or even recreation. We simply need that wild country available to us, even if we never do more than drive to its edge and look in. For it can be a means of reassuring ourselves of our sanity as creatures, a part of the geography of hope.

Very sincerely yours,
Wallace Stegner

MY FIRST MEETING with Dave Brower came after Stegner wrote the "Wilderness Letter." That letter followed a suggested topic, and treatment of that topic, that I had proposed to Stegner in a letter I wrote while I was on the staff of the Wildlands Research Center at the School of Forestry in Berkeley.

The Outdoor Recreation Resources Review Commission was set up in '59 to do this huge study of all recreation resources in the United States. It was funded by Laurance Rockefeller, I think. The Wildlands Research Center had got the contract to do the Wilderness Report for the study. And I was working on that. I wanted to include something from Stegner in the Wilderness Report. I had read Stegner's *Beyond the Hundredth Meridian*, which my mother loved and got me to read.

I drafted a very good letter. I went back and looked at it recently after Phil Fradkin, who was writing his biography of Stegner, asked me about it. I didn't have a copy of my original letter. I'd lost it. Fradkin dug it up in his research and he sent me a copy of what I had written. As Fradkin says, it's amazing what a young man in his twenties was able to conjure up. I mean it was a very thoughtful, analytical, emotional request. I said, "I don't have the skill to write this. Here's what I want it to say."

It took about four or five months before Stegner responded with his letter. He copied Dave Brower on it. Dave wanted to publish it immediately. The Sierra Club held wilderness conferences every year, organized by Dave, with the purpose of getting the Wilderness Bill passed in Congress. He wanted to publish the letter in the proceedings of the next wilderness conference.

In any event, I was offended. Stupidly, I was offended. I thought, *That's my letter! I asked for it, and it's addressed to me. I want to publish it first.* Of course, I was wrong. But I had to deal with Dave over that issue. He was diplomatic. I don't think he was contentious. I was the young upstart, you know, and if anybody was contentious, it was me, not Dave. What he said was, "You know, it's up to Stegner." And Stegner said, "Go ahead, Brower, use it as you see fit." What was important was getting a Wilderness Bill passed. So I lost that struggle, and I should have.

In any event, I finished the wilderness report, with the Stegner letter incorporated, and then I didn't know what I was going to do. A job opened up on the staff of the Fish and Game Committee of the state assembly. This looked like everything I liked, hunting and fishing and environmental policy, so I applied. I was hired by the committee chairwoman, Pauline Davis, the assemblywoman from Portola, up in Plumas County. She had succeeded her husband, who had died in office. I didn't know what I was getting into.

Pauline was this huge, paranoid woman with a towering bouffant hairdo, dyed red. There were only two kinds of people, to Pauline's way of thinking: there were the descendents of old pioneer families, and there were snakes in the grass. One day at the office I would be the golden boy, a son of the pioneers, and the next morning I'd come in, and her office door would be closed, and she wouldn't talk to me. Through the door I'd hear whispering and mumbling. Mumble, mumble, mumble, and then "snake in the grass."

It was a small office. Just two woman secretaries and me in the outer office, and Pauline in the inner office.

The Fish and Game Committee was being lobbied hard by commercial fishermen. There seemed to be an opportunity for me to get some legislation passed limiting logging. I'd done a lot of fishing up there in the north myself, and I'd seen the damage these awful logging practices inflicted on spawning streams. There were people in the Fish and Game Department who were concerned about the same thing, and who had written a good deal about it. And I did succeed in persuading Pauline to hold some hearings on it.

But it wasn't an enjoyable job.

Pauline was in a feud with the Department of Fish and Game over deer-hunting regulations. She wanted more deer hunting, but less doe hunting. Pauline was sure the Department of Fish and Game was cooking the books. She didn't believe their statistics. One day she sent

me over to Fish and Game to count all the deer tags. I was supposed
to refigure the numbers by hand. There were boxes and boxes full of
hundreds of these tags, little pieces of cardboard covered with deer hair
and blood. I had to sit there trying to read what hunters had scrawled
in pencil, in the woods, by the headlights of some truck. The hunter
has to note where the buck had been shot, how many points it had,
and so on. My numbers came out pretty much the same as Fish and
Game's. Naturally Pauline figured that Fish and Game had got to me.
I had gone over to the other side.

It was crazy working for that woman. It was an awful job.

Then one day Dave Brower called and asked me to join his staff.
This was early in 1962. We had not been in contact, I think, since the
episode of the Wilderness Letter, but here he was on the phone. That
was his style. He had a history of recruiting young people on impulse.

Well, this was my chance to get away from Pauline and this terrible
job and come down to San Francisco. San Francisco was a great city in
those days if you were young and single. Here was the chance to work
for the Sierra Club and Dave Brower, who was this charismatic, larger-
than-life figure. So I accepted.

It was never clear what my job was. My degree was in forestry, so I
became the Sierra Club spokesman in Forestry board meetings talking
about revision of the Forest Practices Act. My actual title was "Conservation Editor." The Sierra Club book program was just starting, and
Dave would get manuscripts that he would send me for review. Sometimes I would edit a manuscript, if it looked promising. And sometimes
nobody was quite sure what I was supposed to be doing. Dave wasn't sure
how he wanted to use me. He was a man full of spontaneous ideas, but
he was not a good manager. At the Sierra Club I was a jack-of-all-trades.

It was fun working for the Club. Dave would take us to lunch every
day, or almost every other day. He'd take a couple of selected members
of his staff. He had a favorite little restaurant in an alley there a couple of
blocks from the Mills Tower. And he'd have his martini. We'd all talk.
Tanqueray martini, he insisted on that. You know, we'd just talk about
what was going on in the world. He liked to be surrounded by young

people with everybody having ideas. It paid for lunch! I didn't have much money.

But I didn't know what I wanted to do with my life. I didn't want to work forever as Dave's jack-of-all-trades. I didn't want to work in traditional forestry, either, just managing timberland for cutting. I didn't want to be a "sawlog forester," as Dave called it. That's what I had studied, but I didn't want to practice it. For two summers in forestry school, I'd worked for Southern Pacific marking and cruising timber. It's good, healthy outdoors work, but it was not enough. There was no intellectual challenge.

I was single. I had an undergraduate degree I didn't really like. I didn't know what I wanted to do with my life. And right around then, while I was working for the Sierra Club, I heard about a position as a forestry advisor for the Food and Agriculture Organization in Tanganyika. The idea of being a forester in Africa, that grabbed me. I immediately put in for it. The UN is a terrible bureaucracy, and the paperwork was horrendous. It dragged on and on. But while I was working for the Sierra Club, I processed this FAO application. I took flying lessons, because I was going to have a little airplane in Africa.

Then along came Bodega.

I didn't know anything about Bodega Bay, or Bodega Head, or about the nuclear plant that Pacific Gas and Electric wanted to build there. But Dave, apparently he knew that Bodega Head had previously been listed by the National Park Service and by the State Parks system as a potential coastal park site. So he came to me one day, and he handed me two clippings. One was a marvelous letter to the editor that Karl Kortum had written. Karl Kortum was a sailor, an ocean guy, the founder of the San Francisco Maritime National Historical Park. His letter was an imaginary conversation between a PG&E executive and a local politician, demonstrating the arrogance of PG&E. The other was a column by Hal Gilliam about how terrible it was to have lost this site.

At this point, the Public Utilities Commission had granted a certificate of "convenience and necessity," which was the only permit that

PG&E would require from the state to construct a nuclear plant at Bodega. They still needed to go through the Atomic Energy Commission, but they hadn't started that process yet. In his column, Gilliam treated it as just a lost cause. But Dave said, "Well, go look into this. See what you think." Again, it was the jack-of-all-trades kind of thing. I was hired for *forestry* stuff, and now Brower had me doing nuclear energy.

So I naïvely went over to the PG&E office, which was only a couple of blocks away, just down at 245 Market Street. This was on my own initiative. I went up to the engineering department, on the tenth floor, I think, and it was noontime. There was just a secretary there. And I said, "You know, I'm interested in the Bodega case, do you have a file on it?" *And she handed me this file.*

Talk about just lucking into something! Can you imagine something like that happening today? It absolutely never would happen. She didn't think there was anything wrong with it, just handing me the file. So I started going through it. I saw a whole lot of correspondence back and forth between the public affairs department of PG&E and the board of supervisors of Sonoma County and other public officials, letters where it was just a foregone conclusion that local government would fall in line. They just treated it as if the nuclear plant was a done deal. There were all these indications that PG&E had local government in their pocket. My antennae started to go up. So I copied a lot of this, in handwritten notes. They didn't have copying machines in those days.

That letter Karl Kortum had written, along with the Harold Gilliam column, triggered a political decision on the part of the Public Utilities Commission to reopen the licensing procedure and hold more hearings. Their purpose obviously was to just let the public vent, and then have PG&E get on with the business that they were determined to do anyway. So they held these hearings in the PUC building. They were the most chaotic hearings I've ever seen. Completely wild. Anybody in the audience could stand up, and call to be recognized, and then *cross-examine the witness.*

By this time, we had a small group that had been pulled together by a number of people, Hal Gilliam being one of them, and Joe Neilands, who was a professor at Berkeley and a public-power advocate. It was not a big group, just a handful of early environmental types. One was Tony Sargent, who was a nuclear biophysicist. One was Rose Gaffney, who was the owner of the property that PG&E was condemning. She was a colorful old character. Sort of *looked* like Bodega Head. She was a big, sprawling woman, old frock dress and a loud voice. Just a motley group. There was not really any organized opposition to the plant, but there were a number of issues that concerned the local people. One had to do with the road that PG&E was constructing around the harbor. Just odds and ends of issues.

At the hearing I had the notes that I made when the PG&E secretary handed me the file. We were waiting for the supreme dramatic moment to disclose the corruption—we called it corruption, anyway. The PG&E lawyers started to cross-examine me, and somehow they intuitively decided just to stay away from that topic. I had anticipated that they might not ask me, and so I planted a question in the audience with a member of our motley crew, Tony Sargent. We had these little informal meetings, and Tony was very active in this small group, so I had planted this issue with him. I said, you know, if PG&E doesn't ask me, then you should be ready to stand up, under these bizarre procedures permitted in these hearings, and ask, "How do you know all this?"

I had this black suitcase with two snaps on it, and there was a microphone up on the dais with me. So the moment comes and Tony Sargent gets up and asks, "What authority, what basis, do you have for these accusations?" That was the gist of the question. So I deliberately snapped these snaps to open this suitcase. And the snapping went through the microphone out across the room.

Then I described the circumstances of going up and getting this file. You should have seen the flurry of activity at the counsel table for PG&E. Somebody ran out and got on the phone. Total dismay and chaos on their side of the room. I knew we'd hit a nerve.

Where my sense of strategy and tactics came from, I don't know. I think that's just the way I always think. When you get into a political fight—I don't know that I'd been in any political fights until that time, but I'd paid attention to what was going in the world. I was pretty active. I was an active liberal. My parents were liberal. And I was just a political animal. And one thing a political animal asks himself, as a matter of instinct, is, where's the vulnerability of your opponent? Where's the soft underbelly? It just seemed natural. It also seemed right. It seemed like the right issue, the right cause. I wasn't conjuring up anything. I wasn't just making things up.

Starker Leopold testified at the PUC hearings. I was very disappointed in him. He seemed to believe in the project. He was silent on the dangers, and I don't think he was reluctantly silent. He was on the university's side. He was an administrator by that time; he wasn't just a teacher. I had taken a course from Starker, when I was in forestry school, on wildlife management.

There were several reasons that the University of California was behind the nuclear plant. One—and I wasn't as fully aware of it, then, as I am now—is that the university got a huge part of its budget from the Atomic Energy Commission. The university ran the Lawrence Lab in Berkeley for the AEC. They also got a lot of money from the AEC for the Lawrence Livermore Lab, which was then under construction. And Glenn Seaborg had just been appointed chairman of the AEC. Until then, he had been the chancellor of the university. Seaborg was a champion of nuclear power.

After PG&E pulled out, in October of '64, there was a conference of the Atomic Industrial Forum and the American Nuclear Society in San Francisco that December. So I went to the conference, just to sort of kibitz and see what was going on. I got into an elevator with Seaborg and a bunch of other people. He was about six foot six, very imposing character physically. I said, "Hello, Dr. Seaborg! I'm David Pesonen." He looked down at me, and he said, *"I know who you are."* And the doors opened, and he went out, and I never saw him again.

Later, when I was appointed general manager of the East Bay Regional Park District, he wrote a *bitter* letter to the board of the park district about what a terrible mistake they were making in hiring me. He had retired from government by then, and was living out in Lafayette. This was thirty years later! He just never forgot. He was a dour old dude.

There were three or four days of hearings. When the hearings were over, and after everybody had had their say, the examiner took it under submission, and we were waiting for a decision. In the meantime I'd met this fellow from the state department of geology, who had written a report about Bodega Head. It had been published by the California State Mining and Geology Board, and it addressed the issue of the earthquake fault. The guy's name was Koenig. He was very circumspect, but he said, "You might want to look into my report on this." So I read his report. It wasn't very long, but it clearly showed that the San Andreas Fault ran right through the site. I concluded, correctly, that this was an issue on which we could stop the plant. We could stop it on the public safety question of building a nuclear reactor on a major earthquake fault.

And so I went back to the office, and I told Dave Brower about all this. We started issuing some press releases about our position, about what was going on in the PUC hearings. Dave came to me soon after that, and he said the executive committee of the board wanted to have a meeting about this. So we met in Dave's office there in the Mills Tower, and Dick Leonard was there. It was a small group of officers of the Club—the president, the vice president, secretary. Three or four members of the Club's board and Dave and me. And they asked me to tell them what's going on with Bodega. I described briefly what had happened at the Public Utilities Commission hearings. And then I said, "I think we can stop this thing. But we have to develop, and explore further, the earthquake hazard."

At that point, Leonard just exploded. And he shook his finger at me, and he said, "Don't you dare mention earthquakes. Don't you dare mention public safety. The Sierra Club can talk about scenic beauty, and maybe the loss of scenic beauty, but not about public safety. That's not our job."

I said, "Well, you know, that plant's going to get built, if I can't talk about earthquake hazard." But I was just a little lowly staffer. The executive committee, they just directed me: I was not to mention it, the whole topic of earthquakes and public safety. So I thought about it, and about a week later I quit. I thought, you know, I just can't live with that limitation. Dave never got over feeling guilty about that. That was too bad, because I didn't blame *him* at all.

In any event, I quit. And I didn't know what I was going to do. So I just went and hitchhiked around the West for the summer. I had a girlfriend who was working in a restaurant in Aspen, so I hitchhiked to Colorado and spent some time with her. Then I got back and got a ride to British Columbia, went up there with some mountain climbers. You know, I was just sort of lost. And I was also waiting for this job in Africa to come through. It was delayed forever.

When I got back to Berkeley, I had a meeting with Joel Hedgpeth. He gave me a wonderful book of clippings on the Bodega question. Hedgpeth was a pack rat on that sort of thing. His book of clippings collapsed, into one volume, four years of bits and pieces of press coverage of what had been going on in Bodega. At the time, Hedgpeth was director of the Pacific Marine Station, which was the University of the Pacific's research facility at Dillon Beach, at the mouth of Tomales Bay, right where it opens onto Bodega Bay. Tomales, you know, *is* the San Andreas Fault. The bay is just the surface manifestation of the fault. It's this long, linear finger of water pointing directly toward Bodega Head. The biggest displacement of the 1906 quake that destroyed San Francisco was measured at the head of Tomales Bay, where the road from the Point Reyes Station side of the fault to the Inverness side was displaced by nineteen feet. PG&E wanted to build the largest nuclear generator in the world, a giant 325,000-kilowatt reactor, at the other end of Tomales Bay.

Hedgpeth was a specialist in sea spiders. He knew Ed Ricketts, the model for "Doc" in *Cannery Row,* the Steinbeck novel. He was editor of several updated editions of Ricketts's *Between Pacific Tides.* So he gave me this great book of clippings. When you read it all compressed, the whole story came glaringly clear. This was a big, big deal. It had been a big deal from the beginning. And it had been obscured from the public.

There was a very good reporter on the *Santa Rosa Press Democrat*, a guy named Don Engdahl. He knew what was going on. The paper was in favor of the plant, editorially, but they didn't limit Engdahl in the way he could cover events that were going on as the plans progressed. And Hedgpeth was aware of what was going on. That's why he gathered all these clippings.

From that raw material I was able to write "A Visit to the Atomic Park." I didn't have a publisher in mind. I didn't know how it would get published, but I was just so outraged at what I saw. And I'm a good writer. It was a very good piece. I gave it to Karl Kortum, and Karl was dazzled by it. Karl is a good writer, too, and he was a very skilled publicist. He cut his teeth on fighting Caltrans on a highway project up in Petaluma. He and his brother and his father—his father had run for Congress at some point in the past—they all read the manuscript, and they all said, "This has to be published!" Bill Kortum, Karl's brother, a veterinarian up in Petaluma, gave it to the publisher of the *Sebastopol Times*.

Throughout the whole Bodega thing, people rose at timely moments that furthered the struggle. The publisher of the *Sebastopol Times*, which was just a little weekly, was one of these people. He was a guy named Ernie Joiner, an old Texas populist. He told me that after he read the manuscript, "I wanted that thing like a duck goin' after a june bug." It's an expression I had never heard before. He wanted to publish it.

Well, by that time, I realized it was also suitable for a pamphlet. But I didn't have any money. I didn't have any publisher who wanted to publish it as a pamphlet. So I talked to Dave Brower about this. I proposed that if I got Joiner to print quality galleys before he ran it in his newspaper, then I could cut and paste those into a pamphlet. The trouble was, I didn't have any money to print it.

Well, apparently there was a publisher in Berkeley who Dave had done some favors for, and who owed Dave. He had a printing plant. It was in the basement of the Farm Bureau Building in Berkeley. So Ernie Joiner agreed to all this. Joiner published "A Visit to the Atomic Park" in the *Sebastopol Times* in four different installments. I would go up to Sebastopol, I'd sit down and read the galleys, and correct them, and Joiner would publish them that week. Then I took these galleys and I went to this print shop in Berkeley and started pasting up the pamphlet. Karl Kortum, who was a fine photographer, would pull together the photos for it. And we assembled that pamphlet, down in the basement of the Farm Bureau Building. It didn't cost us anything, because this printer owed Dave for something. He was beholden to Dave, and Dave called in his chips. We printed it, four thousand copies, and then I would put it in the back of my old 1946 Ford and I'd drive around to little bookstores and places. We put a one-dollar price on it, which raised a little bit of money, not much. We got it out. People started reading it. It was a hell of a good story.

Right about then, the job in Africa came through. It had been held up with a security clearance. By that time I was so deeply enmeshed in the struggle over Bodega, and I had done a lot of work on it. There were no elections or anything, but clearly I was the leader. I was looked to by a lot of people as the leader. And they were depending on me. So I turned down the Africa job. I've always wondered what would have happened to my life if I had accepted it.

We kept hammering away on the earthquake question. We had the good fortune to have the volunteer efforts of Pierre Saint-Amand, who was a seismologist. That was another turning point.

It happened this way. We held a big meeting in Santa Rosa to organize protests at the local level. We got quite a turnout. Governor Pat Brown sent his representative, a fellow named Alexander Grendon, who was a retired colonel of chemical and biological warfare. His job in state government was coordinator of atomic energy development *and radiation protection.* A contradiction right there in the title. In any event, he was at this meeting, and he sat in the back of the room. Well, the meeting was starting to get away from me. I was the MC. I could see people starting to get restless, and some people started to drift out. We were losing our audience.

Then somebody asked me a question about what role the Atomic Energy Commission would play in all this. I said I didn't know the answer, but there was somebody in the room who did. I don't remember why I recognized Grendon, but I did recognize him, and I threw the question to him. He was stupid enough to get up, in the back of the room, and start ranting and raving at the audience. He said that they didn't know anything. That they wouldn't be able to bring anything to the Atomic Energy Commission hearings, because they were all stupid. He didn't use the word *stupid*, but that was the impression he left. And he just outraged the audience. People got up and started shouting, they were so angry. It became just a hell of a meeting.

There was a radio reporter in the meeting who taped the whole thing for KPFA. She produced an hour-long program, which was rebroadcast over the Los Angeles public broadcasting station. This seismologist, Pierre Saint-Amand, was listening on his car radio someplace in Southern California, and *he* was outraged by Colonel Grendon. He called me up and volunteered. He wanted to come up and help out. He worked for the Navy out at the Naval Ordinance Test Station, just east of Bakersfield. And he was just a character. He had a beard, nicely clipped, and a funny-looking hat, and kind of a Columbo raincoat that he wore all the time. He was a pilot, he had his own airplane, and he flew up and we went out to Bodega Head to survey the property. He said, "There's *all kinds* of faults out here."

Saint-Amand was pretty well known. There'd been a major earthquake in Chile the year before, a Richter 9, and it killed a lot of people and did a tremendous amount of damage. Saint-Amand had written the definitive report about this Chilean earthquake. He was well known in the profession. He had a good reputation. So he wrote a report on Bodega. I took his report to PG&E, and I said, "You know, we're going to release this, and it's going to be explosive. But if you pull out, I won't release it." They just laughed at me. So we released it. It got a lot of press.

By that time, Harold Gilliam was working for Udall in Washington. He was an assistant to Udall. Gilliam took the report to Udall and said, "You know, we ought to get the Department of the Interior in on this, through the US Geological Survey." So Udall directed the USGS, from Menlo Park, to do their own study. Well, Seaborg, I learned later, was furious. The Department of the Interior was invading what he thought was an exclusive AEC terrain. So two geologists from the USGS went out there, did a survey, and wrote a report. They confirmed the fault.

By that time, the licensing process had reached the final stage, where the staff of the AEC were to issue their own report. And another body, supposedly an independent body—an academic committee made up of nuclear-engineering professors, mostly—issued their report simultaneously. The gist of the AEC report was that while it's difficult to anticipate all safety issues, there comes a point when you cross the line. And this site crosses the line. Whereas the other committee, the academic committee, came out with a more sanguine report saying that we can overcome any of those problems.

These two reports gave PG&E a face-saving way out. They pulled out within two or three days of the issuance of the reports, stating that they had always maintained that if there was any question about public safety, they wouldn't build the plant. The staff of the AEC gave them a face-saving solution to an intractable problem.

And that's the way it happened.

That was my last collaboration with your father. When he was facing termination as the Sierra Club's executive by the board, which was troubled by how hard he fought for things, he asked me to negotiate his severance terms with the board. I was just out of law school, very green. But that's why he was calling on people to help him and his vision—because of their values, not their academic credentials. I helped negotiate his severance terms. After that, we saw each other from time to time over the years, of course. In his speeches, I know, he used me as an example of how one person can make a difference. He included me in the company of Rachel Carson and Wangari Maathai, people like that, which was flattering. I admired him a great deal.

He started the environmental movement. He created it. As I said, he was not a manager. He was a visionary. He had the sense to know it wasn't enough for him to enjoy his vision. It had to be shared. He had a lot of background in publishing, having worked for quite a few years for

the University of California Press. He understood books. He understood
how to deliver a message. And he inspired people. He inspired people
because his vision was out there, all the time. You couldn't be around
him very long without being infected by it. He wore it on his sleeve.

Cathedral in the Desert, Escalante River, Glen Canyon
Photograph by Richard Norgaard

RICHARD NORGAARD

PROFESSOR RICHARD NORGAARD lives in a house built with his own hands, along with some help from the hands of his son, in a ravine of redwoods in the Berkeley hills. The deck looks directly down on the North Fork of Codornices Creek. Downstream, the *V* of the ravine and its redwoods frame a small wedge of San Francisco Bay. Upstream, the headwaters of the North Fork emerge from a pipe. On leaving that ersatz spring they instantly become a real stream again and pass the house babbling in a genuine creek-like way. It is fit that Norgaard has settled in this spot, above flowing water, given the way streamcourses have shaped the course of his life.

The professor is sixty-eight, yet his face is youthful and unlined. It is commonplace for old acquaintances to observe that, save for twenty extra pounds and some gray in his beard, Dick Norgaard looks exactly as he did as a teenage boatman on the Salmon, the North Fork of the Clearwater, the Feather, the South Fork of the American, the Sacramento, the Selway, the Lochsa, the Rogue, the Yampa, the Green, the Colorado, the Canoe, and the Columbia. It must be something in the water.

Norgaard is a founder of the discipline of ecological economics. The words *ecology* and *economy* both derive from the Greek *ecos (oikos)*, "house," an intimate relationship that most economists studiously ignore. Norgaard is one of the handful willing to consider the connection, and he has spent his career contemplating the two derivations where they intersect. The darkest lapse of the dismal science, to his way of thinking, is its failure to question its addiction to growth. Norgaard is in the camp of the Quaker economist Kenneth Boulding ("Anyone who thinks you can have infinite growth on a finite planet is either a madman or an economist") and of Herman Daly ("We treat the earth like a business in liquidation"), and he quotes both these thinkers often. He is far outside the camp of Julian Simon ("Resources are infinite and the economy can grow forever") and Ayn Rand ("Altruism is evil and selfishness is a virtue") and Milton Friedman ("Few trends could so thoroughly undermine the very foundations of our free society as the acceptance by corporate officials of a social responsibility other than to make as much money for their stockholders as possible"). He likes to quote these three putative thinkers, too, just for the depravity of their ideas.

Norgaard had his four children in two batches. With his first wife, Marida, he produced Kari Marie, now a professor of sociology and environmental studies at the University of Oregon, and Marc, now a pilot for Southwest Airlines. With his second wife, Nancy, he produced another girl and boy, the twins Addie and Matt, who are twelve. Kari, Matt, and Addie share the same birthday, December 18, but thirty-one years apart.

The professor's office is a single-room structure at the end of the deck, fifty feet upstream of the house, a distance that allows him some separation while at work from the life of his family. The southeast wall of the office is solid with books, floor to ceiling, on shelves he fashioned himself. Low on the northwest wall are rows of file boxes labeled: Trade & the Environment. Complexity Chaos/Deliberative Science. Amazon World Bank. Climate Change. Millennium Ecosystem Assessment. Promotion Battle/3rd Millennium.

The problems sorted in these boxes are global, except for the last. "Promotion Battle/3rd Millennium" is a personal file that chronicles Norgaard's struggles in the past decade, as maverick economist, for promotion at the University of California—the price he has paid, Norgaard believes, for his apostasy. "I've felt my work should not be controversial by now, but I guess I keep irritating economists in new ways." Earlier file boxes chronicle this same struggle in the "2nd Millennium." The notation "3rd Millennium" is a dark little joke, a rueful reference to how endless the battle seems to have been.

On the shelves above the file boxes are all the editions of *Journal of Conservation Biology* ever published. There is also a complete set of the 1911 *Encyclopedia Britannica*, which Norgaard likes so much he had all the old volumes rebound. "You can't Google this," he says of the *Encyclopedia*. "It's what the world was like. How racist the Brits were, for example, along with everybody else."

We sat for the interview on the professor's deck, above the babble of the North Fork of the Codornices. Now and again a jay called from the redwoods. Redwood forest is normally the province of Steller's jay, but this was clearly the strident, petulant call of a scrub jay. The bird never showed itself in the darkness of the redwood canopy, but it was in there somewhere, interloping, like a crusader in Mecca, or a river runner in the Department of Economics, or Martin Luther in Wittenberg nailing his ninety-five theses to the church door.

MY FIRST ENCOUNTER with Dave was in Hite, Utah, in June 1962. It was a Sierra Club trip through the Glen Canyon, billed as one of the last. Your dad was pretty aloof. People sort of knew that this was David, but he didn't jump out of the crowd too often. He talked quietly with people, but he was mostly just watching. Just watching. We had some conversations and began to know each other. I would have been eighteen, going on nineteen. It was a six-day trip through the Glen. There were probably forty people. A fairly large number. It was not really the last trip through Glen Canyon, but this was the last year before the dam's diversion tunnels were closed and Lake Powell began to fill. So in that sense, it was the last year. We kept running the river through the years the lake was coming up, but to get the whole trip, '62 was the last chance.

I've said Dave was "aloof," but maybe the word is "mournful." He'd lost Glen Canyon and the water was rising.

My family knew the Elliot family, and that was how I got into river running. Lou Elliot was organizing river trips for the Sierra Club. Bob Elliot, his son, was a Boy Scout in my Boy Scout troop. I started as a pot-washer in 1959, running first the Green River, and then the Yampa. Or maybe it was the Yampa and then the Green. They were Sierra Club trips, and in those days the Hatch family provided the boating services, but the Sierra Club lined up cooks and pot-washers, and Lou Elliot signed me on as a pot-washer. I took the oars whenever I could. Then that same season I went on to do the main Salmon, and I got to do more boating there. And finally, at the end of that summer of '59, Lou Elliot ran his first quasi-commercial trip with the American Whitewater Association. This was in Idaho, a combination trip on the Selway, the Lochsa, and the North Fork of the Clearwater, spending more or less two days on each river. He needed a boatman, and I became a boatman about the time I turned sixteen.

So my thing with rivers was certainly in part the coincidence of knowing the Elliots, but also it was just, *rivers*. Water. Water resonates with some of us. Flowing water. Canyons. Just the life of the river. The life of what goes on with moving water. I mean, I'd done backpacking, and casual mountain climbing, but for me the river was just much more attractive. It just took me. It grabbed me, and I said, *Yeah!*

Also, river running—*rafting*, at least—is a way of being out on an adventure with people. You're not panting up a trail. You can relax and talk. It's easy camping. It's a social life that's very comfortable.

Before that first trip in June with Dave, I'd done Glen Canyon once, in spring of that same year, on Easter week, with Lou Elliot. But Lou himself didn't really know the canyon. There were no guidebooks. We didn't know the side canyons. There were rumors that you want to go up Moqui Canyon. And here's how you find Aztec Canyon. And they said that Hidden Canyon is hidden, the entrance to it, but you can get back up into it if you stay on that right side of the Colorado. But our knowledge was minimal on the early trips. Not quite so minimal as it was for John Wesley Powell. When Powell first ran the Glen Canyon, he didn't know anything at all. At least we knew the river had no waterfalls in front of us. We knew it was all easy. Powell didn't know that. If it had been the Grand Canyon, with big rapids, you could say it was more like Powell days, but even with the Grand Canyon, the quality of the boats had improved immensely from Powell's time. His boats were outrageously heavy and uniquely able to destroy themselves. The World War II assault rafts we used were pretty heavy, but they were also pretty indestructible.

On my first trip with Dave, we would talk about what was going on, just normal river conversation. He didn't really open up a lot about Echo Park. I don't think it was till the next Glen Canyon trip, which followed pretty fast on the first one, where I began to get the full story, the history of his campaigns against dams on the upper Colorado. It was on this second trip where he said, "This dam is taller than it would have been, because that's how we saved Echo Park."

It was on the second trip that I got a sense that he approved of me. I think he just thought that an eighteen-year-old who can keep forty-five people running down a river, and the outboard motors running, and the food cooked, was okay by him. I can't remember any deep conversations we had that bound the ties between us. I tend to be pretty quiet myself. So maybe it was just our shared quietness.

Certainly there were times we found ourselves walking upcanyon, and often you end up walking side by side. You don't need to say much. No need for words. When you turn the corner in a side canyon, and a whole new stretch of the canyon opens up! You round that sandstone wall, and it's always something beautiful and new. So I suspect it was just seeing it together. Plus, you have to remember, this was only my second trip in the Glen. And so I was learning it myself. I was saying, "Let's try this side canyon," and then, "Let's try that one."

Dave immediately set up a third trip the next month, July. Your whole family came. Toppy Edwards came—Walter Edwards—a photographer from *National Geographic*. Toppy had been on the June trip, too. He and Dave decided they needed to go back for more photography. This was a ten- to fourteen-day trip, and we took a lot of time on it. Went more slowly. Toppy brought his wife. And Phil Hyde came, another photographer, and Phil brought his wife, Ardis. It was mainly photographers. It was just a photography trip. Dave was thinking about the Grand Canyon fight, which was heating up, and he wanted to document what we were losing in Glen Canyon. This trip was a much more intense experience, because we spent just a lot more time together. I got to know the Browers. Barbara was twelve at the time. Johnny was ten. You were seventeen. I don't remember Bob Brower as much. Another quiet guy. He was fifteen or sixteen. I do remember he was around the motor a lot.

There was an event, either the June or the July trip, where we had broken a whichamacallit, a shear pin, on the outboard motor. I was leaning over the motor, replacing the shear pin, and somehow I dropped the hammer in. I decided I should just fall in after the hammer, and maybe I'd go to about the same place the hammer was going and intercept it. And that worked. Maybe that was one of the things that impressed your dad. I don't know.

Dave himself was really not that comfortable in the water. He wore his life jacket *all* the time. So whenever we went up side canyons, in case we needed to swim, he had his life jacket on. So eventually all of us just said, Okay, we'll just all wear our life jackets. We didn't know what we were getting into in many of the side canyons, and how far we were going to go, and what we might discover. And there were some places where we did need to swim. There's also a lot of slipping and sliding in the side-canyon pools. And also you get cold. So the life jacket is a little insulation against falls and the cold. The side canyons could really get cold.

So the hammer went overboard. I just thought, *Okay, this is our hammer. I'm going after it.* I just grabbed around and flailed about underwater. There's no visibility. This is the *Colorado*, full of sediment, can't see a thing. I just remember, *Ah, it's in my hand, I'm up.* The river was only three and a half feet deep at that point, anyway. The trouble was the boat was going down the river. So I had to swim after the boat.

Or the "raft," but we called it a boat. That was one of these monstrous Neoprene rafts made of smaller rafts twenty-four feet long by six feet wide. Three of them tied together, so we were eighteen-by-twenty-four. Except that we pushed the middle one forward four feet, to make a prow, so it was an eighteen-by-twenty-eight-foot platform. Not much of a craft, but it was perfect for quick exits to go up side canyons. And for throwing stuff on and off. And for camping.

Dave's talk was much more intense and personal on this July trip. He opened up much more on his feelings about the canyon. He began to say, "I've really got to do something here. I've got to try to get the little dam up Bridge Creek built, to save Rainbow Bridge." At the same time, he knew that this cofferdam would not happen—it was not in the cards politically—but maybe it would delay things for a while. Maybe we could keep the lake away from Rainbow Bridge a little bit longer. Maybe, maybe, maybe. So there was a year where he spent a lot of time trying to get that cofferdam built. It was congressionally authorized but not funded. I mean, it was a crazy idea in the first place. Because Bridge Creek floods really heavily. You would have to have a pump big enough to pump floodwater over the dam into the lake. And you couldn't get it all. You'd still end up with a little lake, going up under the bridge. I remember discussions about that. But that wasn't the point. The point was to just gum up the works. And to just make sure that people knew what was happening.

Dave lent me his Hasselblad on a couple of later trips. He liked the Hasselblad for its film size—a medium-format camera where you look down into a ground glass. He lent it on a '64 trip down the Middle Fork of the Salmon, where Lou Elliot wanted me to go just as a photographer. I got very good at changing film in the middle of the rapids. When it was too rough to actually take pictures, I would change film, bouncing around and holding the various parts of the Hasselblad and getting the film in.

David was a great photographer. He liked the resolution of the bigger Hasselblad format, which was two-and-a-quarter by two-and-a-quarter, and he liked the ground glass. A ground glass is better than a viewfinder when you're composing. But he didn't like the square format. He thought the square was the least interesting frame possible. But he actually claims that I was able to do more with square composition than others. He liked my use of square composition.

Back home, he put me on the Sierra Club payroll part time to run the Xerox machine and see how life goes there. Ten hours a week. I helped in sorting out pictures for the Glen Canyon book. In the summer of '66 he hired me part time to help try to get his own Glen Canyon footage into a movie. He also sent me back to the river in '66. He wasn't able to go on one of those trips back into Lake Powell, so he sent me with a movie camera, his Bolex. On that trip, I didn't trip the gate that keeps the film up against the lens and shutter. So all my footage was blurry. I had practiced with someone else's Bolex, a more recent edition, which when you put it together the gate trips automatically. My footage was worthless. It was an incredible disappointment. Dave tried to make me feel better about it. He said I had the *exposure* perfect.

We talked photography a lot. That was something he certainly encouraged. He put some of my Glen Canyon pictures in the back of the Grand Canyon book. In fact, I have the majority of the Glen Canyon pictures in that book. He didn't have to use my pictures. He could have used Philip Hyde's, or his own.

I became part of the campaigns to stop dams in the Grand Canyon. And I decided to become an economist. Not *particularly* because of rivers. Rivers are my first love, but basically all the environmental craziness everywhere is driven by economics. I mean, I would have preferred to be a biologist, or a geologist. My first two publications are actually on fluvial geomorphology. But, you know, *people* were the problem. And people are the problem. It's people's ideas that shape how we relate to Nature and what we do. So I got into economics. To go on the inside. To get at the problem from inside.

It was watching Glen Canyon go under in '62, '64, that got me mad enough to become an economist. You have to be pretty mad to join the priesthood, but not be *in* the priesthood. That has caused me trouble throughout my career. Still causes trouble. I'm reviewed by economists, because I have a Ph.D. in economics. I still publish economics, so I must be an economist. But I'm not an *economist* economist. So I still have trouble.

As an undergraduate student I did not do well. All that river running before I turned twenty, that pretty much explains why I nearly flunked out of Cal. I had to go back for two summers for half of each summer just to do makeup work and get my grade point average up so I could stay in school. It wasn't just rivers. I was just goofing around with other stuff. I would get Fs in German. You had to take languages, and I chose German because it's supposed to be the easiest. But German was also very *Germanic*. It was strict. They said you could miss X number of days. I was going to miss more than X number of days because of being in Glen Canyon in the spring. And I tried to explain that to them, but, nope, they gave me the F. I shouldn't have signed up. There was ROTC at the time. You had to spit-polish your shoes. I didn't spit-polish my shoes. I'd get a D in ROTC. I got all the right bad grades.

In the beginning I thought I wanted to be a math major. All of a sudden that just became too much of an abstraction. It's the time in life when you're just trying to find out what the heck's going on. How are you going to fit in? Who are you going to be? Of course I had this wonderful "who" I could be—a river runner—but I knew it had to be more than that, so I didn't follow Bob Elliot into the river business. There was also the Vietnam War, of course. It was graduate school or the Mekong Delta. The Mekong was not a river I wanted to run right then.

I graduated from Berkeley with low grades, a 2.23, so I went on and got the master's degree at Oregon State. After the master's, I applied to Chicago in geography, as well as in economics, and I was admitted to both. My grades actually hadn't come up that much. For graduate-student grades, I did pretty poorly, but I still impressed the professors. The problem in going to Oregon State for the master's was that there were rivers to run and mountains to climb and beaches to camp on in the middle of winter, and it was too darned nice. I didn't get good grades until Chicago. When you're living in Hyde Park, there's no beaches or rivers or mountains. No hope.

What I didn't know when I went to Chicago was that they admit sixty students and graduate fifteen with Ph.D.s. That's very atypical at

American universities. Students were dropping out like flies. It's just too crazy. Everybody's thinking just economics, sixteen hours a day. It was very intense. But I didn't have any rivers to run or mountains to climb in Chicago, so it was tolerable.

Dave liked the line, "Economics is a form of brain damage." Whose line is that? A woman. She's in Florida. We'll remember her before we're done. Hazel Henderson.

Hazel Henderson is right. Economics *is* a form of brain damage. But I teach it as a form of religion. Basically the economy is our cosmos. It's everything around us. All the signals we get are price signals. The talk about GDP going up, about employment up or down, about stock market up or down. We're bombarded by economic signals that basically don't have any meaning to us. But we somehow try to give them meaning. We have to see the world through this cosmos of the economy. Our working lives, our consuming lives, are all just framed around it. Economics is the way of explaining what's going on. It justifies growing. It justifies consuming. It justifies who gets which wages. It justifies returns to capitalists. It justifies globalization. But not actually—it doesn't do any of those things. If you actually pursue its theory rigorously, you can't get *any* answers. It's just a pattern of thinking. It's assumptions that have the answers come out from them. But from this comes the political discourse we have, a discourse justified by the economists, who are going along with it. The truth is that the basic economics doesn't give answers. And that's been my whole career, just making this point. Economics needs criteria outside of economics to tell the invisible hand where to go.

That's known within economics. But basically since the 1936 Flood Control Act, economists were brought into government to be experts who can help make decisions. Just like a dam engineer, or an irrigation engineer, or a ballistics person, economists were asked to do benefit-cost analyses—to say, for example, whether this dam is better than that one. And ultimately you can't do that in economics. Because the kind of economy you have may not be the kind of economy you want to have. You have to ask questions about the distribution of income, for one thing. But economics today is all about stepping back and *not* asking those questions. The economics profession has rationalized that stepping back, that *not* asking those questions. And yet when it comes to sustainability, when it's about the rights of future generations, you have to ask those questions. When you put future generations into the economic model, it just raises all kinds of questions that economists can't ask, because they're in this role as experts. They've assumed the role of pope. It's a religion. It's a secular religion.

Ecological economics, which I helped develop, grows out of environmental economics, which in turn can be traced back to Malthus and the Physiocrats. But environmental economics really comes to life in the sixties. It's about applying economic theory to environmental problems. In the early days, environmental economists talked about how markets fail, and why you need government to step in and establish stronger regulations. Then in the seventies it evolved into exploring how can you make markets work better. How can you come up with values that the EPA can use to justify its regulations? So environmental economics became much more institutionalized within the system. Whereas when I first joined it, it was a critique of the system. It started as part of the environmental movement and a critique of the market. And it becomes instead absorbed into the economic way of thinking. I think what makes *ecological* economics different is that we acknowledge that economics is a part of the problem. Environmental economists won't say that.

Dave and I didn't talk economics a lot. What I got from David was that what you do in school, and whether you get out of school, maybe doesn't make that much difference. What I got out of him was just reinforcement of determination, and a sense that you can do something to make a difference.

How do you describe the bond? Sharing seven weeks in the Glen with Dave did do something to us. I mean, he certainly made me braver, gutsier, in terms of taking my own course. The boldness quote that Dave liked so much, the Goethe quote, was on my wall, both as a master's student and a Ph.D. student.

"If there is something you can do, or dream you can, begin it..."

89

Dave influenced people by example, just by seeing his determination. Just by his willingness to take on the opposition. Dave was always more radical and trying to get the environmental movement to be more radical, more active. In the expansion from a movement concerned with wilderness preservation to a pollution-oriented, pesticide-oriented, city-oriented, environmental justice–oriented movement, he was way ahead. Compared to organizations today, *he was defending the environment.* Today it's more, "Yes, we need to save the environment, but also save the organization." With Dave there was no compromising. The principles were what mattered.

The Sierra Club's "Sistine Chapel Ad"
Text by Jerry Mander, design by Scott Freeman

JERRY MANDER

P OSTERS OF FULL-PAGE newspaper advertisements covered
the green sofa in Jerry Mander's office, dozens of white broad-
sheets piled in a deep drift. All were the work of the extinct firm
of Freeman, Mander & Gossage. Some were still rolled up as scrolls. Others
had been laid out flat, but these were trying to scroll again, curling up at
top and bottom. Mander scooped up posters from one side of the sofa and
heaped them high on the other, clearing space for his interviewer to sit. His
excavation exposed an advertisement titled "Ecology & War." He paused
to skim the text.

"The War Ad," he said. "That was one that Dave was very excited about,
because he wanted to do something about war. Something relating war
to the environment. He very, very strongly felt that environmental groups
would have to start relating to other movements."

The War Ad was illustrated by a medieval etching of naked men in
hand-to-hand combat with scimitars, axes, and daggers. The text was set
in Centaur, the elegant Roman typeface designed by Bruce Rogers. There
was a lot of copy, as was normal in the political ads that Freeman, Mander
& Gossage produced for the Sierra Club and Friends of the Earth. Even the
headline was wordy:

The need is not really for more brains, the need is now for A GEN-
TLER, A MORE TOLERANT PEOPLE THAN THOSE WHO WON FOR US
AGAINST THE ICE, THE TIGER AND THE BEAR. The hand that hefted
the ax, out of some old blind allegiance to the past, fondles the
machine gun as lovingly. It is a habit man will have to break to
survive, but the roots go very deep. (Loren Eiseley)

The emphasis was Jerry Mander's. The Eiseley epigraph was suggested
by David Brower, who loved the line about the ice, the tiger, and the bear,
and it was Brower who signed "David Brower, President Friends of the
Earth," at the end. But it fell to Jerry Mander, as usual in this collaboration,
to write most of the copy in between. Mander's text conceded that war is
not typically regarded as a concern of conservationists, but that in fact the
laterization of soil by napalm and chemical defoliation of Mekong mangroves
were worthy issues for the environmental movement. The ad urged readers
to support several resolutions then before the Congress: the Cooper-Church
Amendment requiring withdrawal of all American military from Cambodia,
the Repeal of the Gulf of Tonkin Resolution, and the McGovern-Hatfield
Resolution, which required total American disengagement by 1971.

More Friends of the Earth ads surfaced as Mander cleared the sofa.
The Supersonic Transport Ad:

BREAKS WINDOWS, CRACKS WALLS,
STAMPEDES CATTLE, AND
WILL HASTEN THE END OF THE AMERICAN WILDERNESS

The Coastal Drilling Ad:

AGAINST COASTAL OIL DRILLING?
You'd Better Say So Now!

The Fur Ad:

(Important Memo to the Fur Industry)
WE WILL NO LONGER BUY ANYTHING MADE FROM THE SKINS,
FURS, OR FEATHERS OF WILD OR ENDANGERED ANIMALS.

The Fur Ad's opening declaration was in capital letters of Centaur type. "Our goal is to make it unfashionable to wear wild animal skins," Mander's text began. "After only six months of organizing, we have had notable success. The names below represent only a tiny fraction of the total list of women and men who have subscribed to our position and who are spending at least a portion of their time encouraging others to join them." The declaration was signed, among others, by Mrs. Robert Alda, Miss Lauren Bacall, Richard Benjamin, Mrs. Leonard Bernstein, Mr. and Mrs. William Buckley, Truman Capote, Mrs. Johnny Carson, Peggy Cass, Dick Cavett, Blythe Danner, Dave DeBusschere, Mr. and Mrs. Jules Feiffer, Mr. and Mrs. Ben Gazzara, Mr. and Mrs. William Goldman, Huntington Hartford, Mrs. Ernest Hemingway, Dustin Hoffman, Mr. and Mrs. Hal Holbrook, Mrs. Jacob Javits, Danny Kaye, Mrs. Pat Lawford, Mr. and Mrs. John Lindsay, Ali MacGraw, Mrs. Norman Mailer, Mrs. George Plimpton, Robert Redford, Pete Seeger, George Segal, Mr. and Mrs. Neil Simon, Mrs. William Styron, and Mrs. James Wyeth.

The Sistine Chapel Ad, the most famous ad of all—an argument against dams in the Grand Canyon—appeared in the pile. "SHOULD WE ALSO FLOOD THE SISTINE CHAPEL SO TOURISTS CAN GET NEARER THE CEILING?" the headline read.

Below, between the ad's two tall columns of text, like a rope down the shaft of a well, stretched the four-billion-year timeline of the Earth. At the very top, the timeline was marked off by two fine horizontal lines with an infinitesimal gap between. The upper hatch mark was labeled "Age of Technology," and the lower "First Man, 2 million yrs ago." A reader had to peer closely at the two lines to see the infinitesimal gap between. This was the duration of anthropoid history, just a microtome slice of time. Our experience as *Homo sapiens* is the thinnest of veneers on the long story of the Earth.

A short distance down the timeline came "First Elephants, 60 million yrs ago," and then "First Redwoods, 130 million yrs ago." Toward the middle of the page, halfway down the well, came "First Reptiles, 275 million yrs ago." Nearing the bottom was "Grand Canyon, 550 million yrs ago," and then "First Corals, 575 million yrs ago," and finally "First Sponges, 650 million yrs ago." Below that, the spatial limits of the newspaper page and the temporal limitlessness of the geological record required ingenuity on the part of the ad's graphic designer, Scott Freeman. He solved the problem by allowing the timeline to pile up on itself at the bottom of the shaft, like six hundred feet of bucket rope lowered into a one-hundred-foot well.

"Earth began four billion years ago and Man two million," Mander's text began.

> The Age of Technology, on the other hand, is hardly a hundred years old, and on our time chart we have been generous to give it even the little line we have.

> It seems to us hasty, therefore, during this blip of time, for Man to think of directing his fascinating new tools toward altering irrevocably the forces which made him. Nonetheless, in these few brief years among the four billion, wilderness has all but disappeared. And now:

> 1.) There are proposals before Congress to "improve" Grand Canyon. Two dams would back up artificial lakes into 148 miles of canyon gorge. This would benefit tourists in power boats, it is argued, who would enjoy viewing the canyon wall more closely. (See headline.) Submerged underneath the tourists would be part of the most revealing single page of earth's history. The lakes would be as deep as 600 feet (deeper, for example, than all but a handful of New York buildings are high) but in a century silting would have replaced the water with that much mud, wall to wall.

> There is no part of the wild Colorado River, the Grand Canyon's sculptor, that would not be maimed.

> Tourist recreation, as a reason for the dams, is in fact an afterthought. The Bureau of Reclamation, which has backed them, has called the dams "cash registers." It expects the dams would make money by sale of commercial power.

> They will not provide anyone with water.

Jerry Mander was born in the Bronx in 1936 to a Jewish immigrant couple who had escaped the pogroms in eastern Europe. His father, Harry, was typical of this exodus; poorly educated, hard-working, married young, he hustled to stay alive on the Lower East Side, found work in the garment industry, did well—Harry Mander and Company—and moved his family to semirural Yonkers.

"My parents knew nothing about 'gerrymander,' " says Jerry Mander. "They were both eastern European immigrants. They may never have known. The world divides into people who know the term, and people who don't. Some people just start laughing. A lot of people say, 'Well, you should have a political career.' Quite a few people think I made it up. It's been good. It makes me easier to remember."

In the Yonkers outback Jerry grew up playing golf. A star on the links in his youth, he dreamed of a career as professional golfer, but settled instead on a B.S. in economics from the Wharton School of the University of Pennsylvania, then an M.S. in international economics from Columbia Business School.

"Right out of college, I tried to get a job at an advertising agency. That is what I was attracted to. But I couldn't get one. Only after a while did I realize they don't hire Jews. I did take a job with Worthington Corporation, a giant Fortune 500 company. I worked in the marketing department, and I found that very, very, very, very unappealing. Very, very boring. Then I came out West to visit a close friend of mine, who was living out here. I'd never been to San Francisco. As soon as I landed in Oakland and smelled the air, I decided, 'You know what? I'm not going back.' My first job was a Christmas clerk at the City of Paris."

Mander drifted into show-business publicity. His work caught the attention of the advertising guru Howard Gossage.

Howard Luck Gossage was an original thinker whose small San Francisco firm would have large effect. Gossage believed that an ad should be a conversation, an interaction between the adman and his audience. It was for the dialogues of his ads, perhaps, that someone dubbed him "the Socrates of San Francisco." Jerry Mander liked the Socratic method and went to work for Gossage, setting up shop in Gossage's beautifully renovated brick firehouse at 451 Pacific Avenue. The redesign incorporated the firemen's brass pole. If an adman was late for a client meeting, he could leap on the pole for a quick descent to the ground floor. Freeman & Gossage, the firm at "the Firehouse," soon became Freeman, Mander & Gossage.

When Mander was in his late twenties, his hair, which he wore in a big Hebrew Afro, began to turn white, and by forty the change was complete. The white kinky nimbus of his hair made a striking contrast with the youthful face below. At any conference or cocktail party of environmentalists, or indigenous-rights advocates, or social justice activists in San Francisco through the last third of the twentieth century, Mander was instantly recognizable, no matter where he stood in the room. Upon entering you knew immediately whether or not Jerry Mander was there. In the early seventies, one of his clients was the antiwar congressman Ron Dellums, cofounder of the Black Caucus and later chairman of the House Armed Services Committee. Dellums dropped by occasionally to confer at the Firehouse, and it was interesting to see the two men together, the tall Dellums with his big Black African Afro, the shorter Mander with his big White Judaic version. They were like the punch line to some joke.

Another arresting tableau at the Firehouse was the team of Mander, Gossage & Brower, all three men prematurely gray, as they leaned over the table to fine-tune one of their ads. A witness might have supposed that wisdom had descended early on these three white heads, except for the boyish excitement and spirit of play that animated these sessions.

Mander is now seventy-five but looks twenty years younger. This is not the normal fate of an advertising executive. It is as if, in some Faustian bargain—a Dorian Gray sort of arrangement—the adman had assured that most of his aging would be confined to his white mane of hair. Today the mane is less expansive, and recedes more from his forehead, but it remains his signature look.

Almost from his start in commercial advertising, Mander began easing himself out of the game. In 1971 he founded Public Interest Communications, the first nonprofit advertising agency in the United States, and then the Public Media Center, an outfit with a similar purpose. He wrote books: *Four Arguments for the Elimination of Television. In the Absence of the Sacred: The Failure of Technology and the Survival of the Indian Nations. The Case Against the Global Economy and for a Turn Toward the Local. Indigenous*

Peoples' Resistance to Globalization. The SuperFerry Chronicles, an account of successful efforts by Hawaiian activists to halt the operation of the giant, fast, whale-unfriendly catamarans that once raced between Oahu and Maui.

In 1994 he founded the International Forum on Globalization and established its office in the Presidio of San Francisco, which the US Army had relinquished to the National Park Service that same year. The Presidio, a military post since Spanish times, occupies priceless real estate at the northern tip of the San Francisco Peninsula, with intimate views of the Golden Gate Bridge. On its incorporation into the Golden Gate National Recreation Area, a number of the Presidio's barracks and officer's quarters and mess halls were made available to nonprofits like Mander's. He set up his Forum on Globalization in Building 1009, a former army hospital ward. In 2009, Mander retired as executive director of the Forum on Globalization, but he continues to serve on the staff as distinguished fellow, and he keeps an office in Building 1009.

On the day I dropped in on Mander, he was writing at a stand-up workstation against one wall. His MacBook monitor displayed a page from a nearly finished book on capitalism that my interview had interrupted. *The Capitalism Papers: Six Fatal Flaws of an Obsolete System* was the working title, subject to change. Few of the chapters had been written here at the Presidio. Mander does his best writing at home, to the north across the Golden Gate, in the coastal hippie refugium of Bolinas, where he is safe from intrusions like mine.

He writes standing up, Hemingway-style, not because, like Papa, he crashed small planes in Africa and has problems with his back. "I just feel more awake," he explained. His workstation is compiled of books. Atop the basement rock of a gray steel file comes this stratigraphic succession: *Workers,* a photo book by Sebastião Salgado; *Migrations,* also by Salgado; *San Francisco Album; The Cultural and Spiritual Values of Biodiversity;* and finally, *The Corporate Reapers.* These titles and thicknesses bring his keyboard to the correct typing height.

"Jerry-rigged," I joked of his system. Mander laughed.

On the wall by the window was a joke full-page advertisement done in the Mander style.

"Interviewed on his 60th birthday, Savant Jerry Mander reveals WATCH-ING GOLF ON TV IS MY PATH BACK TO NATURE!" ran the headline.

Portraits of Einstein and Mander, side by side, illustrated the ad, both photos featuring big white signature hair. Einstein's hair is the wilder. "Before Conditioner," Einstein is captioned. "After Conditioner" is Mander. When I laughed at the ad, Mander turned to it. "They even have Centaur type on it," he said. "Centaur is beautiful!"

DAVE CAME TO US. He wandered into the office, talked to Howard Gossage at first, and Howard called me in. Dave had noticed that a lot of Gossage's ads used Centaur type. He was looking for an advertising agency willing to use Centaur.

I had just started. I'd been working with Gossage for about six months. Until then I hadn't even been in the advertising business, just in the publicity business. Theatrical publicity. One of my clients had been The Committee, which was this outrageous comedy review. It was a satiri-cal comedy review—a *political* satirical comedy review—and they started this campaign against the Vietnam War. They invented what they called "The War Toy of the Week Competition." People were encouraged to bring in their war toys. The Pentagon had announced that to pacify the villages in Vietnam they were going to do *friendly* things. They were going to drop toys on the villages they had just recently invaded and killed a lot of people, just to make everybody feel okay. The Committee was asking, "Well, what sort of toys would be appropriate?" *War toys,* obviously. So The Committee decided they would have a competition and encourage people to bring their toys in. The War Toy of the Week. We gathered this mountain of war toys in the lobby. The idea was to get a helicopter and drop them on the Pentagon. We wanted to give the Pentagon an idea of how it felt. So we did a series of ads about that, and it got enormous response.

I don't know if Dave ever saw those ads, but Howard Gossage saw them. He called me and asked why didn't I come to work with him.

The War Toy Ad, it was a kind of new idea of how to approach information, a kind of iconoclastic approach to things. I had been working with Gossage for about six months when Dave wandered into the Firehouse. When Howard asked him, "Why did you come *here?*" Dave said, "Oh, because you use the kind of typeface that I like." Brower was a fanatic on this. He loved Centaur type.

So that's how he came in the door. And then we got talking. He talked about dams in the Grand Canyon and how outrageous it was. The Grand Canyon dams had already been okayed by the Congress. Stewart Udall was in favor of them, and Lyndon Johnson was in favor of them. It was a done deal. Dave was desperate. He said, "We've got to do something about it. The public doesn't even know what's really happening here. We need something to get the public engaged." Gossage liked the idea and he thought I could do an ad on it. So I worked with Dave on the copy.

Dave had already written an ad. We didn't think it was good. We encouraged him to just let us write the ad. He said, "No, no, no, this is what I want to say." Somewhere I have his original ad, and I have my version of it. He would not let go, so we had a big argument. Right away! Within the first few weeks, we had a big argument and we couldn't agree.

Well, in those days, *The New York Times* offered something to advertisers, which was called a split run. If you wanted to try out two different versions of something, each hit of the paper would be one ad or the other. So we convinced him to do a competition. We said, "We're going to do a lot better than yours, because…" I don't quite remember what the issues were, but Dave had more of a "companions-on-the-trail" approach. A sort of Sierra Clubby approach. And we said, "You've got to get more urgency in it." So in our ad, the headline was "NOW ONLY YOU CAN STOP THEM FROM FLOODING GRAND CANYON FOR PROFIT." And we had all these coupons. Dave didn't see the point of the coupons. Afterward he loved them. They were Gossage's invention, those coupons. They hadn't been in an ad before.

And so *The Times* agreed to run our ad in one hit, and then his ad, and then ours. And we got at least two-to-one more dialing response and mail response than he did. I think that first Grand Canyon ad got about five thousand responses. Which had never happened before. Stewart Udall said that he'd never seen that many responses. We had a coupon for readers to send to Udall, the secretary of the interior. And I think this was the first time when the IRS problem came up. The IRS said the Sierra Club can't do this and keep its tax-exempt status. That response came very fast. The IRS notified the Sierra Club that this was lobbying, and you can't do this and stay tax exempt. The coupon element was the thing they were angry about. But Udall was very, very impressed. He understood that something important was happening.

Anyway, we won the competition on the ads, and Dave said, "Okay, you guys do it." And then we did another ad in that Grand Canyon series—I can't remember what the second one was—and then we did the Sistine Chapel Ad, which was the very famous one.

I can tell you a story about that ad. At that point, I was only vaguely connected to environmentalism. I was much more directly political. But I was learning from Dave, because he would talk about what it all meant, you know. In the ads, we would try to narrow it into political-action elements. Anyway, after the first ad, we talked about what else we could do. We wanted to show a relationship between people and the Grand Canyon. We already thought of the Grand Canyon as this very important ecological, historical place. But Dave had really big visions about how he wanted to talk about it.

We had a period of hanging out together in New York, actually. You know how he'd always go to the Biltmore Hotel and hang out under the clock? One time we got really pissed. Drunk. Under the clock. And he started talking really beautifully about the history of human beings and how the human beings would sit at night around a fire, and experience each other, and experience Nature, and it would be quiet. He started talking about that whole experience. And then he said, "You know, the feeling of human beings sitting around a fire right now, *it's the same as human beings sitting around a fire back then.*" And then he says, "That's what we've got to get at. We've got to get at showing that we're still connected to that entire history of human beings and our relationship to Nature. And bring that forth again."

That really changed me. I've said it before, but that drunken night at the Biltmore Hotel actually changed my heart and head. From then on I started looking at these issues more deeply and broadly. It really informed the way I went about doing the writing on the ads. And that big vision was definitely Dave's thing. He was *always* doing that. We had thirty ads or more with Brower—thirty, forty ads. Each time, I would always take the lead from him, in terms of the conceptual framework, including on the Earth National Park Ad, and the War Ad—all the ads. He always had a deeper conception of it. He wanted people to grasp the ecology of it from a very spiritual and historical perspective. Not only in the moment—not just from a concern with whatever river or forest we were trying to prevent from being destroyed—but he wanted all this to be related to bigger things.

The Sistine Chapel Ad was our idea, but it came from Dave. He was talking about the natural world, and how it evolved. Stuff like that. He talked about how human beings have just barely arrived on the scene, when you consider the whole history of the planet. In the ad, on Scott Freeman's chart, the age of technology is just barely visible, and human beings are just as narrow as a line.

The heading "Should We Flood the Sistine Chapel?" was not my line. It was from Hugh Nash, who worked for Dave as editor of the *Sierra Club Bulletin*. Hugh delivered that line at a congressional hearing, testifying in response to Floyd Dominy, director of the Bureau of Reclamation, who had said the flooding from the dams would be great, because it would bring the tourists closer to the walls. Hugh said, "Well, should we also flood the Sistine Chapel so the tourists can get closer to the ceiling?" Tom Turner may have called my attention to that line. It was just a little thing in his testimony; nobody made a fuss about it. I thought it was just a great line.

With the Grand Canyon dams, we probably did about ten or fifteen different ads, I don't remember exactly. We got very excited about this kind of advertising, and we wanted to keep doing it. We did a campaign for the Sierra Club to establish the Redwood National Park in Northern California. We did a series of ads about that. We had a similar chart in one showing the old-growth redwoods—how many there were once, how few are left now. It was a pretty dramatic chart, too. And then we did ads for North Cascades National Park.

I was new to the advertising business. I was having a good time. Howard Gossage had just brought me aboard after seeing my war ads for The Committee. And I did some other ads that were sort of like that. Gossage really spotted those. He said, "This is good. This is what I like, this approach to ads." He had done some similar ads himself. He liked the idea of doing public statements.

Howard was a very different kind of guy. He didn't like advertising. He was just ashamed that he was in advertising. He tried very hard to lift advertising out of its doldrums and take on only certain kinds of clients. He loved to quote some guy from some big ad agency who quit advertising: "One day I woke up and I didn't give a shit whether they sold more of their product than we sold of our product."

Howard Gossage was a very important mentor, too. I still quote him all the time. I think about things he told me. He was very, very handsome. Beautiful-looking guy. With big gray hair. A very beautiful young wife. The offices themselves were very beautiful. He was a very elegant guy. A great writer. An elegant writer. His heart was just not in advertising. He always was trying to break out into something new. He was very, very happy that we got into this whole Brower business.

For my part, at that time, I was happy to learn about advertising. I didn't come with a big political background. The Committee and then Brower were my radicalizing elements. And of course once I started doing this kind of ad, I did more and more and more of them, and it was through that process that I engaged in political action. This was the sixties, you know. All kinds of things were starting to happen.

I fought with Brower all the time. He was a very buggy guy, your dad. *Buggy.* He would call in the middle of the night. This would be two days before the ad was to run. We'd already shipped the ad off to *The New York Times,* but he'd say, "We gotta change that paragraph!"

I'd say, "We *can't* change the paragraph! It's already in New York."

Of course, we had already discussed the copy with him many times. He had corrected us when we got things wrong. Or he'd say, "I'd rather say it this way than that way." And we'd fight about it. Sometimes he would prevail. Sometimes I would prevail. But basically he went along with our approach. He was very supportive. But he would bug me in the sense that he'd always get a new idea, and there was never an end to the process. If he got a new idea at 4:00 a.m., then he'd call at 4:00 a.m. And he'd say, "We've got to change the ad. Because it's really better if we say it this way rather than that way."

I'd say, "We can't change the ad! It's already at *The New York Times.* It's gonna run tomorrow. They're going to start printing it tomorrow!"

He'd say, "Well, call the composition room."

It was very expensive. In those days they didn't do it on computer. It was hot type. We'd have these carefully typeset ads, and they would be on these...boards, these big white boards. Repro proof? I really don't remember now, I forget what it was even called. These boards would ship very fancily, very expensively. At *The Times* they photographed them and shipped them onto their page. Sometimes the ads would already be in *The Times* composing room, and the paper was ready to run the page, by the time Dave called me and asked to change something. I'd say, "We can't. We can't do that." And he'd say, "Yeah, you can. Just call *The Times.* Ask for the composing room. Talk with the actual people who are physically doing the composing."

Well, on a couple of occasions I tried to do that. And it was very, very, very difficult. Or I'd say to Dave, "Listen, if that word is no good, *if you don't want to use that word,* then we'll just rap that word out. We'll just have a blank space. But we can't set a new word and paste it in, that will slow down the whole thing. And in a couple of instances we actually did that, rap out the word. Or we'd fix it so that a word was deliberately made unreadable. Because he, he, he…Because there was something wrong with that word.

He was very much a loose cannon. But I totally admired him. We argued, but it was never an angry argument. As I've said, he changed my worldview. My life. And it hasn't changed back. He got me to understand the roots of the environmental movement, and the deep concerns that he had, and what we've lost in this society. And I also respected—even though it was irritating to me—I respected his nonstop fanaticism. Because I realized that's what really works. That's what unique people do, people who are just going to go nonstop, no matter what happens. They're going to just keep doing it. And he was that way. He just was like…he didn't care. If it bugged you, he didn't care, he would just keep doing it if he felt it was necessary to do it.

And also he was so responsive. He was *so* responsive. The idea for the Earth National Park Ad, I'm not sure now, but I think that was my idea. But it came only because he was talking about it all the time. He was constantly talking about how we've got to find a way to stop all this excess development. On the whole planet. We've got to start thinking of the whole planet as a conservation project. We can't just do little bitty things about watersheds, or rivers, or lakes, or mountains. We have to do the whole thing, because the whole thing has been so overrun. And he was talking to me about that all the time. Finally I said, "Yeah, we really ought to make an ad. Now we have space travel. Pretty soon we'll be headed for other planets, so probably we ought to designate Earth as a conservation district in this part of the universe." And he immediately said, *"Let's do that! Let's do that!"*

But then he had a second thought. "Let's talk about it," he said. "I'm not sure I can do that, unless we also talk about the books." The book budget was a different budget from the campaigning budget. So that's why we had the books in the ad. Because then he thought he could justify it out of the budget. So we had to put a lot about the books in the ad, a list of the Exhibit Format books and the others he had done at the Sierra Club. It was unfortunate, because they detracted from the ad, in a way. We talked about Earth National Park, we talked about the concept, and then we had to turn to the books. I had no idea that he didn't have permission to do this ad. I had no idea. I didn't have any idea of how any of that internal stuff worked at the Sierra Club.

When the Sierra Club fired Dave, he moved into the Firehouse. It was Howard's idea. "Dave has been fired. We have this office downstairs, we're only using a couple of desks down there. We'll bring those desks upstairs and let Dave have that." Dave was immediately for it. He started Friends of the Earth downstairs. I think that space was free. I don't think we charged him anything—not for a while, at least. It wasn't a big space. It was enough for a couple of offices, basically, with a little central workspace. So Friends of the Earth started at the Firehouse. From there it spread all around the world, fifty or sixty sister organizations everywhere.

Dave could really work. He was on it all the time, nonstop. And he had a nice, gracious way about him, too. He would be buddy-buddy, invite you to lunch, and have a bunch of drinks, tell jokes, and have a good time. He'd always be gracious, and he'd give credit. He always spread the credit around.

He remade the Sierra Club. What had formerly been a companions-on-the-trail hiking club was now a very potent environmental movement. The membership of the Sierra Club increased enormously. Stewart Udall credited Brower, and the ads, with creating a new kind of movement, a new environmental movement, which was much more active. But Dave wanted it to be still broader. He was the first environmentalist who really wanted to see it hooked to economic issues, to military issues, to social justice issues, to race issues. And he was very eager for that to happen.

When I quit commercial advertising, I decided to do this kind of thing for the rest of my life. Five years after I met Dave, I was no longer doing any commercial work at all. I was completely devoted to non-profit work of one kind or another. Some was environmental work, but also a lot of other stuff. I started to do similar ads for Greenpeace, and for indigenous groups. When I first got involved with indigenous peoples, it was also in the sixties. I got approached by a woman named

Marie-Hélène Laraque, an Arawak from Haiti. Wonderful person. Very, very active in indigenous causes. She got me involved in it, and I did a lot of indigenous ads. We had a lot to do with helping the Cree in their fight against the James Bay Hydroelectric Project, up in Quebec. We did ads with the Maya Indians against the government of Guatemala, which was screwing them over.

And I started doing women's movement ads. Abortion rights. We did the original abortion rights campaign that got abortion legalized. In some ways, as important as the Sierra Club ads were, the Grand Canyon ads, and so on, I think probably the abortion rights ads had as much influence. Not in terms of public consciousness, maybe, but from a political point of view, it was successful. Those ads were very powerful. And they achieved something. They changed something. A lot of these ads *changed* something.

The ads I've done have probably been more influential than the books I've done. Books influence people, but they don't start movements. Books change people's heads, but ads are written on specific issues. Some of these ads, when they appeared, they would just stop the thing cold. They'd appear, and that would be the end of the problem, whatever it was.

The first ad I did in this whole line of ads—the start of this whole kind of ad making—was the first Grand Canyon ad I did for Dave. I'm telling you, Dave was the man. He got me turned on. Dave had a lot to do with the rest of my life.

David Brower and Tom Turner at Point Reyes
Photograph by Patricia Sarr

TOM TURNER

TOM TURNER, recently retired as senior editor at Earthjustice, writes now at home, having converted his son's old room into an office. On the day of the interview, his alto saxophone rested on a music stand near his desk. In the low illumination of the room, the horn gleamed golden. The brass captured most of the available light, then burnished and reradiated it. If this were the Egyptian wing of the museum, then the sax was Tutankhamen's mask. Sheet music on the stand was open, as it happened, to a composition called "Cleopatra's Dream." On the windowsill, backlit by the late-morning sun, grew an orchid. Alongside, in a blue vase, was a spray of pale-gold rattlesnake grass from Point Reyes National Seashore.

Above Turner's desk, framed on the eastern wall, was a poem by Gary Snyder, a copy handwritten by the poet himself. The title was Snyderesque: "Why log truck drivers rise earlier than students of Zen." Beside the poem, framed too, was a letter to Turner from Pete Seeger. "Dear Tom, *Not Man Apart* is a 10-times better publication whenever you are writing it. Please, please do not resign without letting all the members of Friends of the Earth know. We will get in there & fight for you."

Beneath these words of encouragement, Turner's computer screen was aglow with notes toward a biography. His desktop was piled with materials for this project: a life of David Brower, his boss at the Sierra Club and Friends of the Earth.

Turner is sixty-nine, a middleweight of middle height. For most of the past half century he has been bald, and for much of that period he has worn a thick compensatory mustache. The mustache may also owe something to his stint in the Peace Corps in Turkey. In his youth it had the dark, bristly luxuriance through which a Turkish male, raising with fingertips the hot, handle-free demitasse of his *fincan,* strains his morning coffee. Turner's salaried career divides into four parts: Peace Corps, Sierra Club, Friends of the Earth, Earthjustice. He never goes by "Thomas," not even on the mastheads of the environmental journals he has edited, or on the title pages of his books. In those books, *Sierra Club: 100 Years of Protecting Nature,* and *The Sierra Club Legal Defense Fund and the Places It Has Saved,* and *Justice on Earth: Earthjustice and the People It Has Served,* he is credited as just plain Tom. His salient virtues are steadiness and calm, traits that served him well through the many years he worked with David Brower—traits, indeed, that made those many years possible.

On the north wall, beyond the saxophone, was a broadside designed by the great typographer Bruce Rogers and set, under Rogers's direction, by Mackenzie & Harris, the San Francisco type foundry that typeset almost all the books that Brower published at the Sierra Club and Friends of the Earth.

"CENTAUR AND ARRIGHI," read the headline, in giant letters of Centaur type. The text began, in Venetian Renaissance style, with a rubric—a big illustrated initial—in this case the letter *I.* The illustration within the rectangle of the rubric was by Bruce Rogers himself, a line drawing, vaguely medieval, that rendered the *I* as an ionic column rising among the trees of a forest. Standing four-legged under the boughs, reaching up to pluck fruit, is a centaur, half man and half horse. "IT IS NOW EASY TO OBTAIN Centaur Roman of Bruce Rogers & Arrighi Italic of Frederic Warde in foundry metal, in all the existing sizes."

Foundry metal!

How time flies. The 4800 years between the invention of cuneiform writing and Gutenberg's invention of the printing press were less eventful, technologically, than the fifty years between the first Sierra Club photo books, set in foundry metal, and the computerized printing of today. The Sierra Club's pioneering large-format books are of nearly Mesopotamian antiquity.

The text of the broadside was written by Robert Grabhorn, of San Francisco's legendary Grabhorn Press. It begins in tiny six-point type, the smallest Centaur available. At first this seems a perverse choice. Grabhorn's opening, his "Call me Ishmael" or his "Arma virumque cano," looks like literature for ants. But the fine print is effective. The typographer speaks so softly in six-point type that the listener must lean forward to hear.

THE STORY OF THE MAKING OF THIS CENTAUR TYPE PROPERLY BEGINS IN VENICE IN THE fifteenth century, in spite of Bruce Rogers' years of application to it in the twentieth; for in 1470, Nicolas Jenson's fine roman made its first appearance. It was the third, or possibly the fourth, pure roman, and was undoubtedly a type rendering of a very fine humanistic manuscript letter. Jenson's type brought forth lavish praise in his own time even from himself; but how much of this acclaim was due to the merits of the type itself and how much to Jenson's superb craftsmanship as a printer is material for conjecture that could be just as fruitfully applied to Rogers and his Centaur.

Tom Turner's boss was married to Centaur. David Brower and the typeface were fused at the waist, like the centaur himself, the horse-man of Bruce Rogers's broadside. My father despaired of ugly fonts. He particularly hated what he called "studhorse type," the heavy, inelegant, sans serif fonts offered up by typographers who have forgot that type is supposed to be beautiful. Having discovered Centaur and Arrighi, he saw no need to try anything else. He sometimes claimed that if someone ever showed him a cleaner, more eloquent font, then he might consider switching. Nobody ever did.

Part of his enthusiasm for Centaur surely had to do with its evolutionary history. My father was a big fan of evolution. In his youth, after the blindness and death of his mother, he lost his Christian faith, and his sense of the numinous settled instead on Creation, in particular on the infinite artistry of natural selection. As Robert Grabhorn suggests in his six-point paragraph, Centaur traces back in its phylogeny to 1470 and the Roman typeface introduced by Nicolas Jenson, which was in its turn a rendering of older manuscript letters, which is to say that Centaur is the wormhole through which Bruce Rogers tumbled back to the era of the Old Norse sagas and found himself in the company of the Icelandic scribes who set those sagas down on sheepskin, in ink boiled from willow and bearberry, using quills they carved intricately from the flight feathers of ravens, eagles, geese, and swans, plucked from the left wing, preferably, as those were believed to rest easier in the hand. Centaur is a font that has stood the test of time. As such, there is something like organic truth in it.

If, as David Brower once suggested to Jerry Mander, we experience our campfires exactly as our Paleolithic forebears did, if it is true we really are the same people—our fronts hot from the blaze, our backs cold from the night, the tribe gathered in a circle of fire-tinted faces, the vast dark universe beginning just beyond the reach of the firelight, each face mesmerized by the glow, reciting or listening, watching our tales and tropes and creation myths take shape in the flames—then we are also the stonemasons who chiseled the first Centaur-like letters in the marble pediments of Rome.

What my father saw in the Bruce Rogers broadside—what he saw in Centaur and Arrighi on any page—was craftsmanship that lived and breathed. In the handset display type of the title pages and chapter heads of the big Sierra Club books, the typesetter, in loading his composition stick, had "leads" to space out the lines vertically. He had quads and spacers to vary horizontally the distance between letters and words. He was a kind of blue-collar poet scanning the lines of our books. Even when he sat at the keyboard of the monotype caster, typing out sentences as a single slug, he had latitude in how to justify the line. The human eye wants to harmonize. The machine doesn't care.

My father had framed copies of the Centaur and Arrighi broadside in his house and office. I have always kept one in mine. My brother Bob, who was drafted into service doing "mechanicals" for the Exhibit Format books and for the Friends of the Earth monthly, *Not Man Apart,* had one, too. Tom Turner liberated his copy long ago from the Friends of the Earth office in New York, where some philistine had removed it from the wall and stashed it under the staircase.

In Turner's pile of research materials for his Brower biography was a nine-by-twelve-inch broadside called "A Gift from the Tree." Produced in 1969, shortly after my father and Turner were fired by the Sierra Club, the broadside was sent out to charter members of Friends of the Earth, my father's new organization. Stapled to the bottom in a tiny clear envelope

was the seed of a giant sequoia. The text was by David Brower. The seed
had been collected in the Sierra Nevada by Turner.

A

GIFT

FROM

THE

TREE

(and from Friends of the Earth)

One day, about two and a half millenniums ago, when things were
just right for it, a small seed began the process of putting together
the exact amounts of air, water, soil, and solar energy to form what
would be the Wawona Tree.

Most of the seed was a wing, to carry it far in the wind. Within
the seed itself was a wealth of vital, unique, secret information,
packed with great efficiency in very little space. It would inform
the tree and all its parts, specifying the thickness of bark near the
base and the thinness near the top, the number of branches, the
density of foliage, the suppleness in wind, the process of pumping
water nearly three hundred feet above the ground, the insulation
against heat and cold, the resistance to fire and disease and drouth,
and placing and depth of roots, with notes about which food they
were to select, the adaptability to varying sites—a long list of things
a tree ought to know, each essential, none superfluous.

And the seed was also told how to produce a cone with seeds
in it, each of them containing life directly descended from the first
life on earth, some to germinate quickly and some slowly, and very
few to succeed fully.

By the time of the first Christmas the tree was a handsome young
giant, perhaps fifteen feet through and two hundred feet tall. Nearly
nineteen hundred years later (in 1864) President Lincoln signed the
bill including the tree and its grove in the nation's first park.

People journeyed to the grove from all over the world to mar-
vel at the tree. As more people came, it was inevitable that some

would wonder what to do with it, and one visitor advocated cutting a tunnel through it to demonstrate how big it was. The tunnel was cut four decades ago, and horse-drawn stages and internal combustion–driven vehicles passed through it, as everyone who has read a geography book knows quite well. Thanks to man, the tree became the most famous of all.

Then somehow cars became longer and wider, with more space inside and less space outside—so much less that there was often not enough room for the tunnel. What with its imminent obsolescence, the National Park Service built a new road right over the downhill roots of the tree so that wide-car drivers could see it and pass it by.

Sometime in the big-snow winter of 1968–69—the kind that the tree had often weathered and had withstood even after the tunnel was cut—the big tree fell and shattered. Its fragments blocked the tunnel road but not the side road over the roots. So many people wanted to stop to see the fallen tree, however, that even that road had to be blocked off. Last summer people by the thousands parked their cars and walked half a mile to see the tree that fell because the seed it came from did not tell it how to cope with the automobile.

A seed shaken from a cone lying among the fragments of the Wawona Tree's crown is affixed here. It can produce a tree that will live beautifully for three thousand years or so. If it fails to do so, please return it.

I'VE TRIED TO figure out when this all began. And it began with my birth, because Anne Brower and my mom were good friends. Your mom babysat me before she was married, I think. In fact, I know she did. The two of them worked together at the Admissions Office and the Registrar's Office at the University of California before your mom was married, and probably before my mom was married, too. Mine got married in '36. So I would have met Dave as soon as he came back from the war.

Anne and Dave Brower used to show up at Christmas cocktail parties. I didn't know them very well. There was one such party in 1964, when I was just about to graduate from Cal, finally, and I was talking to Dave. We were standing in the living room at my folks' house, talking about—I don't remember what. But all of a sudden your father interrupted me and said, "You have a nice speaking voice, would you consider narrating a film for the Sierra Club?" And I said, "Sure."

It was a surprise. It was out of left field. Nobody had told me I had a good speaking voice. The film was a slide show of Glen Canyon put together by Phil Pennington and made into a movie by Larry Dawson. We went to Dawson's studio, and I remember almost having to trot to keep up with Dave, swinging his long legs. He was in very good shape then. So I did the original narration. Later they wanted to make some changes, but I was gone into the Peace Corps by then, so they got a guy from KQED who was a pro. The version that was distributed most widely didn't have my narration on it. But I did the first one.

Dave paid me with three Exhibit Format books. Two copies of the Glen Canyon book and one copy of the Grand Canyon book.

Then in 1965, on spring break, we all went to Glen Canyon. The reservoir, Lake Powell, was half full or so, and the only place you could go anymore was the Escalante River and its side canyons. We could go into the Cathedral in the Desert, and Davis Gulch, and Hummingbird, and Coyote Gulch, and so forth. Dick Norgaard organized that trip. Lou Elliot and at least one of his daughters were the boat people. My whole family was there. Your whole family was there. And the photographers, Phil Hyde and Dave Bohn, and their wives. The proposal to build two dams in the Grand Canyon was being considered then in Washington. Your dad would give little pep talks around the campfire after dinner every night. He said, "You see what's going on here, this flooding. We can't let this happen in the Grand Canyon." It was very moving. I think that was it for me. That's when I really first thought that if I could figure out a way to participate in this sort of work, I would sure like to do it.

Then I went out to Turkey with the Peace Corps and spent two years in a village in the eastern Black Sea region, and afterward I traveled around Europe for three or four months. From London I wrote a letter to Dave Brower saying that I would love to be of service to the Sierra Club somehow. I don't know biology. I don't know photography. I'm no writer. I don't have any particular talents to offer, except enthusiasm and energy. And he never answered, of course. Correspondence was not his strong point, to say the least. But he remembered that letter, because he mentioned it later.

So I got back to America and got a job at Head Start headquarters in San Francisco, through a Peace Corps connection. It was just a low-level, menial job. There was a fellow there named Martin Schweitzer, who was also working for Head Start. He was a photographer in his spare time, and I thought a very good one. Martin and I backpacked a little bit together. He took close abstracts of Nature, mostly. We were down at his house one night looking at his slides, and I thought they were really wonderful. I said, "You know, I know David Brower a little bit." And his eyes lit up. The Sierra Club books were then the only game in town. I mean, if you were a Nature photographer, that would be your ideal—to get something published by the Sierra Club.

Martin said, "You gotta introduce me to Brower! You gotta get him to look at my pictures!" And I thought, *Oh, Jesus, what have I got myself in for? Brower must get appeals like this all the time.* And he did.

I kept putting Martin off, but he nagged and pestered, and I finally said, "Okay, I'll see what I can do." I phoned the Sierra Club and talked first probably to Linda Billings, who passed me off to Ann Chamberlain, Dave's secretary, who made it clear I wasn't getting through to Dave Brower unless I had a better story than I'd come up with so far. So that afternoon I got home from work and I called the Brower house. And your mom answered. We chatted a minute. She said, "Dave isn't here yet, but I'll have him call you when he gets home." And I said, "No, no, no, no! No, I'll call back. Never mind."

Well, a couple of minutes later, Dave did call. He said, "Before you tell me what you want to ask me, why don't you come up here? There's somebody you might like to meet." So I did. And the somebody was Norman Clyde. The great old climber, the grand old man of the Sierra Nevada. Norman was in town for a cataract operation. He was eighty-three then, as I recall. And he was scared. He was going to have his eye operated on at Alta Bates Hospital and he was worried about that. He was up at your folks' house to get a little courage and support. So we got to talking. Norman started telling stories about his first ascents and his rescues. He was pushing salt shakers and things around on the table, saying, "Well, this is this such and such minaret, and this is the Palisades," and so forth.

At one point he stopped and said, "Dave, when are you going to publish my book?" And Dave said, "That depends on whether I can talk Tom here into coming to work on it." Well, I'd never, ever done anything like that in my life. It was Dave coming out of left field again. I'd hardly ever written anything, except for school, and letters, and so on. And so I said, "Sure. Okay."

Norman had done a lot of writing for magazines and kept journals and so on. And the idea was to put together a selection of his writing. It was to be Norman's story as part of the history of the Sierra, and of California. Well, your dad through the evening kept my glass full of scotch. So I was really plastered by the time we got to this point. Finally, at the end, Dave said, "What is it that you wanted to talk about?" And I told him, "Well, I have a friend who I think is a really good photographer." I could see Dave sort of deflate a little. I think he was disappointed that I had asked him that.

Anyway, I was drunk enough that I had to call up the next day to make sure that this job offer was really for real. And it was. And so I gave notice at Head Start, and went to work at the Sierra Club in the library. I didn't get an office for a while. Dave had a whole box full of Norman's magazine articles and journals. I read them all and tried to pick out a representative sample. The problem was that they were all the same. When I got the selections made and a few chapters put together, Bob Golden, the general services manager of the Sierra Club, did a mean thing to me. He just read aloud the first and the last paragraphs from each of them. There wasn't any difference. Norman always started with something like, "I set off down the path with the rosy dawn licking the tops of the mountains." Norman was not a great writer.

One day, I'll never forget, I was working in the library and it came to be lunchtime. Dave came and said, "Would you like to have lunch?" I said, "Sure." We went to In the Alley, with Hugh Nash and Bob Golden and Cliff Rudden. They all ordered a martini. So I ordered a martini. And then they all ordered another martini. By the time lunch was done I went back to the library and put my head down on the table and slept all afternoon. It takes a little practice to do this.

The Sierra Club never published the Norman Clyde book. It was a casualty of the battle that was just getting underway then between Dave and the board. Eventually Scrimshaw Press did a much shorter version of it. But I did my version of the Clyde book. It was a real toss-you-into-the-deep-end sort of experience, because I didn't know what I was doing. And then the terrible battle over Dave's tenure at the Sierra Club began, and I spent a lot of time trying to help with that effort. Six days after Dave resigned from the Sierra Club, I got fired, along with Hugh Nash, the *Sierra Club Bulletin* editor.

In his resignation speech Dave announced the new organization, as yet unnamed. With this new outfit, he said, he would be doing the things the Sierra Club didn't want him to do, like publishing and international conservation. That was in May of '69. There were a lot of people who wrote to him and said, "Okay, what are you going to do? We want to help." I had just moved into this house, actually, and I remember typing letters downstairs, answering people, saying, "Well, thank you, we'll put your name on the list, and we'll let you know when the announcement is ready."

It was around then I made my drive up to the Wawona Tree.

The Wawona Tree, the "Tunnel Tree," was a famous giant sequoia in Mariposa Grove in Yosemite. It had fallen sometime in the winter that Dave got chased out of the Sierra Club. It was 90 feet in circumference and 227 feet tall. In the 1880s, a tunnel was carved in it, and the road passed through. In winter of 1969 it fell under the weight of a big snow load.

On the front page of the *Chronicle*, on the morning Dave was forced to resign, was an Ansel Adams photograph of the Wawona Tree when it was still standing. There's an old Pierce-Arrow parked by the cut and a man beside it. The figure is too distant to make out. He's not identified in the picture. It's David Brower. The picture was taken decades before Dave's resignation, by his chief adversary, or one of them, Ansel Adams. John McPhee writes about this in *Encounters with the Archdruid*, and he says it's likely that on the day of the resignation, only two people in the room, Ansel and Dave, knew who that figure was. The *Chronicle* caption was "A Fallen Giant."

So Dave got the idea of writing this essay, "A Gift from the Tree." It was to be a thank-you note to charter members of Friends of the Earth. My then girlfriend, Trish Sarr, and I drove up to Mariposa Grove in my MG. I can't remember whether Dave asked us to do it, or we volunteered. But certainly when the idea came up, I would have volunteered immediately. I mean, it was a great trip. There was still a lot of snow on the ground, especially around the tree.

It was an amazing coincidence. The tree fell and then Dave fell. The tree fell that winter, but no one saw it, so it didn't make any noise. But the *Chronicle* had it on the front page the day Brower resigned from the Club. I never heard Dave say so in so many words, but all this could have been somewhere in the back of his mind—fallen giants—when he wrote this piece. I don't know.

We didn't have to put chains on the MG or anything. But it was cold. Lots of snow. I can't remember whether the convertible top was up or down. We had to hike quite a ways to get up to the tree. It had shattered when it fell, and it was in many pieces. It was easy enough to find little cones, and we just tapped the cones and picked out the seeds, until we had hundreds of them. I mean, it was a felony, I suppose. It was certainly a misdemeanor. And then we came back. I don't remember whether Dave had already written the essay. But it got written. And then somebody got little tiny plastic bags, and we stuck them in, and stapled the bag to this one-sheet essay, and sent them to charter members of Friends of the Earth, of whom there were a few hundred.

• • •

Friends of the Earth was incorporated on July 11, 1969, but it wasn't announced to the public until September or maybe October. The announcement said, Brower's back. His new organization is going be bold, and uncompromising, and active, and it will be soliciting members. The thing that caught the attention of the media was the announcement that a division of Friends of the Earth was going to be called the League of Conservation Voters. With LCV, Dave was going to try to rally conservationists to get involved in the political process, and make sure that decent candidates ran and were elected to office. That was new. The rest of it was not quite so new. It just reemphasized what Dave had always stood for. So LCV led the news that day.

After about six months or so, we got up to a thousand members. The early money for Friends of the Earth came from book advances Dave got from McCall Books. He got an advance to do ten or twelve Exhibit Format books in what was called The Earth's Wild Places Series. He got a good piece of change for that, so we got on the payroll. George Alderson came on as the representative in Washington. Dale Jones pretty soon comes on in Seattle. Almost all these first people had previously been with the Sierra Club.

The first Friends of the Earth newsletter was called *Muir and Friends*. After the third *Muir and Friends*, we started talking about doing something more substantial. Dave sent out a memo suggesting various names, and he then decided by himself that it was going to be called *Not Man Apart*, which had been the title of a Sierra Club book. He brought Hugh Nash in, the former editor of the *Sierra Club Bulletin*, who had been unemployed since being sacked by the Club. Dave asked Hugh if he would be editor of *Not Man Apart*, and he made me the managing editor. My girlfriend, Trish Sarr, was an assistant.

We were in the Firehouse then, Engine No. 1, where Freeman, Mander & Gossage was upstairs, and Warren Hinkle was in the back, working on a magazine called *Scanlon's*, which lasted about a year. I remember one time at the Firehouse, right at the beginning of Friends of the Earth. There was a little patio out behind the back office. It had a fountain and a little pool, a goldfish pond or something. Somebody called and said a baby bird had fallen into the water and was about to drown. Your dad raced back there and picked it up and cupped it in his hand. And just comforted it and let it dry off. And talked to it for fifteen or twenty minutes. And there were phone calls coming in all the while. He said, "Oh, I'll get back to it," and he continued conversing with this bird.

Dave did have a habit of impulsively looking for talent that often worked out well, but sometimes not. At one point, there in the Firehouse, this young guy walked in the front door, and introduced himself as Chris Condon from Seattle, who worked on a paper called the *Northwest Passage,* which actually was a pretty good weekly. Dave was away on the road. Turned out that your father had been up in Seattle giving a talk, and as usual he went to the bar afterwards to continue the talk with anybody who was interested. Chris was very interested. He started bending Dave's ear about how Friends of the Earth really should have a proper newspaper, magazine, whatever you called it. One pitfall of conversations like that is that people can come away with different understandings of what has been agreed to. So Chris came into the office and said, "Well, Dave Brower has hired me to be the production manger of a new magazine, and I've just rented space from *Rolling Stone,* can you please give me a check for three thousand dollars?" And I said, "No, I can't. I don't have it. And I wouldn't do it anyway. I don't know you from Adam."

Dave still wasn't back yet. When he did come back, he said, "Well, no" to the magazine. Maybe we would start something, but it would have to be a lot more modest than that. So Chris was taken on as production manager of *Not Man Apart.* Now it was Hugh Nash and me and Trish and Chris Condon. And Chris was a disaster. He lasted for two issues. He was always late, couldn't meet a deadline. He'd come in at four in the afternoon and work all night snortin' coke and stuff. Bob Brower was hired to do the production work. Hugh Nash moved to the country and became senior editor, and I became the editor.

Very soon new Friends of the Earths began springing up internationally. Sister organizations began incorporating overseas. The first one was in France, Les Amis de la Terre, in 1969. Then came in England in 1971, and then Sweden. There are more than seventy now, but those three were the start.

In late '71, Dave Brower and Teddy Goldsmith got together somewhere. Teddy was publisher of *The Ecologist* magazine, which was new. He and Dave decided, either together or independently, that it would be a good idea to publish a daily newssheet at the Stockholm Conference on the Human Environment, which was to be held in June of '72. They got together and decided to make it a joint publication. This was the first *Eco*. It was mostly staffed by people from *The Ecologist* and from Friends of the Earth in London, which was going great guns by then. So we put this thing out every day for two weeks. There were two editors-of-the-day, and they would rotate back and forth. One day it would be Robert Allen and Mike Allerby from *The Ecologist,* and the other day it was me and Amory Lovins from Friends of the Earth. It was great fun. Your dad was making suggestions and contributing pieces.

The cartoonist Richard Wilson was on the crew. More than anyone he was responsible for the look of *Eco*. He's brilliant. He's absolutely brilliant. He would hover around and ask, "What stories have you got going today?" He'd read them, and then he'd disappear. Half an hour later he'd come back with four or five finished cartoons. He was incredibly fast. Just wonderfully talented.

We put this thing together in a school, not in central Stockholm, but someplace out by the outskirts. Lennart Daléus, who was cofounder of Jordens Vänner, the Swedish Friends of the Earth, had arranged it. He went on to become the leader of Sweden's Center Party and now he's general secretary for Greenpeace in Sweden. At the Stockholm conference, Lennart recruited a lot of volunteers from Jordens Vänner to distribute the *Eco*. This was all done on manual typewriters, with Letraset headlines. And these typewriters were Swedish, so the letters were in the wrong place. It was really a bitch to get type set that was clean.

The Stockholm delegates were trying to put together a green declaration. They wanted a document such that if they got nothing else out of this conference, at least they'd have something that they could take home with them. It was assumed that it would just be passed on a unanimous voice vote. But about halfway through, the Chinese said, "Just a minute, we would like to offer an alternate declaration." The Chinese had just joined the UN. In fact their joining had caused the Russians—the Soviets—to boycott the Stockholm conference. So now the Chinese wanted to be heard. There was a secret session, a plenary of one delegate from each country, closed to the press, closed to the public, where the Chinese introduced their alternate declaration. It said, in essence, "Man is the most important species and everything else is in service to him. So, be a little careful about all this touchy-feely ecosystem stuff."

Well, we had a spy. I'm sworn to secrecy, so I better not tell you who. But we had a spy in there, and we got the full text of the declaration, taken down by shorthand. So the spy came back and transcribed the declaration, and somebody else wrote a commentary about how stupid it was—how foolish the Chinese draft was, and how it missed the point. And we sent it off to the press. We just couldn't sleep. We were up all night, just waiting for this thing to come back. Teddy Goldsmith had rented an apartment—he had endless money—and so we all went over there and drank and talked and waited for the delivery of the paper. It came at about five in the morning. Dave was there. Amory Lovins and Walt Patterson were there.

It was just so exciting. We had scooped the world. There were something like twelve hundred journalists there, from every country, *The New York Times* and *Asahi Shimbun*, all the big papers. And we had beaten them all. With this big banner headline, "China Declares..." I went to three or four press conferences afterward, and that was all any of the reporters wanted to talk about. They'd say, "Is this report in *Eco* accurate?" And delegates said, "Yep, yep, that's right." All of a sudden *Eco* was the first thing everybody wanted to read in the morning. We were flying high after that.

Eco continued for a long time. We published *Eco* at various meetings and conferences through the years. Later that same summer, 1972, Henry Kendall, who was a physicist at Harvard, and also a wealthy guy—he had a family foundation that saved Friends of the Earth more than once—Henry was very concerned about nuclear power plants. He and a guy named Daniel Ford had started the Union of Concerned Scientists, and one of the early things they did was to force the Atomic Energy Commission to hold hearings into the emergency core-cooling systems of reactors. Kendall and Ford were worried about the possibility of the very disaster that just occurred in Fukushima. There was some question, back then, about whether the tests of the emergency core-cooling systems had been run properly. It was a very, very technical and complicated matter. But Kendall had forced the AEC to hold hearings and listen to people like himself and Dan Ford and John Gofman and the other critics. This is when Ralph Nader's interest in nuclear safety peaked, as well.

Well, Henry called up and said, "Dave, we can't get any publicity for this thing! Nobody's paying attention to these hearings." *The Times* sent somebody who stayed there a couple of hours and left. Dave Brower decided we should do an *Eco* there. So he called me, and he got Amory Lovins and Walt Patterson to come over from London. Richard Wilson came out to do his cartoons. We published an *Eco* three days a week for the three weeks of the hearings. We had to pull all-nighters. I stayed up ten nights out of eighteen. I was younger then. It was brutal. The hearings were out at Bethesda, but we worked at the Friends of the Earth office, which was on Capitol Hill. It was D.C. in summer. Ninety degrees and just foul air. We scrounged up mailing lists. There was nobody to distribute it to, really, so we scrounged up mailing lists from all the antinuclear groups and mailed out two or three thousand copies of this, and tried to get reporters interested. It helped.

You got to keep pushin' and pushin', and something's going to spark somebody's interest. One thing that I learned along the way is that you can work your butt off, and do research, and write a story, and it disappears. But if it fires up one or two people it can be worth it. This particular *Eco* encouraged little groups here and there, people worried about nuclear safety. They came to believe there was somebody out there who understood what they'd been talking about, somebody who was working toward the same end.

Then *Eco* went to the International Whaling Commission meetings. In 1977 the IWC was held in Canberra. I was in Auckland, New Zealand, on sabbatical. David McTaggart of Greenpeace called up and said, "You got to get your ass over here, we need coverage of what's going on at this meeting." McTaggart had heard about the Stockholm *Eco* and the emergency core-cooling *Eco*. So I went to Canberra and the IWC meeting and we did an *Eco* there.

In 1978 the IWC meeting was held in London, and we had another scoop-the-world moment.

The IWC Commissioner from Panama, Jean-Paul Fortom-Gouin, had persuaded the Panamanian government to let him propose a resolution for a ten-year moratorium on commercial whaling. Fortom-Gouin was a French citizen of Moroccan extraction, and he was now a resident of Florida and the Bahamas. He had business interests in Panama and sometimes lived there. It had been five years since any whaling moratorium had been proposed at the IWC. Because there was no hope. The Japanese were just going to roll everybody. But Fortom-Gouin had introduced it. And then one day he came to us, at the Friends of the Earth UK office in Soho, where we were busy organizing the first issue of *Eco*. Representatives from about a dozen environmental groups, mostly English and American, were in there, planning demonstrations and plotting strategy.

"I've been dismissed as chairman of the Panamanian delegation," Fortom-Gouin told us. He said that the Japanese had threatened Panama over sugar contracts, or something like that. The ambassador had informed him that the new commissioner, who was to be the ambassador himself, would be withdrawing the moratorium resolution as soon as the IWC meeting began. Everybody wanted to go straight to the press with this, but I said, "No! No! Let's save it for *Eco*." And again, we scooped the world. This really, really got attention.

Not Man Apart went from monthly to fortnightly starting in '74. It was a killer. We got one extra position. Dave wanted it to be weekly. That was his goal for a long time. Never quite happened. After a couple of years, I was just beat. I mean, you finish one and you're late for the next one. Producing a journal every two weeks, when you have only about six people working on it, it was just crazy.

It didn't last too long. We were hurtin' for money. We were always hurtin' for money. Pretty soon it went back to monthly. But by then I was beat. I remember we were out at lunch and I said, "Dave, you know, I've been working here seven years, more than seven years, and I'm exhausted. I think I should get a sabbatical." He said, "Well, you've been reading my old speeches." He had given a talk at the Commonwealth Club in the early '60s saying something to the effect that universities shouldn't have a monopoly on this great idea, the sabbatical. A sabbatical makes sense for almost anybody. Work for six years and then take a year off—six months or a year—and recharge your batteries and think about new things. So we agreed that Trish and I would go on a sabbatical.

The formula we worked out was that we would spend six months at two-thirds pay working with an existing Friends of the Earth group, or trying to get one started somewhere else. Your folks had just come back from New Zealand. Your mom said that if she were to consider living anyplace else, she would think about living in New Zealand. She loved it. So we offered our services to Friends of the Earth New Zealand. We flew over there, got off the plane, and thereby doubled the size of their staff. The one detail that your father had neglected to do anything about was getting approval, or funding, for this. When the executive committee of Friends of the Earth heard about this, they said, "We don't have money for something like this! Are you nuts?" So our pay was taken out of Dave's speaking fees. Not for the first time, or the last.

David Gancher was to be the acting editor of *Not Man Apart* when I left. He was going to do it for six months. The plan was for us to stay in New Zealand for six months and then travel the rest of the way around the world, stop in Turkey, and maybe even try to get something going for Friends of the Earth in Turkey. But around about April, David Gancher took a job on *Sierra* magazine, earning twice as much money at the Sierra Club. Your Dad, I think without consulting anybody—certainly without consulting me—went and asked Stephanie Mills to edit *Not*

Man Apart. Stephanie had been working writing fundraising letters for a while. I didn't know anything about this hire. Well Natalie Roberts, the administrative director of Friends of the Earth, called me up and said, "I think you should know that Dave has offered Stephanie the job as editor of *Not Man Apart*." I was pissed.

Not terribly long after that, Natalie resigned. I don't know why. She was just tired, I guess. Your dad called me in Auckland, and said, "I need you to come back and take over as administrative director." I told him I didn't know whether I'd be any good at that, but I'd do it on the condition that I could return to *Not Man Apart* after six months, if he was unhappy with my performance, or if I was unhappy with my performance, on the new job. He said okay. For once in my life I had the presence of mind to write this down, and sent him a letter, and Natalie a copy, saying, "Okay, agreed today, orally on the phone," and I spelled it out. So now Stephanie Mills was really bummed out, I'm told, and I can certainly believe it.

I came back and tried to be administrative director, but I was no good at it, and I didn't like it at all. So I went to your dad and said, "I can't do this anymore. I want to get back to *Not Man Apart*, that's what I like the best." He didn't want to hear that. So we worked out this deal where I would become Executive Director of Friends of the Earth and editor-in-chief and publisher of all Friends of the Earth books and *Not Man Apart* and all the rest of it. I actually drafted a letter for his signature, announcing this, and never sent it. It just was crazy.

Then, right about that time, spring of '78, Stephanie cracked and quit. It was too much pressure. Here I was looming over her, so she quit. So I was back as editor of *Not Man Apart*.

Dave's diplomatic skills were not his strongest suit.

As a talker before a crowd, Dave could really inspire. He could get people believing that they themselves could make a difference in the way of the world. And he could make them want to do it.

He was usually a good listener. When I had suggestions to make, he would hear me out. He was always trying to find ways to make things work. And that was a big strength. Of course, it also sometimes happened that these things manifestly weren't going to work, and it was time to cut your losses, and not spend any more time on them. He was not so good at that. Cutting losses was not one of his strengths. Every once in a while he would come up with some idea that I thought was just *impractical*, to put it charitably. Just not serious. So I'd nod and grin and talk about it, and then forget about it. Sometimes *he* didn't forget about it. He'd say, "Tom, you can't just ignore these things!"

In some instances he was a little bit too open, I think. He got hooked up with some people I thought were just bullshit artists. Not to be taken seriously. They would try to take him for a ride. He was very open to people.

He was very, very quick to forgive. If not forget. I remember at the beginning of Friends of the Earth, we would have lunches up at Enrico's. It was Hugh Nash, Jack Schanhaar, sometimes Ron Keller, and me. And all we wanted to do was bitch about the Sierra Club, but your dad wasn't interested in that. He wanted to move on. He eventually reconciled with Ansel Adams, and Dick Leonard, I think, and Ed Wayburn. He made up with a lot of Sierra Club people who had said really nasty, foul things about him.

He was an amazing pack rat. He wouldn't throw anything away. When the Friends of the Earth office was on Commercial Street in San Francisco, there was a basement storage area, and we had cubic yards of *Not Man Apart*, bundles and bundles of the paper. The space filled up, and we needed more. So we decided we would recycle most of these things. We hauled it out and stacked it along the sidewalk. Your dad came by and said, "This is valuable stuff! We should give it to libraries, or something." And he made us take it all back downstairs again.

He wasn't very good with people he disagreed with. He wasn't a good politician. It got him in trouble at the Sierra Club. It got him in trouble at Friends of the Earth. I've heard a lot of people say that if only he had spent more time trying to work out compromises, or explore differences of opinion and misunderstandings. But he just didn't seem to have time for that.

The old friends who became his enemies thought he was reckless in defying the board, or in not following the board's orders, not checking things with the board. In his oral history, Martin Litton, his strongest ally, says that Dave's tendency was to take things so far down the road that it was too late to turn back before he would seek permission.

Sometimes I felt appreciated by Dave. Sometimes not. Somewhere in this stack of papers I came across a letter, I don't know if I ever sent it to him. But it said, "Have I done something wrong? You haven't invited me to lunch for six months." I used to go to lunch all the time, when he was in town, almost every day. I don't think I was in the doghouse particularly, but he could get distracted or go off on some project or another.

Once, early on, when I was at the Sierra Club, my back went out on me, and I had to have surgery for a slipped disk, which was a much bigger deal then than it is now. I let my beard grow. When I came back to work at the Club I had a beard. Dave bitched about it to your mom, and she mentioned it to my mom, who mentioned it to me, and I said, Screw this, if he wants to give me trouble about my beard, he can do it himself. I left it on for a long time, probably just out of stubbornness.

He changed my life, and all for the better.

The other day I was talking with Edwin Matthews, who succeeded Dave as president of Friends of the Earth. When I told Edwin I was thinking about writing a biography of Dave, he said, "Can you be objective?" He reminded me of an episode, and he remembers it the same way I do.

The background is that Edwin came to take over as president in '79, on the tenth anniversary of Friends of the Earth, at your dad's request and instigation. He uprooted himself from Paris and got transferred to San Francisco by his firm, Coudert Brothers. But it just didn't work. Edwin was trying to hold down a law job and run Friends of the Earth at the same time. He would say, "Okay, we're going to have a staff meeting at four o'clock on Friday afternoon." People would grumble and not show up.

Part of his problem was Founder's Syndrome in Dave. Friends of the Earth was Dave's organization, his baby, and he could not cut loose emotionally, take his hands completely off. He was hovering over the operation. But Dave was right to be concerned. It just wasn't working out with Edwin. Then it was getting down to the endgame, and the board was considering whether to sack Edwin or extend his contract for another year. It was a contest between Dave, the chairman, and Edwin, the president. Edwin called me over to his place—he was living in San Francisco—and he said, "I need your support on this. This is not working, and it's not fair, and I'm not being treated right." And I said no. I said, "I don't know all the details. I don't want to know all the details. But I'm a Brower guy. That's where it begins and ends. He plucked me from oblivion. I've worked for him all my working life. I'm not going to stop now."

Huey Johnson

HUEY JOHNSON

H UEY JOHNSON, for nine years the western regional director of the Nature Conservancy and then president of that organization, went on to become the founder of the Trust for Public Land, the Grand Canyon Trust, the Green Belt Movement International, and the Aldo Leopold Society, among other organizations, and he was secretary for resources for the State of California in the first administration of Governor Jerry Brown. He now runs the Resource Renewal Institute in Mill Valley, California.

On his office walls are trophy photographs, scenes of local landscapes that Johnson has snatched from developers through acquisition by his land trusts. One shows a sign, "Marincello," at the gateway to what was to have been fifty high-rises and a city of thirty thousand on the Marin Headlands, at the northern end of the Golden Gate Bridge. For $6.5 million, Johnson and the Nature Conservancy bought the site out from under the developer and transferred it to the Golden Gate National Recreation Area, which had just been established. Another photograph shows Kent Island in Bolinas Lagoon, which the Marin Audubon Society and Johnson's Nature Conservancy bought in a coup, thereby removing the centerpiece of a plan to fill the lagoon with restaurants, hotels, and a 1600-boatslip marina, while turning the two lanes of coastal Highway 1 into a four-lane thoroughfare.

On another wall is another sort of trophy, a rack of elk antlers. Johnson, a dedicated and unapologetic hunter and fisherman, shot the elk on the ranch of a wealthy tycoon he was cultivating. "I have it there as a symbol," he told me. "It's for PETA members who visit me. It rattles them."

In a back room with a copy machine is a wall dedicated to photographic portraits of Huey Johnson's heroes: Aldo Leopold towing firewood on a sled in what must be Wisconsin. Edward Abbey squinting into the sun in the Southwest. David Brower gesturing with a stick.

Beside the entrance to Johnson's inner office is an elegant little broadside called "Credo," a set of beliefs in capital letters, signed by David Brower:

> THERE IS BUT ONE OCEAN THOUGH ITS COVES
> HAVE MANY NAMES; A SINGLE SEA OF ATMOSPHERE,
> WITH NO COVES AT ALL; THE MIRACLE OF SOIL,
> ALIVE AND GIVING LIFE, LYING THIN ON THE ONLY
> EARTH, FOR WHICH THERE IS NO SPARE. WE SEEK
> A RENEWED STIRRING OF LOVE FOR THE EARTH.
> WE PLEAD THAT WHAT WE ARE CAPABLE OF DOING
> TO IT IS OFTEN WHAT WE OUGHT NOT TO DO. WE
> URGE THAT ALL PEOPLE NOW DETERMINE THAT AN
> UNTRAMMELED WILDNESS SHALL REMAIN HERE
> TO TESTIFY THAT THIS GENERATION HAD LOVE
> FOR THE NEXT.

FIRST ENCOUNTER with Dave, mine's a classic. I was raised in the Midwest and came out West after graduate school. I was really burning with passion. When I got out of school, I applied to fifty environmental organizations and didn't get one answer. So I drove to Michigan to start a doctoral program. I was there just a few weeks when they pinned up a job announcement. A job in San Francisco. "Nature Conservancy." I had never heard of it. I stepped in a phone booth and I applied. They had these things called "phone booths" then.

They flew me back to Washington. I was the eighth employee of the Nature Conservancy, and the only one west of the Mississippi. They said, "Okay, you go out West and do this work, raise money." This was a new concept. I had been a kid in a rural community, post Depression. We didn't know we were poor. We were in rural America, there's plenty of food to eat, but if you were *employed*, that made you the elite of the town. I didn't know that people gave money away. But I took the job with the Nature Conservancy. The organization was on the edge of bankruptcy, they told me when I went out the door. I arrived out here and I thought, *Gee, how am I going to raise money?* The story of how to do that still goes on. But I figured it out, for the time being, and I survived.

In California one thing I really looked forward to doing was meeting David Brower. The moment came at some cocktail party, which is still a fashionable thing in San Francisco. Environmentalists show up at various fundraisers and you get to see old friends. It's about the only time anybody ever has time to slow down and say hello to anyone. So I waited and I went up and I said, "Mr. Brower, I'm Huey Johnson and I'm with the Nature Conservancy." He kind of looked down and he says, "Nature Conservancy, what's that?" I said, "Well, we save land with its various life-forms." He said, "If any land needs to be saved, the Sierra Club will do it." He turned around and walked away.

I don't know what was wrong that day. Over the years I would introduce him to other people, and he was always very charming. I suppose he must have just lost a donation to some foundation like us. We were rather new, so he didn't know us. There's a saying, "If you want to roast an Irishman, you get another Irishman to turn the spit." Fundraising drives people to frustrated extremes very often. A proposal you've worked on for a month gets rejected because they decide they're going to give it to somebody else.

But time went on, and Dave and I became friends, and he became just the most important inspiration to me. And I think an inspiration to our movement, a central figure of success in an era of environmentalism which may be ending, I fear, not to be revisited. I was constantly inspired by Dave and things he did. His boldness. That always impressed me. It was an example for me and for a lot of others. You know, to be courageous enough, and to believe what you're doing enough, that you get your principles straightened out and go forward.

Before I got to know him well, I'd seen him at a couple of events. One, we were in Washington for some big conference and he was debating Mo Udall. Dave was so glib, and so in command of the facts, and so skilled with humor that he just killed in debates. I wouldn't want to have ever had to get up and debate him, if he was serious. Nobody could touch him. He was just gifted beyond belief, and he chewed up Mo Udall. Mo, Morris Udall, was a congressman from Utah, the brother of Stewart Udall, the secretary of interior under Kennedy and Johnson. Stewart was called "Stewdall," and Morris was "Modall." So Dave just chewed Mo up. He had bits of Modall flying out. Modall got mad and said something like, "I can't stand this," and he turned around and just walked. This huge auditorium, he just walked out.

One of the most important experiences I had with Dave was when Jerry Brown wanted me to be secretary of resources for California. And I didn't want to be. At the time I was head of a nonprofit, The Trust for Public Land, which I had thought up and started, and it had been in business nearly five years, and we had eight million dollars in land assets, as I remember, and several million cold cash in the bank, and I was potentate of the place. I was chair of the board and operating officer and I controlled it. I hired, fired, did whatever I wanted to do. The boardroom was made up of my friends. So it couldn't have been much better. And Jerry said, "I want you to come to Sacramento." I said, "I don't want to come to Sacramento."

Finally, Dick Baker, head of the Zen Center here, arranged for me to have dinner with Jerry Brown. I'd never met him. Dave Brower was around, and I said, "Would you like to come along?" So we went together to this first meeting with Jerry Brown. We sat there and talked about what ought to be done in California. Before this meeting, Jerry had asked me what I thought of his operation, and I said, "Well, you're lucky to get a C for your environmental program. Right now I'd probably give you a D, because the people at the moment aren't doing anything." It turned out Jerry really liked that kind of thing.

Well, Dave was at this first meeting, and it was a wonderful meeting because, between the two of us, we could set Jerry up. Jerry said something about a proposal on his desk right then from someone wanting to import turtle meat, of all things. Sea turtle meat! He asked us what he should do about importing turtle meat. My response was, No, this turtle farm they were proposing would just be a cover for all kinds of poaching. So that was the first decision we influenced. Jerry said, "Okay, I won't do it."

Dave and I talked to Jerry about wilderness and a lot of the other issues we cared about. Dave said, "Governor, if you appoint Johnson, he's going to be tougher than the people you've got in here now, you better understand that." Jerry liked that. So Dave really set it up. Dave said he had hoped I would take the job, and I did.

There were major things that I did as secretary of resources. Wild Rivers. I wanted to save twelve hundred miles of wild rivers, and in the end we accomplished that.

Then there was RARE II, the Wilderness Roadless Area Review and Evaluation. This was a program to determine which national forest areas should be considered in the National Wilderness Preservation System. There were millions of acres of federal land that were to be described in final-use apportionment. I started getting calls from honorable, honest Forest Service employees saying, "We're being ordered to provide in-depth descriptions of the condition of thousands of acres of land, and we've never been over it. We don't have any *people* to go over it. We don't know anything about it, and they want to make final decisions about it." The evaluation was all being done with a computer, not with feet on the ground. It was just this phony thing that these forest people had been ordered to do. So I filed a suit against it.

I had to get the attorney general's signature. The attorney general at the time was George Deukmejian, the future governor of California, a conservative Republican who did not like me, and vice versa. We disagreed over environmental matters. My problem was that Deukmejian had to sign off in order for me to sue. One of our attorneys said, "I've got it all ready to go. I'll get it done, just don't ask me any questions." Well, what he did was, he had a girlfriend in the attorney general's office. She knew Deukmejian's routine. He would come in the mornings and he'd have a tall stack of papers to sign. At first, he would read each one conscientiously before signing, but after a while he'd notice the clock, and he'd look at his schedule, and he'd start flipping through and signing them fast. So this girlfriend took a chance. She made the sacrifice of sticking our document in the stack, down toward the bottom. Deukmejian could never understand how he had signed off on this thing.

RARE II was such a big deal. I started getting a lot of pressure on it, including from congressmen calling me. One of the most intense was Phil Burton, whom I'd never met. He called me, he's very loudmouth, a tough guy. He said, "You son of a bitch, I've been working with these stupid green buddies of yours for six months, and we got everything all set, and you're screwing it up by threatening to file this lawsuit." I said, "Mr. Burton, I *am* going to file a lawsuit." And he swore a while and then said, "Do me a favor and I'll do you a favor. I want you to let that goddamn thing alone." I said, "Mr. Burton, I'm not going to do it." Well, then he just unleashed. "Son of a bitch" was the least thing he said. He shouted, "I'll tell you this, you son of a bitch"—or whatever word he was using by then—"you better win that goddamn suit!" And he slammed the phone down.

Well, the moment came, and the judge ruled in my favor. The first call I had was from Phil Burton. "Mr. Secretary," he said, "this is your protégé, Mr. Burton, calling to congratulate you." That was a big win because it concerned millions of acres. The Forest Service then sued us back. They lost again, so it took in the whole list and stopped millions of acres of wilderness from being lost. That was probably the most important decision of my time as secretary of resources. So Dave had a hand in that.

Dave had so much energy. I remember the Earth Summit at Rio. I was racewalking in those days, for exercise—competed for many years at it—and at the Rio conference I'd get up early and do it. One morning on the beach I saw a figure coming around the shore of this huge bay. It was your father, at four or five in the morning, photographing for *Eco*, his conference newspaper. He was eighty. He had that kind of energy. He'd stay up late and get up early.

He had this wonderful habit of going out with college students after lectures and conferences and drinking martinis till he closed the place. He'd sit there with these kids and have some wonderful talk and ideas.

His ability to communicate reached us all. He didn't care whether he was addressing an audience of ten thousand or a lunch table of five. His writings were impressive. They certainly impressed me. I loved his introductions to books. He published so many books himself, and wrote so many forewords and introductions to books published by others, that I guess the introduction was his main form of literary expression. In fact, I have put a proposal together. I would love to edit a collection of his introductions to the Sierra Club Books. He introduced a book I did; it's one of the most precious things I have.

Dave was solidly certain on what he stood for. If you asked him, he had the answer before you had the question finished. He could present it in the best way. He had this unusual blend of human characteristics: the blessing of intelligence, the blessing of being able to think on his feet, and the blessing of a sensitivity to people. He knew exactly what the principles were. He didn't compromise them. He didn't worry that he was going to step on the toes of the Chamber of Commerce, on the one side, or the Audubon Society, on the other. He just dealt with issues honorably and honestly and directly. He was willing to risk his jobs and friendships for what he believed was right. So very few leaders are able to do that.

The Wawona Tree, Mariposa Grove, Yosemite

PATRICIA SARR

T RISH SARR AND her husband Keith live thirty-five minutes north of Wellington in an old beach cottage enlarged by
amateur additions over the past sixty years. The house is ugly
outside, she admits, but she likes it inside, all books and wood. Out front
is a huge veranda. For the interview she sat at the kitchen table covered by
oilcloth—red strawberries in a bright yellow field. On top was a blue vase
filled with daffodils, irises, and tulips that Keith bought for her farther north
in New Zealand.

The windows look out on two large, flat picnic areas in Queen Elizabeth
Park and beyond to the sea. American soldiers were billeted on the picnic
areas during World War II, and village legend has it that tanks and other
gear lie buried under the grass. The next-door neighbors, digging to sink
new pilings under their house, struck a lode of military ore, so maybe the
legend is true. Queen Elizabeth is a big park, two thousand acres. In summer,
the seaward paddocks of the park beneath Sarr's window fill with Pacific
Islanders, members of church groups arriving early in the morning in school
buses. They stay all day, singing, playing tug-of-war, and running noisy three-
legged races. Sarr is struck by the mixing of generations. Young adults play
with children. Teenagers flirt with their gray-haired elders as they bring them
plates of food. Old men in lavalavas join in the games of cricket.

But that is in summer. Now in New Zealand, Sarr's adopted country, it was southern winter, summer having shifted up north to her native hemisphere. This morning in her kitchen she looked out on empty picnic grounds and the winter ocean of July, sparkling in the crystal light that strikes her as peculiar to New Zealand.

IT SEEMED TO me in 1969 that the world was about to end. That's how it looked to me, anyway, at the age of twenty-two. *The Population Bomb* had been published and the first Earth Day was being organized. I was doing a year of premed at Berkeley, studying a lot about biology, life, and death. I even did a course called "Atomic Radiation and Life." It seemed there was no reason to keep on studying for work in a world so obviously on its way to the cliff.

About then, a friend invited me home to meet her flatmates. Among them were Lloyd Linford and Tom Turner. They had both worked at the Sierra Club. They talked about their former boss, and it was with respect and affection and a personal commitment. They said Dave Brower believed we could, and we must, change the course of human history. I remember feeling that maybe there was another course, and maybe I could help. I fell in love with both Tom and Lloyd. We danced and we talked. I fell in love with this sense of hope, and principle, and intelligence.

Soon after, Tom took me to meet Dave, who lived just up the hill. Tom's mother, Beth, and Anne Brower had been lifelong friends. Tom had worked for Dave for years, and he had been thrown out of the Sierra Club alongside Dave. Tom wore cutoff beige shorts and a white T-shirt with a spring neck. I can't remember what I wore except that I thought very carefully about it. I was embarrassed by Tom's informality.

The family monkey, Isabelle, was on the porch when we arrived. She grabbed for Tom's pocket and took a bite out of his pack of cigarettes. I was not reassured. We were welcomed by Anne. You know, I still wear the pendant Anne gave me after she'd visited Holland, her old country—a fragment of blue tile in a simple silver frame. Do you remember she used to say of me that my nondrinking was "the only flaw in an otherwise sterling character"? Can't you just hear her? Anyway, that day she rescued us from the monkey and left us with Dave. The three of us sat in the living room at 40 Stevenson Avenue, Tom comfortably on the sofa, me uncomfortably on a chair. I remember the talk being almost exclusively between Dave and Tom. But at the end of the afternoon I was approved. I had a job at Friends of the Earth. Of course I'd offered to work for no pay for some months and then for almost no pay, which may have helped.

In due course I moved in with Tom. He and I commuted each day on the F Bus to San Francisco. We'd then walk across town to the office, which was first the Firehouse, and later on Commercial Street. Dave said he'd figured out a route from the bus station to the Firehouse totally off-street, through alleys and parking lots and parks. It was so like him. Somehow we never got him to show us. There were only four staff in San Francisco then, as I remember it. Tom, me, Joan McIntyre, and Connie Parrish.

Dave spent quite a lot of time out of the office. The organization was brand new, and it was Dave Brower who was its heart. He traveled and talked and talked and talked. Big audiences, campuses, little gatherings of environmentalists. Often when he would come back to the office, he'd bring with him someone he had discovered. Sometimes we rolled our eyes, other times not. One of those Dave brought home was Amory Lovins.

When Dave came into the office, the energy in the place intensified. But there was also an unease. In our first office, the ground floor of the Firehouse—this old firehouse in San Francisco—Dave worked at a stand-up desk which he turned to face the wall. I know now he was shy. But all I knew then was that you had to approach him carefully and not intrude.

He lit up the hearts in the room, reminded us of the purpose. This was never in staff meetings, which we never had, or in speeches to staff, because we didn't have those either, but through him telling us stories of his travels or about something he had seen that day. I'll never forget the morning he came into the office rather late in the morning. He dragged an office chair into the small space between desks and he stood on it. He looked up and with both hands he flung leaves at the ceiling. They didn't fall. They spun and twirled and floated and eventually came gently down to earth. We cheered. He picked up several of the leaves and did it again, and again. Then he talked for a few moments about the magic of the leaves, and then went back to his desk.

Dave lived in the world he inhabited. He saw things, he celebrated them. He caused those of us around him to do the same. To see with a child's eyes, wide open.

Working with Dave was not all sunny, of course, nothing like it. He was shy. Tom and I were among those who hosted dinner parties with potential major donors. Dave would work his magic over the meal, then excuse himself while we made a pitch for money. I don't think Dave was ever comfortable with women. When a woman was acting as secretary, okay, but basically I saw him as a man who was uncomfortable with women. He was shy, and he was of his generation, certainly, so it's not fair to judge him in hindsight. But at the time I felt strongly the discomfort that he radiated when around women, including me.

I only remember winning one argument with him. I was editing copy for *Not Man Apart*, and he had written something about our energy policy being akin to the woman driver who goes ever faster to get to the petrol station because she discovers her tank is running low. I went upstairs to see him, quite anxious but determined. I asked, why couldn't it just be "a driver"? He said, "Because the joke is about a woman driver." We talked about it for a few minutes, and I let it go and walked back down the stairs. As I reached my desk one floor down, the phone was ringing. Dave said only, "Change it."

In those days, and maybe still, the various movements were in separate cells: environmentalists, feminists, unionists. We worked vertically but not horizontally. Dave could name the paper *Not Man Apart*, he could write about women drivers, because he might never have been exposed to feminist ideas. This is maybe 1972, and I barely had been exposed to them myself.

One of Dave's admirable, rare qualities was his ability to change. He talked openly of how he used to advocate nuclear power before he saw the light. And he called me that day and said "change it."

There were shadows, but my time with Dave was without doubt a blessing in my life.

I came here to New Zealand on sabbatical from Friends of the Earth. Dave always said that everyone, not just academics, should have sabbaticals, so when Tom Turner and I had done seven years with Friends of the Earth we invented a sabbatical program. You had to leave the United States for at least half the time—we were trying to internationalize Friends of the Earth then—and you had to do something environmental for half the time. So Tom and I came to New Zealand. There was a new Friends of the Earth here, which, in a coalition with unions and locals, had reputedly stopped a multinational PVC plant. They spoke English here. It was reported to be a multicultural paradise in the South Pacific, and it was the first country to have given women the vote. Sounded good!

After several months, Tom was asked to go back to take over as administrative director of Friends of the Earth in San Francisco. I stayed on to help lead a fight against a major dam project. I remember sounding quite convincing when I told people that of course we could stop a dam on the Clutha River. Dave Brower had stopped dams in the Grand Canyon, hadn't he? But Friends of the Earth New Zealand wouldn't take it on. Keith was one of the cofounders of Friends of the Earth in New Zealand, but the organization said we would never win. So Keith and I formed up a small group, printed new letterhead, and became "Clutha Rescue." In the heat of the campaign, Keith and I were married near the proposed dam site. The wedding was on the news that night. PROTESTORS MARRY IN LOWBURN. We lost the fight. I had no idea how deeply dams and "progress" were wedded in the New Zealand heart. We argued that the country didn't need the electricity, and we lost. But it was a good fight. Special legislation had to be passed for the dam, and did so by only one vote. There have been no more large dams built since that time.

Keith and I moved to Wellington, the capital, near the end of the campaign, in the hope of getting more attention from national politics. And here we have stayed, more or less. I went to work in unions for fifteen years. I worked in unions of truck drivers, shop assistants, storesmen, and bank staff. I ran campaigns for women's employment rights. At the end I was in the Central Organisation, our version of the AFL-CIO, doing policy and research.

Then a new, conservative government was elected with the specific aim of "deregulating the labor market." The core labor laws were changed, and I resigned. Having worked in unions amounted to roughly zero on one's CV. So I went to university to "launder my experience," as Keith put it. With no bachelor's degree, I talked my way into a master's degree course in public policy based on my experience, publications, and blarney. I won the Prime Minister's Prize at the end and rescued my CV. I also took some time out to help form an Oxfam in New Zealand, and to travel to Rwanda for Oxfam, near the end of the genocide, helping in refugee camps near Goma.

Then came about fifteen years in the public service, working in policy. I began with constitutional issues surrounding the place of the indigenous people here, the Maori. I co-led a review of our court system by the Law Commission. Then, inevitably, I went to the Department of Conservation, where I led a team developing a long-term direction and supporting strategy for the Department, which is responsible for managing one-third of New Zealand.

You know, back in California I worked for Dave for seven years, never reaching beyond layout and copyediting of the paper. I know now, from my experience of myself in senior roles in New Zealand, and thanks to encouragement from managers and friends, that I could have given much more. I didn't put my hand up. But Dave never saw the possibilities. He might not have noticed my hand, even if I had put it up.

I loved him, I hope that comes through, though he drove me nuts sometimes.

My last job here was at the Ministry of Education, thinking about the place of education in the Maori language within a public education system. I left that job last December and haven't yet looked for anything else. At home, I'm baking our bread, growing a beautiful garden of irises and artichokes and garlic and oregano. I meditate each day. I'm trying to learn what it is to be content without being responsible in my own mind for saving the world.

The Wawona Tree! I remember that trip so clearly. It was Dave's idea. The Wawona Tree had fallen that winter he was fired from the Sierra Club and started Friends of the Earth. He wanted seeds from the cones to give charter members of FOE. Tom and I immediately volunteered to go. My memory is that we wouldn't have let anyone else do it—it was *our* job. We went in Tom's sports car, the MG. We had the top down while we were crossing the San Joaquin Valley, but I remember there being snow around when we finally got up to Mariposa Grove and began fossicking for seeds. So the top had been put up by the time it got so cold in the mountains. I remember the long shafts of light, the sense of silence and peace. That's such a strong memory. It was very cold, but that just made the world seem more silent and sharp edged.

When we got there it was not so simple, because there were so many trees, standing and fallen. The Wawona Tree had been so large that identifying her crown and seeds, among all the tree debris, was a bit hit-and-miss. But we decided that it really was not important. A pedant, Dave was not.

I also remember sitting in the Firehouse at the big, long wooden table, dropping one little seed into each glassine envelope, carefully stapling the envelope onto the sheets that had Dave's message, in elegant type. That was Dave's hope and optimism. A giant sequoia seed for each charter member of his new organization.

I still have my copy.

"A Gift from the Tree," it was called. And Dave ends it, "A seed shaken from a cone lying among the fragments of the Wawona Tree's crown is affixed here. It can produce a tree that will live beautifully for three thousand years or so. If it fails to do so, please return it."

That was Dave's humor. And now he would have been one hundred! His centennial! When I knew him he was so full of life I could never imagine him dying. I find it odd to be celebrating the life of someone who still feels so alive to me.

Keiko, the killer whale, freed to the wild, breaching in Taknes Bay, Norway
Photograph by Mark Berman

DAVID PHILLIPS

THE INTERNATIONAL Marine Mammal Project, IMMP, has its headquarters on the fourth floor of the David Brower Center, a new office building for environmental and social justice organizations in downtown Berkeley. The Brower Center in its design and construction is exceedingly Earth friendly—it was given a LEED Platinum rating, the highest bestowed by the US Green Building Council. Across the street are the University of California and its track stadium. On Saturdays in springtime, at irregular intervals, like a jolt of caffeine, startling any drowsy environmentalist working through the weekend, comes the crack of the starter's gun.

IMMP's proprietor, David Phillips, generally works in sunlight by the window on a Mac. Along his windowsill, porpoising in single file, is a procession of carved dolphins from around the world, a few realistic and identifiable as to species, but most half-imaginary, some of wood, others of stone. The marine mammal that Phillips's International Marine Mammal Project most often finds itself defending is this one, the dolphin. The dolphins on the windowsill all leap westward toward San Francisco Bay, the nearest saltwater.

The day of the interview was a Thursday in May. It was track season, but there was no meet underway and no intermittent gunfire from the stadium. Phillips's staff was all traveling on various missions, a rare circumstance, and the IMMP office was unusually quiet. The environmentalist had the place to himself until the interviewer arrived.

Phillips is fifty-six, a compact man, bearded and balding. Haircuts are not an obsession with him, and what remains of his hair is longish and always a little unruly. He often has the look of rumpled absentmindedness or preoccupation you might see across the way in one of Berkeley's theoretical physicists. His Macintosh has a twenty-four-inch monitor. Considerable fragmentation is built into Phillips's workday, and the big screen is necessary to display all the various ongoing concerns of the moment.

Phillips is both the director of IMMP and one of the two co–executive directors of Earth Island Institute, which has its offices on this same fourth floor, and to which he commutes periodically by foot down the hall. IMMP is one of fifty-five "projects" of Earth Island Institute, an incubator organization for environmental start-ups founded by David Brower in 1982. After my father was fired by Friends of the Earth, Phillips and other loyalists from that organization followed the boss into exile and helped him set up the new outfit, which would be his last. As executive director of Earth Island, Phillips is his own mentor and overseer at IMMP. He is constantly switching hats, sometimes several times in the course of a minute. He spends about half of each workday, he figures, in either job.

The interviewer, it happens, had been witness to David Phillips's beginnings as a working environmentalist and marine-mammal advocate. In 1978, a few months after my father hired Phillips fresh out of college to work for Friends of the Earth, he sent his new employee and me to London to cover the annual meeting of the International Whaling Commission. Under the editorship of Tom Turner, we were to help put out *Eco,* a daily conference newsletter dedicated to reporting the undercurrents at the IWC to the participants.

Delegates arriving at the convention site, the Mount Royal Hotel, were greeted by demonstrators. On one side were antiwhaling pickets waving placards. REPRIEVE FOR LEVIATHAN, said one. PEACE FOR THE WHALES, said another. LET THE WHALES RECOVER, said a third. One placard was illustrated by a drawing of a whale in whose bleeding back the flags of Japan and the Soviet Union—the only two remaining whaling superpowers—had been implanted by harpoon. AS GO THE WHALES, SO GOES THE SEA, this placard predicted. On the other side were pro-whaling pickets, members of a Japanese seaman's union, whose placards protested the environmentalist threat to their livelihood.

Demonstrating at the entrance to the Mount Royal was a killer whale who offered each new arrival a flipper to shake. Most accepted the flipper with a smile, even the delegates from Japan. The cut of the killer-whale suit was remarkably true to the shape of a real animal, until you looked down. Protruding from beneath the black-cloth flukes was a pair of bare male feet. The feet were extraordinarily long and thin. They were very pale, testifying to the sunlessness of English summer, and they were dirty, testifying to the grime of the Underground. To me the feet spoke of the sordid London flats where Phillips and I were flopping, bare, dim apartments in which man's inhumanity to whale was decried, through a haze of hash smoke, late into the night. The pale feet were incongruous, as feet were the first appendages discarded by ancestral whales when they returned to the sea.

This was David Phillips's first close encounter with a killer whale. The flipper shake at the entrance to the Mount Royal Hotel amounted, then, to an augury. Intimacy with killer whales, one orca in particular, lay in Phillips's future.

A large contingent of Alaskan Eskimos attended the IWC that year. Eskimos are the planet's first whalers, having begun the practice four millennia ago. To the 1978 meeting they brought a model of an umiak, the skin boat in which the Inupiat, as the Eskimos of Alaska's north coast call themselves, have pursued bowhead and gray whales from time immemorial. Eskimos are great artists, and the miniature vessel was exquisite. The covering of the model was the real thing, sealskin, stretched drum-tight and translucent over a framework of wood. The crew of dolls was dressed in miniature fur parkas, cunningly sewn. Each man stroked with a tiny leaf-bladed paddle, driving the umiak across a sea of pro-whaling literature piled on a table outside the conference hall.

Eskimos still hunt whales in these lightweight craft. No sea creatures are more acoustically aware than whales, and any motor-driven vessel would be much too noisy for a hunt in the leads of the spring pack ice as it breaks up.

Few issues at IWC meetings in the 1970s were so divisive as the debate over Eskimo hunting of bowhead whales. The controversy divided the Eskimos from the environmentalists, two groups normally better aligned. It split the environmentalists themselves. The Greenpeace Foundation was for an immediate cessation of Eskimo bowhead whaling. Friends of the Earth, Inc., the mother organization in the United States, was for allowing a limited subsistence hunt by North Slope Eskimos. Friends of the Earth, Ltd., the British daughter organization, was against such a hunt. The controversy made for strange alliances, as well. In London the Eskimos found themselves on the same side as the Russians, their old enemies from the days of Baranov.

The Eskimos in London for the IWC that year had two distinct approaches to international diplomacy. The older Inupiat were unfailingly polite. The younger were almost invariably angry and rude.

John Oktollik, a veteran whaling captain from Point Hope, was representative of the first group. He was a stocky, gentlemanly, bespectacled man missing his lower incisors. "I'm fifty-eight," he told us one morning, in the lobby outside the conference hall. "I've been exposed to whaling since I was a seven-year-old. At first I had to stay in the tent. It was cold—the first part of April. I was getting snow to make water, or cutting up some blubber for fuel. Later, when I was twelve or fourteen, I started getting a little bit of training. When you first go out in the boat, it's very exciting. It's sort of scary—going after that monster in a small boat five to six meters in length. Sometimes, when we take people from the outlying villages, and they see the whale, before they know it they're paddling backwards."

Oktollik said that when he took novices from inland villages out on the hunt, he liked to watch their faces as the bowhead surfaced to blow. The bowhead whale, *Balaena mysticetus,* is distinguished from the two other members of the right-whale family—the northern right whale and the southern right whale—by a white blaze on its chin. Everywhere else on the body, the bowhead is all velvety black. The "bib" or "vest" or "shirtfront" of the blaze is the first thing you see rising underwater, green tinted, like a motorized ice floe with a mind of its own. The spout is bushy and explosive. The whale's hot breath and a mist of atomized water blasted from atop its blowhole condense instantaneously, with a rainbow shimmer, in the cold arctic air. Then comes the endless curve of the black back as it follows the blowhole back under the slush ice. Finally, the whale shows its black flukes and is gone.

"They say, 'Aaaaahhhhh!'" Oktollik said of the novice whalers. "That's their expression, you know, at the bigness." The sound, as reproduced by Oktollik in London, was remarkably like the blow of a whale, only a much less mighty version. "Aaaaahhhhh!" exhaled the novice Eskimos in amazement, and then, at Oktollik's command, they dug in with their paddles, pursuing the object of their wonderment.

Billy Neakok, a youthful whaling captain from Barrow, was representative of the second, younger group of Inuit, practitioners of a much less measured approach to diplomacy.

"The questions you ask show how ignorant you are," he told me one morning in the hotel coffee shop. "It is impossible to explain it to you."

Neakok was dressed for the London fog in a white parka, a bone necklace, and dark glasses. His wore his hair long and parted down the middle. He was especially angry this morning, because yesterday the IWC technical committee, most of whom had Nordic faces like mine, had recommended a bowhead quota of just twenty-four whales for the Eskimos. The Eskimo contingent had promptly walked out of the session, declaring themselves free of IWC jurisdiction.

Neakok had a low opinion of the US scientists who had conducted this spring's bowhead census. The scientists had counted 1734 whales and had estimated the world population at between 1763 and 2865 bowheads. They had spotted only 19 calves, from which they extrapolated a total of only 29 calves—an alarmingly low recruitment figure.

"There was a May 1st cutoff of the count, just when the calves start coming through," Neakok told me. "The mothers and calves usually come by when it's most difficult to hunt them. It's hard then because the ice is dangerous. The ice is rotten, disintegrating from the heat. It's shaved by the current. Sixty-centimeter-thick young ice can get shaved to two centimeters in an hour. We can live on the ice when it's only ten centimeters, and you can see through to the waves underneath. For a hundred thousand years we've been compiling information. We don't have to use figures. The language has names for all these ice conditions. We evolved in that manner. We can't express it. It's racially uncommunicable.

"The people doing the count were from National Marine Fisheries. They had brand-new snow machines and gear. But they didn't know how to live on the ice. They didn't understand the danger. We had to tell them when to go inland. After they finished the land count, they started a half-assed aerial count. Airplanes are noisy. Everyone knows—every Eskimo, even a child—knows that a mother and calf react to noise. Of course NMF didn't count many calves. We have our own research program. We're going to educate the scientists. The Eskimos and the whales are here because of the success of Eskimo management."

Rising, my coffee finished, I asked Neakok how he liked London. For a moment he did not answer. Clearly he found it another of my foolish questions.

"It's like any White man's town," he said, finally. "More barbaric than the place we come from."

On the final day of the 1978 meeting of the IWC, a group of radical environmentalists commandeered the chairman's dais in protest. The demonstration was peaceful at first; then one of the demonstrators, an Australian, poured blood on two members of the Japanese delegation. Several Japanese men shouted and seized the Australian, at which a detachment from the antiwhaling faction came to the man's aid, which in turn brought more Japanese reinforcements. The aisle was instantly jammed with people—a good thing, in the end, for no one could free a hand to throw a punch. Hotel security officers led the Australian away. "You're barbarians!" he yelled at the Japanese. "Whaling is barbaric!"

"You!" a Japanese woman shouted back, weeping. "You are barbarians!"

Welcome, young Dave Phillips, to the politics of whaling.

Now, in the International Marine Mammal Protection office thirty-three years later, Phillips put his Mac to sleep for the interview. At this point in his career he had dozens of annual IWC meetings under his belt. On the west wall of his office hung a large poster advertising *The Cove*, which won the 2010

Academy Award for best documentary. One of Phillips's employees at IMMP, Ric O'Barry, was the protagonist of that movie. (O'Barry, a former trainer of the 1960s television dolphin Flipper, had a change of heart and went over to the other side, where he is now a relentless activist against dolphin capture and captivity. For *The Cove,* O'Barry, IMMP, and the filmmakers went undercover to expose the horrors of dolphin slaughter at Taiji, Japan.)

On the east wall hangs the very placard, "text DOLPHIN to 44144," that Ric O'Barry held up suddenly on the podium as he and his team accepted their Oscar. By texting, the viewer joined a petition to US and Japanese government officials to stop the dolphin slaughter at Taiji. It was a subliminal message at the time, for the cameras quickly swung away; yet forty thousand readers with photographic memories texted after Oscar night.

Several posters in the room advertise the movie *Free Willy,* as well as the several documentaries made on Keiko, the killer whale who played Willy in the movie. For a time Phillips and IMMP owned this whale. It was Phillips who negotiated Keiko's release from the tiny tank in Reino Aventura, the Mexican theme park where the movie was filmed and where the whale suffered, near death from inadequate space and poor diet, his body covered by papillomas from water that was much too warm. When the Keiko project grew too cumbersome for IMMP, Phillips founded the Free Willy-Keiko Foundation, through which he finessed the construction of a new $7.5-million facility for Keiko in Oregon and oversaw the whale's rehabilitation and eventual return to his native waters off Iceland.

Never before or since has a captive killer whale been released to the wild. One photo by Phillips's desk shows the huge Air Force C-17 that flew Keiko from Oregon, a picture snapped moments before touchdown in Iceland. The plane's crew had presented Phillips a copy signed in felt pen. "Good luck Keiko," wrote Major Tim Harris. "Finally!" wrote Captain Randy Huiss. "Enjoy your freedom, Keiko!" wrote Lieutenant Colleen Lehore.

The bookcase is dominated by books on whales and the ocean. *Sea Change,* by Sylvia Earle. *In Defense of Dolphins,* by Thomas White. *Freeing Keiko,* by Kenneth Brower. *The Smile of a Dolphin,* by Marc Bekoff. And so on. The top of the bookcase is stacked high with canned tuna from all over the world. Thunfisch—Salat, Texas mit würsigen. Supreme Thon Rose,

Product of Thailand. Bonito Del Norte en Aceite de Oliva, Hijos de Jose Serrats, Bermeo, (España). No Name Shredded Tuna. Wild Planet Troll Caught Wild Albacore Tuna. Ocean King, Trader Joe's, Mareblu, John West, Dardanell, Progresso, Heinz Greenseas, Nixe, California Girl, Pinocchio, Gran Coche, Fortuna, Solomon Blue, Ayam Brand, La Sirena, Rio Mare.

These companies are clients of Phillips's. He and IMMP led the campaign against the tuna fleets of the Eastern Tropical Pacific, which were killing 150,000 dolphins annually as bycatch in their purse seines. Phillips went so far as to put a spy with a video camera aboard a Mexican seiner. The resulting video of dolphin kills swept the world, and IMMP forced a change in industry practice. They succeeded, in fact, almost too well, for the organization is now saddled with running a monitoring program employing observers all over the world to assure that the "Dolphin Safe" label is deserved. The cans of tuna are sent in by IMMP observers.

On a middle shelf, under a half ton of tuna, is a framed quotation from Goethe. It was a favorite passage of David Brower's. Almost everyone who ever worked for him learned by heart:

> If there is something you can do,
> Or dream you can, begin it.
> Boldness has genius, power, and magic in it.

IT WAS AT COLORADO COLLEGE. I was very involved with all sorts of environmental activities there, and one of them was putting together an Earth Day extravaganza on campus. I was one of the organizers. We brought out Amory Lovins, who was already in Colorado, and we brought out Dave Brower. They were both willing to come. We had small travel honorariums, and the two of them were to give a speaking engagement and a lecture. I didn't know anything about Dave Brower. I had learned a little something about Lovins. There were some professors there somewhat involved with environmental stuff, anyway, so we brought Dave Brower out. He was at Friends of the Earth at the time.

Basically, my first meeting Dave was hearing "the Sermon." And this was Dave at his best. In front of a college audience, a bunch of young people, enraptured, and at the end, it was, like, just people streaming forward, asking, "What can I do to save the planet?" And I was just bit by that. The first time I saw him. And that was actually in my junior year, that would have been 1976, so that was the first time I ever met Dave.

I was a biologist, so I was studying the natural world. But I was also getting caught in this issue of whether I want to be, like, a Ph.D. biologist that just goes and studies something, or do I want to get involved with actually trying to change things? Should the work be about saving things? I was right in that crux. And that was where Dave was. Dave was all about how you could make a difference, and how much making a difference was needed. That was the part that spoke to me. How the world really needed people to step up.

A year later, when I was getting ready to graduate, I was still in that mix. Do I want to go to grad school, or do I want to work for an environmental group? What do I want to do? I had one advantage in that whole scene. It was that my dean was Richard Bradley, and Rick had all sorts of familial connections to Brower. So it was getting on towards time for my graduation. I went to Rick Bradley, and I said, "Will you call Dave Brower for me?" And he said, "Yeah. What do you want me to say?" I said, "Tell him I want to work! I want to work for him!" And so Rick Bradley called him up. Dave Brower said, "Oh, yeah, yeah, I think I remember him."

Sure he did. He remembered me? I don't think so. But Dave told Rick, "I'm going to be in Missoula, Montana, in about three weeks. Have him come up and meet me."

So I trundled myself up to Missoula, Montana. Dave was giving lectures at the University of Montana. I went and knocked on his hotel door beforehand, and he was very gracious, and we went out and had coffee. He was very interested in what I was doing, and it was Dave again at his best. "So what do you do?" he asked me. I said that I'm a biologist. I've been studying endangered species. I did my thesis on the Abert's squirrel, this black, tufted-ear squirrel that lives in the ponderosa pine forest. And I've done a month on the coral reefs. And I've done a month with gray whales. So I was interested in megafauna. And minifauna, too. And he was, like, "We have to have that! We totally need that. You *must* come and work for Friends of the Earth."

There was a little wrinkle to that, of course. Which was, in Dave's inimitable style, he hadn't told anyone I was coming. I arrived at Friends of the Earth in San Francisco, thinking that since he's said you *must* come to work for us, and he's the chairman and the president of this organization, that he was hiring me. But apparently it didn't mean to Dave the same thing that it might mean to someone else.

After that trip to Missoula, I had gone back and graduated. Everybody asked what I was going to do. "I'm going to work for Friends of the Earth. I have a job. Dave Brower." And when would I start? "Well, I'm not quite sure about that." And what were my, like, terms of employment? "Not really sure about that. We'll just figure that out when I get out there." So I got out to Friends of the Earth, at 124 Spear Street, this little brick building in San Francisco. I remember the first time I ever rode up the elevator, it was with David Chatfield, who was the director of Friends of the Earth International. And he said, "Who are you?" I said, "Oh, I'm Dave Phillips. I'm going to be working here." And he was, like, "*Okaaay.*" I kind of imagine Chatfield had a blackboard back there someplace, and each time someone like me came in, he would add a mark.

When I arrived, Dave was out on the stump. He was traveling very extensively then. It was probably a week or so before he came back. There were some desks in back, intern spaces, and they found a desk for me.

So the reality was, what I had was a desk and the enthusiastic support of Dave Brower.

That was my job. No money. But you know what? That was enough. It turned out to be a build-your-own job. Find a way. Dave kept saying, "Just keep working, we'll figure out a way to make this happen." And within six months of the time I arrived, he got some funding and gave me the money to go over to the International Whaling Commission meetings in London. So it was, like, *experience.* It was learning. It was like the School of Environmentalism. It was like Brower University. It was more valuable than anyplace I ever could have gone. In terms of learning the environmental movement, how could you learn it any other way? If I'd just tried to put my résumé in to a bunch of places, they would have been, like, "Who are *you?*" It was unconventional, but that was Dave. I got roped in. But I was already roped in. I was willingly roped in.

And it wasn't just me. When I was in Missoula for that first meeting with Dave, there was a journalist there, Jim Robbins, who Dave also kind of roped in on that same night. So I had another compatriot. Jim was, like, "Yeah, now I'm going to be working on an environmental newswire service with Friends of the Earth." Dave was out collecting future activists. Some of them could find a way to make it work. Others dropped out and did other things.

With Dave it was, like, invent your job. Write your own job description. Find your way. Because we *need* that, whatever it is you're going to do. If I'd said I was an environmental economics person, he probably would have said, "We need that!" The fact is, though, he really did feel that Friends of the Earth was short in the wildlife department.

So I became "wildlife coordinator" for Friends of the Earth. And I jumped right in, and ended up, fairly quickly, concentrating on California condors, Mono Lake, and whales. Those were all hallmark Dave Brower campaigns. He liked campaigns like that. Because they were David and Goliath. They were long shots. Mono Lake, it was a little group of ornithologists against Los Angeles Department of Water and Power—just a few bird people against this giant utility, which for decades had been diverting water from the lake. And on the condor question, too, it was fighting huge institutions. I mean, on condors we had to fight the zoo establishment, and the Fish and Wildlife Service establishment, and much of the environmental community. Audubon, for example, was full on board with the captive-breeding program. We were against it. We were for wild condors.

Even whales were pretty much a long shot, back then. There were a lot of countries that were whaling. And also some of the positions we took on whales were difficult. We ended up supporting the Alaska Eskimos fighting for their right to take bowhead whales, at a time in which that was heresy in the environmental movement.

Friends of the Earth had a couple of Alaska representatives up there at the time, and an Alaska office, and we had been quite involved with the Alaska lands bill, trying to protect wilderness up there, and trying to stop oil drilling on the North Slope. Along the way, Friends of the Earth got to feeling that we needed the Eskimo communities in order to fight these fights. And we did some *listening* to them. Clearly whaling was the cultural tradition up there. For us it was about the difference between commercial whaling and subsistence whaling. There was no question that the bowhead whale was an important part of the cultural and nutritional reality in these villages. And the Eskimos were raising big questions about the role of government in setting the quotas, and of government scientists knowing what the whale numbers really were.

Dave was iconoclastic. He was not hung up on the positions of the other environmental groups on the matter. If he felt like he should be sticking with Eskimos, that the Eskimos were right, then it didn't matter that Audubon, or Sierra Club, or all these groups were critical of him. He was not afraid of being a lightning rod.

So I got my trial by fire in a set of issues that was all about boldness, about being willing to take a contrary position, about trying to outflank bigger, better-financed adversaries. I jumped right into the method that Dave was really known for.

On condors, our position, which was to oppose the captive-breeding program, was influenced by our connections with a group of habitat guys down in condor country. Some of them knew Dave, or knew about him. So we had the McMillans—Eben McMillan and Ian McMillan—these two brothers, ranchers, who had lived their whole lives down in San Luis Obispo and the Carrizo Plain and had written about condors. And Carl Koford, who had written *The California Condor*, which is *the* book about condors. Steve Herman. John Taft. Roland Ross. These folks, they *knew* condors. Koford was a Cal professor, he lived in Berkeley and he knew Dave. Koford was trying to find some ally to stand up for what he perceived to be this raid on the wild condors.

I very quickly knew whose side I was on. I was running interference for Friends of the Earth on condor matters up at the state Department of Fish and Game and the Fish and Game Commission. The people that were sent out to defend the capture position were obnoxious and holy and so wrong. They wanted to capture all the remaining wild condors for captive-breeding purposes, in zoos. Their approach was so manipulative, so disdainful of anybody like Koford. "Ah, Koford, he's an old-timer." They were all into the modern trapping, zoos, captive-breeding, radio telemetry, invasive biological management. They were awful. And the people they hired to run the program were awful, too—very disdaining of any opposition or any criticism. *They* were the experts. How could anybody get in their way?

My first trips with Dave were to talk condors at meetings of "the hook and bullet boys," as he called them. The hook and bullet boys were the people from the US Fish and Wildlife Service, the California State Department of Fish and Game, and from groups like the National Wildlife Federation, Ducks Unlimited, the Isaac Walton League—these big hunter groups. Dave was no hunter, but these people had an interesting kind of appeal to him. And for their part they liked Dave. He knew all of them. I don't know how he knew them.

Dave and I had some good times down at Eben McMillan's ranch. We would go down there for Fish and Game Commission hearings on the condor. Eben was this great old guy. He had roadrunners in his yard. Once when Dave and I were there, the roadrunners showed up, and Eben told us not to look. "Do not look at them at all. Don't even look in their direction." He somehow managed to get these wild roadrunners to stay on his place. So we were busy looking everyplace but at the roadrunners. It must have been hard for Dave. He loved roadrunners.

Dave got along with the Fish and Game people, but he held most dear the scientific and conservation types rather than the wildlife "managers." He liked the Ray Dasmanns, the Leopolds, the Kofords, the McMillans.

The observers rather than the manipulators. The Les Pengellys. Les Pengelly was a wildlife specialist in Montana and for a while he was president of the National Wildlife Society. It was Les who described the Forest Service Smokey the Bear campaign as "anthropomorphic ursininity." And he was the author of a quote Dave liked and used all the time: "You cannot reason prejudice out of a person because it didn't get in that way."

Dave was up to his eyeballs in condors. He was very involved. He was extremely loyal to the habitat and to a more natural approach to wildlife management. The Koford approach. The McMillans. John Taft. Roland Ross. Les Pengelly. That was Dave's tribe. The Fish and Wildlife Service, not so much, though these were people he had known and worked with. The hook and bullet boys, the technocrats, the whole government's approach to condors—catch 'em all, put 'em in zoos—that had no allure at all for Dave. Captive breeding, the whole manipulative side of it, the more we looked at it, the worse it got.

The American Association for the Advancement of Science met every year, and for years Dave would go to keep tabs on scientists, bureaucrats, environmental leaders, and so on. I went with him to several AAAS meetings, and they were occasions where the condor wars burned hot. Not so much on the official agendas, but in the hallways, *a lot*. That is where Dave hung out.

I remember going up to Sacramento with Dave on condor business. Huey Johnson was resources secretary for the state and Kirk Marquald was his assistant. Huey was on our side on condors, but Fish and Game, Charley Fullerton, and the Fish and Wildlife Service were not. Kirk Marquald told me afterward that when we showed up, they were just, like, "Oh my God, here comes Brower." They were fearful. Kirk said he thought Dave Brower was the most effective lobbyist he had ever seen in his life. We would storm up there, and they would just duck for cover. I kind of imagine it would have been that way with Floyd Dominy, at the Bureau of Reclamation, and at other federal agencies that Dave harassed, and with all the secretaries of the interior that Dave pushed and prodded over time. When they saw Dave coming I think they all were saying, "Oh my God, batten down the hatches, here comes Brower."

I still think we were right about condors. But I also think that some compromise, some sort of middle-ground strategy, might have worked. When they determined that, *if carefully done*, the birds would double-clutch—that if the first egg was lost or removed, the condors would lay a second egg—the program could have built a captive population without sacrificing the wild population. They could have let the wild population slowly rebuild by protecting its habitat, while still building a captive population. Carefully done; that I think would have been the key. There could have been focus on the habitat issues that are still unresolved. Lead poisoning in the condor's home range is no better now than it was when we blew the whistle on it. The captive-breeding people just had given up on the habitat. They basically didn't care. If the release of captive birds didn't work in California, they figured, then they would just release them in the Grand Canyon, or in Mexico. They didn't care about the condor's home range in the way that we did.

We lost. They captured all twenty-one remaining wild condors and put them in cages in zoos and breeding programs. They've had mixed success. They've raised a lot of birds. But the birds that they've released have had lots of problems. They swoop down on picnic tables and grab people's sandwiches. Wild condors would never do that in a million years. They sip antifreeze in puddles. Things that no self-respecting wild condor would ever do. I still think we were right. I still think that the program's failure to concentrate on the habitat has hurt us in a lot of ways. The emphasis they give to the zoos as the places to save endangered species—what a misguided message! To think that we're ever going to solve the problems of extinction through zoos!

In the bowhead-whale debate, we were bailed out by luck—by the fact that the whale counting was so inadequate at the time. We were sticking up for the Eskimos taking bowhead whales at a time when the population was thought to be extremely low. I mean, just in the hundreds. And the Eskimos told the scientists, "This is crazy, your numbers are wrong."

And all the scientists said, "Yeah, *right*. We're scientists with helicopters, and you're Eskimos standing on the side of the ice floes. So who is going to better know what the bowhead population is, us or you guys?"

When all was said and done, the population was probably ten times, maybe twenty times the low estimates that the scientists gave. The Eskimos turned out to be right. Which gave them margin such that they could take a limited number of bowheads and have a population still increase. And that's what's happened. They've taken a limited number and the population has considerably increased. So we were saved by the numbers. If there had only been twelve hundred bowhead whales, and the Eskimos kept taking the numbers they were taking, it was going to lead the population to extinction. We would have been seen as just going along with the extinction of the bowhead whales. Which would have been very, very tough.

One spring I went up to Barrow for the bowhead hunt. With a couple of other Friends of the Earth staffers, I went out on the ice and camped on the edge of the shore where they were taking the bowhead whales. We were the first group ever invited to watch the bowhead hunt, out on the ice floes. We were invited because we had been open about advocating for the Eskimo position.

There are Browers, you know, up in Barrow, Alaska. Eskimo Browers. They're descended from a White guy, Charley Brower, who married Eskimos. Before I went up, Dave said, "You've got to meet my other family up there, the Browers of Barrow, Alaska." So I was up there with this small group from Friends of the Earth. They took us in to meet the mayor, and the mayor says, "All you people who come to see us, what I would like to do is take you all out and throw you in the ocean." Not the friendliest start for a meeting.

A little later, somebody else came in, and I had a chance to say, "Well, I've been sent up to meet the Browers. Maria Brower and the Brower family, because my organization is headed by David Brower." So the mayor and everyone were, like, "David Brower! Oh yes, *David Brower*." And it turned into this lovefest over the name. Dave had somehow connected with them previously over the Brower name. Like they were family. It was a lot better than being thrown in the ocean.

Dave really liked my Keiko project. He went up to Oregon and saw Keiko in the water. He had a lot of interest in the oceans and the whales. He saw the symbolic importance of this one killer whale, Keiko, and how Keiko focused attention on all whales and on the problems of the ocean generally. Dave was a storyteller. He is intrigued by big stories, big efforts to tell the story about the world and how to save it. Keiko was a big story.

With Keiko there was a very dark time for me in which the finances were really tricky. We ran out of money at the Free Willy-Keiko Foundation. Enough had come in to move Keiko from Mexico and build a facility for him at the Oregon Coast Aquarium, using Warner Brothers money and funds we raised ourselves. We got Keiko to Oregon, but by the time we got him there, there was no more money. No money to take care of him, or to think about what we were going to do if we got him home to Iceland. Warner Brothers had bailed at this point. Craig McCaw, the cell phone billionaire, had stepped in. He was the financial benefactor. He took over the board—he had a majority on the board— and he had the bank account, and his lieutenants did the staffing. He decided he wanted to have his own people running the Foundation.

Well, *I* had been running it. So I was, like, at sea. I had been the person who had negotiated Keiko from Reino Aventura to Oregon. I had a lot invested in it, a lot of hard work. The idea of just sort of shuffling off and letting somebody else in was really difficult. So I said to Dave, "What do you think I should do? Should I stay in and try to fight it out? Or should I, like, just bail? Should I figure that I did my part, so let them do their part? I have so many other things I could be doing! Maybe I should just let this thing go." Dave said, "No, no, no, no." He didn't really offer advice that often. But he said, "Oh, you should definitely stay in. You're just going to have to outsmart him. You can do that."

So Dave thought there would be a way to actually sort of outsmart Craig McCaw, or work with Craig in a way that we could move him. So

I stayed on the board. Craig's people told him, "Dave Phillips knows a lot about this, he's got all the connections with the environmental groups, which you don't have, and he's got all these connections with Iceland, which you don't have. We've worked with him and he's been straight up with us. We think you ought to keep him." And Craig did.

Afterward, Craig McCaw's lieutenants told me, "Do you realize you are the first and only person that Craig has ever retained? In every other organization that Craig has taken over, every single holdover has been ousted. He doesn't leave people from the old regime. You're the first."

And in fact Craig and I got along very well. There were a lot of issues where Craig and I agreed and others we didn't. And then, in the very, very end analysis, when Craig lost several billion dollars and had to pull out of the Keiko project, he called me up and said, "Now I'm out, and I'm ready to give this thing back to you." So it came back around to me. We were running the Free Willy-Keiko Foundation again. It was on our watch that Keiko joined wild whales off Iceland and swam across to Norway.

Earth Island Institute is consciously designed to favor the Dave Brower style. Not just his style, but his philosophy. It's all about finding people who have an idea and giving them a place to try to make that idea into something that really works for the planet. At a time in which the environmental movement isn't doing that.

Part of what formed Earth Island is what happens to people arriving at the doors of, say, the Sierra Club. They've come up with a great idea, only to have the Sierra Club say, "Oh, well, you know what? We've already done our priorities for this year and next year. The year after that, if the conservation committee thinks what you're doing was a good idea, we *might* be able to do something." And the person is feeling, *Oh my God, there's nothing here for me.* It's same at these other organizations that have gotten big, after starting off at the grassroots. Environmental Defense Fund, or Natural Resources Defense Council, or Audubon, these are big, huge institutions, and big institutions move more slowly. Earth Island was set up to try to avoid that.

But with a little bit more structure than what Dave provided origi-nally. A little more than just the desk in the corner, and "You're on your own, raise your own money." We wanted to try to help people get to where they want to go faster. And so the whole idea of Earth Island is to do that. To help train them, to help them with their finances, help give them an office if we can, or help with publication, to get the word out about what they're doing.

What Dave was about, what Dave *loved*, was when one person, or a small group, could outdo these big institutions. Jim Harding, for example. Dave was, like, "Jim Harding has stopped five nuclear power plants himself!" Or Rachel Carson. Or Dave Pesonen. The nuclear reac-tor they started to build at Bodega Bay is still just a hole in the ground, all because of Pesonen. One reason Dave liked this was because it had been *his* style. David Brower and Goliath. He started developing that style in the campaign to stop dams in the Grand Canyon. What he kept pointing out is how against an institution, with the right perseverance and pushing the right levers, one person could change something big. Somebody like Randy Hayes on the rainforest. All these groups were working on the rainforest, World Wildlife Fund and the others, but Randy, an individual, could get in and outperform huge groups. And Dave loved that. That was, like, his favorite thing. Dave loved the notches in the belts of the people who had gone after things. Amory Lovins, of course, that is totally what Amory is about, how he can outthink all these experts in big institutions.

Dave was always really skeptical about bureaucracy, and about pro-cess—about anything that could get in the way, anything that could come between the idea and the action. So at Earth Island we try our best to do that. We try not to get too hung up on all the bureaucracy of things.

In the shop we have this saying, "What Would Dave Do?" It's still important to think about that. I ask myself that especially when we have a new project that comes in and wants to join Earth Island, and there is something kind of different in the idea behind it. Dave was really big on "big E" environmentalism. He was thinking about war and environment, trade and environment—everything and environment—

back when other people weren't. He was open to the different facets of the environmental movement beyond the classical definition. So we'll see something that comes through the door, and, well, it doesn't look like other things. But this is probably something that Dave really would have been attracted to, *because* it's different, and maybe risky, but it's worth a try.

And Earth Island reflects Dave's thing with young people. Young people are a huge part of Earth Island and a huge force. It's so powerful, the idea of young people thinking about the future of the planet. And stepping up in different ways, confronting the institutions that are not doing anything. This has the potential to be so huge. The energy and the commitment. In fact, it's maybe the only way. The other way, the way of the mainstream groups, has got some real, grave limitations.

One of the things that Dave did which was incredible, and especially incredible to youth, was that he really spent time with young people, and was *of* them. I used to hear people in Friends of the Earth complain, "If he'd stop spending all this time with young people and get out with the *funders*, and get out with the foundation people, we could *run* this outfit." No. That wasn't what Dave was going to do.

"He's such a bigger-than-life person!" they'd say. "If Dave got on the phone and called people and did the 'ask,' brought in some money!" But he didn't do much of that. He didn't glad-hand with the corporate guys at all. I think he was too mavericky. He didn't want to feel like he was getting close to the seats of power. He didn't want to cut deals.

If you had an idea at a college campus, and the Dave Brower lecture was over, and he was sitting with you, having a beer, he was, like, *really there.* And he was listening. Do you know how empowering that is for a young person? To have the head of a big organization, a guy who's done all these incredible things, actually engaging one-on-one, personally, with you? Eager to hear your ideas? Or to give you the sense that you could do it?

It just doesn't happen. So that was a huge gift. He would take that gift all over the country. You'd say to him, "I have this idea, I want to do this." He would answer, "You can do it. You really *have* to do it! I'll try to raise you a little money to do it. You want to go off to a conference in Zimbabwe to save…whatever it is, the thing you want to save? How could you *not* do that? The Earth *needs* that. What can I do to help?" He would *empower* people to feel they could do something way beyond what they thought they could do.

The Fate of the Earth Conference, for example. Dave decides we'll do a conference on the fate of the Earth down in Nicaragua. We'll trundle down there and invite all these people. The people who organized Fate of the Earth—Dave Henson, Josh Karliner, a few other young people— none of them had done any of this stuff. But here they were with Dave getting behind it, *and people would just work all night.* They'd just do everything to make this happen. It was because of the trust he put in them and the support he put into them. He had this never-ending faith in young people to dig in and make a difference. *Never-ending.* I mean, inexhaustible. Wherever he was, he'd be the one closing down the bar, the last person out. A lot of these lecturers come in, give their lecture, head back to their hotel, or whatever. Dave would just move it to the bar and keep the ideas coming there.

Sometimes, if you're going to do that—adjourn to the bar and get excited by ideas—you're going to make mistakes. He would support some harebrained things. But only a few. He was willing to believe in people in ways that I really have never seen. I don't think people realize the power of that kind of mentorship. When you look around at the people he influenced, what a list! There isn't anybody whose hit off of Dave was anything other than his unbending support for what they were doing to help the planet. And where do you see that? I don't see that.

At the time of the turmoil at Friends of the Earth, I was the staff representative on the board. I came to wonder how it was that Dave would get himself into the trouble he did, first with his Sierra Club board, and then with his board at Friends of the Earth. I think Dave never understood why people couldn't follow where he was going. That they didn't see the value of what he was doing. He just couldn't see how they were not getting it. I also think he didn't believe that people were going to stab him in the back as much as they often did. Some of the people on his boards. Your mom and I would see it. Anne Brower and I, we would be, like, "How can you trust Alan Gussow? Or Dan Luten? Or Paul Burks? Or Phil Berry?" Dave would always assume that those folks would come around to his way of thinking.

Of course, he was also a big advocate of the lifeboat scenario. He was always thinking a little bit about the next step. If the organization was not in sync with where he was going, he was more interested in thinking about the next step than in preserving the status quo. Toward the end of his time at the Sierra Club, he saw the writing on the wall, and he had begun planning the birth of Friends of the Earth. And then, in his latter days at Friends of the Earth, he was already thinking about Earth Island Institute. He was more willing to take the risk of something new than he was to try to patch together something that was either not working, or just had gotten antagonistic.

I don't think we had an argument in my entire life with him. I literally don't even think we ever had an argument. Not a real one. I remember this one time, the harshest words I ever had with him, it was in the elevator riding up to Friends of the Earth. He had been traveling, out on the stump for a long time. We were going to sue on the condors, and we had some lawyers doing it pro bono. In the elevator Dave says, "How come you haven't got together the lawsuit yet? I've been waiting and waiting for this." Well, he'd been out on the road, and I'd been home taking care of business. I said to him, "You know what? I haven't just been sitting and twiddling my thumbs!" And that was all! In thirty years, that was the only time. It wasn't even very harsh.

We saw eye to eye. He really trusted me. You know, it sounds really corny, but I really worked to create Earth Island around having an organization that would be the last organization that Dave Brower was part of. I would have considered it a huge disaster to have him feel he had to leave Earth Island and create something else. Or to feel that Earth Island had turned on him in some way. It's hard to keep organizations from turning on people. Anyway, I thought, you know, he's been through enough, let's not have Earth Island go in a direction that turns out to be bad for him.

Ray Dasmann was a big admirer of Dave, and vice versa. Dasmann was this great field biologist and environmentalist, and Dave loved his thinking. It was Dasmann who described this distinction between "biosphere people" and "ecosystem people." People of the global culture, on the one hand, versus traditional, tribal people who know one ecosystem really well. Dasmann coined a phrase that made it into all of Dave's sermons: "We are already fighting World War III, and I'm sorry to say we are winning. It is the war against the Earth." Dave and Dasmann worked together on a number of things. Ray called Dave up one time, or sent him a note, and it just said, "Dave, I've thought about it for a long time, and I've decided. You were right."

Ray meant it as a general principle. It wasn't about anything specific. It was generic.

And it's true. Dave has proved right about so many things. I think that Dave was right about how the environmental movement ought to be structured. I don't think that's the way the environmental movement *is* structured now. Parts of it are structured okay, but a lot of it isn't. Recently somebody did a little sting on Conservation International. Some people purportedly from an arms company went in and said, "Oh, we want to work together with you and see if you can fix our image." Conservation International said, "Yeah, yeah, yeah, no problem. We'll have you adopt this African eagle. We'll put out all this stuff for you." It was a complete greenwash snow job. Accepting huge money from this bad corporation doing bad, bad things. Basically they were willing to dress up anybody for money.

I'm not saying that the whole environmental movement does that—not at all. But I do think that the movement has gotten very institutionalized, bureaucratized, run by MBAs, and there's something really lost in that. Dave aspired to have a movement that was more green, and young, and vibrant, and less compromise oriented, and more about fundamental change, and willing to take on adversaries. And that's what he stood for.

French nuclear test, Mururoa Atoll

PETER HAYES

PETER HAYES, the executive director of the Nautilus Institute,
divides his time between the organization's offices in San Francisco,
Australia, and South Korea, with forays into North Korea, as well.
Nautilus, which Hayes cofounded, is a think tank concerned with problems of
sustainability, security, and nuclear proliferation. His book *Pacific Powderkeg:
American Nuclear Dilemmas in Korea,* published by Free Press in New York
and Han-ul Press in Seoul, suggests one of his principal preoccupations. In
Australia, Hayes is a professor of international relations at the Royal Mel-
bourne Institute of Technology. In California, where he spends about half
the year, he is an activist and keeps a small adjunct office on the ground
floor of his Berkeley home.

Hayes is a big man, six feet five, and his home office does not leave him
a lot of room for maneuvering. A tall steel weight machine occupies much
of one wall. A disk, L3, has gone out in his back, and the weight machine is
to stave off surgery by strengthening his core. He works it every day. The day
of the interview, I squeezed by a table piled with books and found a seat.
On a narrow ledge running around the wall, a surprising number of digital
and analogue devices were recharging. The metronome of the family dryer
clunked softly from the next room. Given the size of the room, there was no
need for either of us to leave his seat for Hayes to give me a tour of his walls.

"That is a scroll from South Korea," he said. "I can't remember the exact translation, but it's words to the effect of, 'Moon, sun, and calm repose.' It's a gift from a Korean colleague. It's beautiful." A satellite photo on the wall showed the stretch of the Victoria coast where his family had their farm. Next was a pair of portraits. "That's my father. And that's my mother. She's still alive. She's out on the farm. They were both agricultural scientists."

"Which one is responsible for your size?"

"He was six-two. Mary's five-eleven. So I guess I get it from both of them. It's genetic, and also from drinking milk growing up on the dairy farm. Actually, my parents always said my height was from walking in bare feet in the chicken shit, collecting eggs. It's dry, the chicken manure, but it's very high in fertilizer."

He pointed to a small stand-up desk.

"That was another thing I picked up from Dave. Standing writing. This little table is brilliant. I spend about half my day standing up writing. He always stood up typing, and I was struck by that."

Hayes picked up a nicely shaped rock and showed it to me.

"You remember Dave used to collect rocks? I used to bring him bloody rocks all the time. I don't know what he did with them."

What Dave did with them, I explained, is fill up his house. My father's rock collection covered every horizontal surface in the place. It drove my mother crazy. Rocks from Glen Canyon, Sierra Nevada rocks with yellow lichen, Canadian rocks with orange lichen, limestone rocks with fossils, river-rounded stones, rocks from all over the world. Hayes laughed.

"I remember bringing Dave a piece of cinder from the top of Mount Stromboli," he said. "Which is an active volcano. Carried that bloody thing all the way around the planet for a couple of years before I gave it to him. And I gave him a couple of pieces of black basalt like this one here, which I lugged off the hill above the beach where I grew up in Australia. Small offerings."

M Y CONNECTION WITH Friends of the Earth began in England, in London, in late '72. I went there to organize protests against the French nuclear-weapons tests in the South Pacific, on Mururoa Atoll. In London I met Richard Sandbrook and Tom Burke, who were cofounders of the English branch of Friends of the Earth. Then I went on to Paris, which was obviously ground center for demonstrations against the French tests. I was introduced to Les Amis de la Terre, the French branch of Friends of the Earth, and I met Brice Lalonde, the founder. Brice essentially took me under his wing. He became political mentor for the rest of my life. I learned so much from Brice about politics and organizational strategy. He had been president of the National Student Union of France at the Sorbonne in the 1968 student revolt against de Gaulle. He was a man who knew how to organize. He was a big friend and ally of Dave's. Later he ran for president of France on the Green ticket and eventually he became environment minister of France.

I was living with Brice in an attic apartment that he controlled. I stayed for quite a long time, working with Les Amis de la Terre, organizing protest walks from London to Paris, and the occupation of Notre Dame, and various sorts of fairly spectacular activities. At that point, the union in Australia and the South Pacific had cut off all telecommunications and trade ties with France, so these protests were not just a sort of side issue. They actually had salience. In Paris the government was paying attention, no doubt of that. The National Assembly reps from Polynesia were involved. Some wonderful people. We sent a group to Mururoa: Jean Toulat, who was a French Catholic priest. Jean-Jacques Servan-Schreiber, the author of *Le Défi Américain,* "The American Challenge," and editor and owner of *L'Express* political magazine—a very rich man. General de Bollardière, who was the actual on-the-ground Resistance leader during World War II. And Brice. Brice came up with this strategy of boarding ships at sea. This group went out to Mururoa and were arrested by the French Navy.

I kept very much in the background, doing a lot of very silent organizing work. And then someone called my parents in Australia and said that I was going to be killed if I stayed in Paris. At that point, we'd gotten through the summer. So I left. This threat, they weren't just screwing around. I consulted with knowledgeable people who said it was time to go, so I did. So that all happened with Friends of the Earth in the UK and Les Amis de la Terre in France before I even knew that Friends of the Earth in the United States even existed. I literally was completely unaware.

Until leaving. At which point Brice suggested that there might be some interest in setting up an affiliate, like-minded entity in Australia. Friends of the Earth Australia. To me, Friends of the Earth had a very attractive style. The combination of the deep research that was going on in the UK—that's when I met Amory Lovins for the first time—with the political organizing philosophy of the French. So I went back, stopped in Thailand, then Australia, and then went to New Zealand, and in each of those three places I started little fires and laid the name Friends of the Earth. In Thailand and New Zealand—particularly Thailand—I found the people that started Friends of the Earth in those places. In Australia I was very directly involved.

Setting up Friends of the Earth in Australia was a very complex story, intertwined with the national environmental politics of Australia. In Australia, members of unions were deeply involved in urban environmental conservation, and in wilderness conservation, as well. Workers would directly put down their tools, put a green ban on the site of a bad project, and say, "We're not doin' it." Then there was a national-government-backed Nature conservancy organization called the Australian Conservation Foundation, whose job was basically to stab the more activist groups in the back.

It all came to a head over the Lake Pedder campaign in Tasmania. Lake Pedder is really where the modern environmental movement in Australia began. It was a lake in the middle of the wilderness, just the most beautiful area. A glacial alluvial lake, brown water, with a white-sand beach three hundred meters wide by three kilometers. No actual surveys were ever done, but there were at least thirty species that were endemic to that lake. The hydroelectricity commission, which at that point had more than half the budget in the state of Tasmania, wanted to dam and flood the whole valley, and then dam and flood the valley next door, to build hydro plants for which there was no demand. *They had a vision.*

There was a huge clash. The lake was flooded in 1972—we lost that one—but the Australian conservation movement began. And, as of last year, we have the Greens, who were really born in that struggle, in the cabinet running the government of Tasmania. The hydro is being dismantled. The whole culture has been transformed. It's taken a generation to do it. Federally, the Greens hold the balance of power in Australia and they're quite influential in Australia. In the Lake Pedder campaign, the Australia Conservation Foundation really knifed the Lake Pedder activists in the back, politically, so several groups—genuine Greens—made a concerted effort to take over the ACF. And they succeeded. The Australian Conservation Foundation has now become a credible organization.

We set up Friends of the Earth Australia at this crucial time, late '73, because we didn't trust the power structure. We wanted a parallel, autonomous networked strategy, combined with research that could stand up and speak truth to power. So that's what we did. The first action of Friends of the Earth Australia was to send a boat out to Mururoa. The second action was to start a campaign to save the mountain Baw Baw frog. We wrote a letter to the minister, threatening to occupy the ski lift that would destroy the frog's only remaining habitat. We succeeded.

The problem is the frog is now gone, a victim of the global amphibian crisis.

We began an anti-uranium campaign. It was at this point, finally, that I started to send letters back to the Friends of the Earth network. "Say, what's going on internationally? Are there resources? Are there speakers? Are there publications that we could draw on? We need stuff on nuclear power. We're starting to find uranium here." At that point, Australia was actually exporting uranium to France, where they were putting it in bombs and bringing it back to Mururoa, blowing it up, and irradiating us.

So that's when I finally got in touch with the San Francisco office of Friends of the Earth. The mother organization. About time, I guess. As a result of that contact, I was invited to go on the Governing Council of the United Nations Environment Programme in Nairobi in October of 1974. That's where I met Dave. And that's where Friends of the Earth International really was set up. This was the founding year of UNEP, and it was UNEP's first governing council. All the NGOs turned up. Huey Johnson was there. And some guy from Audubon. His name isn't coming to me, but he was terrific.

So at that meeting they were trying to figure out what to do. I made a suggestion, which was adopted by the whole assembly. It was that we set up a secretariat, made up of all NGOs, which would be called the Environmental Liaison Center. That went forward and was adopted by the assembly and we all went home. We got a mandate that Friends of the Earth in San Francisco, essentially Dave Brower, Barbara Belding, and a few others, would run the secretariat. Later that rotated to different Friends of the Earth organizations around the world.

The following year there was a bit of a crisis at the meeting. They couldn't really find a candidate to actually run the thing in Africa—no candidate who was going to be acceptable both to the South and to the North. It turned out that an Australian was sufficiently chic, if you like. Not American, but acceptable to the North, yet *from* the South. Sort of acceptable, anyway. So I went to Nairobi for a year and set it up. In May of '75, I came through San Francisco, saw Dave again, and then went out to Nairobi. Dave himself came out that year to Nairobi for the Governing Council meeting in 1975.

This is when I first really talked to him in any depth. There was a local who had a house outside Nairobi where we were having dinner one night. And that's where I connected with David in a sort of very spiritual and personal level for really the first time. It was a very poignant moment. We were standing outside, the blazing Southern Cross and the whole Milky Way above us, on the equator. I can't actually remember what he said, but I do remember it was quite inspirational. It was just a few words. He basically said, "I trust you and I'm convinced you can really do something to save the planet." Whew! Really? I can't tell you how much that meant.

We invited him to come out to Australia and speak. He did. We had small numbers to hear him, but he had a big impact. These were the local Australians who were organizing regionally. They were *very* local. Some of them were very experienced organizers, and others had, you know, *some* experience, and had traveled. But their concerns were almost parochial. They were concerned about uranium mining, but weren't necessarily concerned about the whole nuclear fuel cycle. What they cared about was the Kakadu Wilderness, Aboriginal land rights, uranium—it was all very parochial. But Dave reached all of them. They were all moved.

There was one character in particular, who was from up north, his name was Strider—that was his nickname—and he was about as close to a hippie organizer as you can imagine, but *just tough as nails.* Strider had an ability to move people, and to work closely with Aboriginal people. He was about as hard a nut to crack as you can imagine. But Dave did move him. I still remember Strider spending hours looking through those bloody Exhibit Format books that Dave produced. This is someone, Strider, who lived in Kakadu, which is one of those places Dave's books were about. If Dave had made a book about Australia, it would have been a book on Kakadu.

There just aren't so many people in your life that had a saintly kind of aura around them. Dave had that. That was the charisma of the man. We all know he had faults. Many faults. We can talk about them, if you like.

Well, one of them had to do with his failure to control the budgets of his organizations. I mean, hands-on control, in two respects. One is, always respect the budget. In the sense that, yes, take risks, but take risks that you have under control, so that if the worst happens you have a backup. Dave didn't do that. He went the extra distance out there on the precipice. And of course, when he fell, there was no one there to catch him.

The civil war at Friends of the Earth, to me, it was like a great tragedy unfolding. The players who were in combat, at that point I really didn't understand what was going on, but I just knew it was wrong. Of course, the same thing had happened at the Sierra Club. It was a syndrome with Dave. At some point, he just didn't care about money. And he was right. But he was also wrong. It was a flaw of his, and it was an unnecessary flaw. I think you can take enormous risks, but that those risks are better taken when you have a sense of where the spongy terrain is. Before you stand on it. At least that's what I found.

I'm constantly updating. I mean, I can tell you to the month how far away forward we're funded. For one thing, it's kind of looking after the people you have working for you. Because they don't necessarily have the big picture, from where they sit. If you really want them to go the extra mile and do the extra hard yards, you owe it to them. They have kids they have to raise.

I keep going back to the night in Nairobi, when Dave and I had our conversation, the sky just blazing with stars. Had I not had that conversation, I think I probably would have gone into a much more political career in Australia, and never left the continent.

Dave's inspiration and direction, or not *direction*, but guidance, even without intending it—I don't think it was particularly intentional—it had a way of orienting you so that you saw that there was much more possible. Much more that could be done. And here were the steps. His brilliance was to be able to envision an outcome, and convince you that it was so important, and so necessary, and feasible. It was just a matter of finding a pathway. If you can envision the outcome, and if you can envision the pathway, you can do it. And it's true. You can! That was the brilliance of the man. He got you so focused, so *committed*, that you were going to be able to do anything, provided it was legal. Well, legal didn't really matter; provided it was ethical. But he never really told you how to do it. He probably wouldn't have known. But he convinced you that it was plausible, feasible, possible, and necessary to do it. So you then just did it. He was completely fearless. As a result, so were his protégés. He would ask the questions and they would go find the answers. You did things that were apparently impossible. If you'd asked yourself, at the time, are they possible, you probably would have said no, and stood back, and not tried. But you did not stand back. You tried.

On Glyder Fawr, North Wales
Photograph by Amory Lovins

AMORY LOVINS

ALMOST EVERY YEAR Amory Lovins leaves his Rocky Mountain Institute in Colorado, or departs whatever continent, island group, corporation, government, or military high command he is advising at the moment, and he travels to Northern California to teach a workshop at Esalen Institute on the Big Sur coast. At the most recent of these workshops, in a break between sessions, Lovins and I sat at a bench that looked down the rows of Esalen's large vegetable garden, out past cliffside cypresses, and across inshore kelp beds to the Pacific horizon.

The dark cypresses stood in lovely Maxfield Parrish light. Against the shine of the sea, the kelp stipes, fronds, and flotation bladders showed in sharp Edward Weston resolution. We talked about Lovins's youth, about his most influential mentor, and about the range of miniature yet haunting mountains where his life path took the turn that led to where he is today.

The miniature mountains are called Eryri, which derives from the Welsh for "eagle," or perhaps just "highlands." They make a landscape out of Tolkien. A shepherd in Eryri once spoke to Lovins of "*mynyddoedd yn llawn hiraeth,*" mountains full of longing. The young Lovins understood this in two ways: the peaks feel a sorrow for things gone, but longing is also what you feel for these mountains whenever you are somewhere else.

Where Lovins is today, after following that path diverging in enchanted mountains, is securely positioned as the planet's foremost expert on energy efficiency.

He is the winner of MacArthur and Ashoka Fellowships, the Mitchell Prize, the Right Livelihood Award, the Lindbergh Award, *Time* magazine's Hero for the Planet Award, the World Technology Award, the Heinz Award, the National Design Award, the Happold Medal, the Benjamin Franklin Medal, the Blue Planet Prize, the Volvo Environment Prize, the Zayed Prize, the first Aspen Institute/*National Geographic* Energy and Environment Award, the first Delphi Prize awarded by the Onassis Foundation, and the Nissan Prize, awarded for his invention of superefficient ultralight-hybrid automobiles. He has taught as lecturer or visiting professor at the universities of California, Stanford, British Columbia, Colorado, Dartmouth, Oklahoma, St. Gallen, and Peking. He is the author of 31 books and more than 450 articles.

In 1982, he cofounded the Rocky Mountain Institute, which he describes as an independent, entrepreneurial think-and-do tank. The mission of RMI is "the efficient and restorative use of resources to help create a world thriving, verdant, and secure, for all, for ever." RMI has offices in Snowmass and Boulder, Colorado, with a staff of around eighty and an annual budget of thirteen million dollars.

Lovins's clients at RMI have included Accenture, Allstate, AMD, Anglo American, Anheuser-Busch, Bank of America, Baxter, BorgWarner, BP, HP Bulmer, Carrier, Chevron, Ciba-Geigy, CLSA, Coca-Cola, ConocoPhillips, Corning, Dow, Equitable, General Motors, Hewlett-Packard, Interface, Invensys, Lockheed Martin, Mitsubishi, Monsanto, Motorola, Norsk Hydro, Petrobras, Prudential, Rio Tinto, Royal Ahold, Royal Dutch Shell, Shearson Lehman/American Express, STMicroelectronics, Sun Oil, Suncor, Texas Instruments, UBS, Unilever, Walmart, Westinghouse, Xerox, and more than one hundred energy utilities. His public-sector clients have included the Australian, Canadian, Dutch, German, and Italian governments, the US Congress, the US energy and defense departments, and the United Nations. In 2009, *Time* named him one of the one hundred most influential people in the world, and *Foreign Policy* named him one of the one hundred top global thinkers.

Amory Lovins is, in other words, a force of Nature.

"I've recycled I don't know how many hundreds of his lines," Lovins told me, on the garden bench at Esalen, as we spoke of his mentor David Brower. "And probably some vice versa."

Definitely some vice versa. Lovins was the protégé at the start, perhaps, but afterward the two men would continually swap that role, even as they recycled each other's lines.

"In the absence of a hierarchical command, leaders developed faster," my father once wrote, in musing on his experience in nurturing leadership. "I finally put my philosophy in words I spoke gently to myself: find good people, delegate authority and responsibility, talk things over if serious mistakes are made, and try to make fewer yourself. This is not a commercial, nor is it an objective view. Check it out with the victims. Try Amory Lovins first, and see if he can remember my directing him to do anything when he was Friends of the Earth's United Kingdom representative. I spent most of my time listening and marveling."

A T SIXTEEN I started at Harvard, and then halfway through my undergraduate course I transferred to Magdalen College, Oxford. Harvard wanted me to specialize too much. They had not only plugged all the loopholes behind me, but they were plugging loopholes ahead of me, trying to get me to concentrate on something. So I became a grad student at Magdalen, pronounced "Maudlin."

Meanwhile, to help strengthen defective knees, I'd been starting to hike a lot and do some guiding in New Hampshire in the White Mountains. I had written a monograph on wilderness safety, which I needed to photocopy. Photocopiers were rare in those days. This was 1968. At Oxford there was one of these precious machines in the physics department. I was nominally a physics grad student, because they didn't know what else to do with me. The photocopier kept breaking down and had to be operated by a technician. Philip Evans was the guy, the technician at the Oxford physics lab. He happened also to be probably the top color landscape photographer in Britain, but was essentially unknown. Philip and I got to talking, because the copier was so slow we got to read each page as it went through. We talked about mountains. He wanted to introduce me to *his* mountains, in northern Wales. Really? *In Wales?* How tall are they? Well, the tallest is just 3560 feet. But they really look and act like real mountains.

There was a cabin in Wales that belonged to the Oxford University Mountaineering Club, a stone hut in the Ogwen Valley, so we started going up there. Philip and I were hiking and scrambling and photographing. He'd been doing photography much of his life, and I had done very little photography, but he got me started and taught me some things. After a while, when we had photographed quite a lot, mostly separately, sometimes together, we began talking about the need to cover our film costs. Kodachrome and processing it were fairly expensive, and we were both running out of money. I thought we should send our chromes to the *National Geographic,* because I heard they pay well. The *Geographic* courteously responded, one of their senior editors. "This is beautiful work," he said, "but it's really too atmospheric for us. It's not representational enough. We want pictures that are more in the style we publish, not so much like fine art. But you might send it to Dave Brower, he likes this sort of thing."

Of course, Philip and I had always been in awe of Dave's Exhibit Format books, and thought, well, there's no harm in sending in some chromes. Maybe he'll have some advice about where we can make some money off them and pay for our film. We sent a bunch of them to him at Friends of the Earth in San Francisco. We didn't hear anything for a long time. Eventually, I contacted Dave again. I didn't think they'd been lost in the mail, or anything, but I just wanted to check. Dave said, "Well, as it happens, I'm coming to London next week. Can you meet me in London?"

So we did. It turned out to be the organizing meeting to set up Friends of the Earth in the United Kingdom. In a sidebar to that big organizational conversation, Dave asked Philip and me if we could photograph in more seasons, because we didn't have much winter. He also asked if I could write something about the area. I was a fairly novice writer at that point. So we said, "Okay, we'll do that. And we'll send you some more chromes." Dave said he liked our photography. He gave us some hints about what to do more of or less of, including teaching us Brower's Sky Rule: "Everybody knows the sky is there. So don't show it unless it's doing something interesting, and then show a lot of it." In other words, point the camera somewhat down or somewhat up, but not horizontally. Good rule.

We spent that winter photographing, and I sent Dave a couple of essays. Apparently he read them on the plane coming back to London and he was laughing much of the trip. He liked them. When we met in London, now for the second time, he went through our chromes for a half hour or so, holding them up to some improvised light source. Then he thought a little bit, and said, "You know, I've got this contract with McCall for a dozen Exhibit Format books on the Earth's wild places—the Earth's Wild Places Series. One of my authors just got sick and dropped out. So I have one slot available, and I'll give you a half hour to decide whether you want to do an Exhibit Format book for me about North Wales."

We were, of course, I believe the British term is "gobsmacked." We had thought he was just going to advise us of a potential market for our chromes, so that we could actually start paying for our film. I tried the usual objections, like, *But I've never written a book.* "Well, it's time you did. You're a good writer. Oh! And by the way, I'd want you to lay out the book, too." *But I've never laid out a book.* "Well, it's time you learned." So Philip and I huddled and decided, What an opportunity! Of course we've got to do it. We accepted. We then spent the next year and a bit shooting some more in all seasons, and I did a lot of writing. And that was the beginning of our book, *Eryri, the Mountains of Longing.*

Photographing in those mountains in winter, we would go out with about half a dozen cameras between us. I was using a little Rollei 35 that had been run over by a car but still worked, and a Pentax H1a, which was from the 1950s. It was so sloppy in tolerance that it wouldn't freeze up. We had usually a Hasselblad and a couple of Pentaxes. With the combination of condensation and freezing we'd get frozen condensate inside the camera and it would gum up the works. We'd be lucky to have one or two bodies working by the end of the day. Later I switched to the Rollei SL35, perhaps the best predigital mountain camera because the mechanism was all unlubricated slippery stuff like Delrin, and the wonderful Zeiss lenses had bayonet mounts you could work quickly with gloves on, keeping snow out of the body. You can't do tripod stuff up there, because you're right off the North Sea. The clouds move very fast, and the light just blinks on and off. You've got to grab the shot. It's worse than wildlife photography. It was technically quite an adventure, dealing with the cold-weather conditions and the very dynamic light, which of course was generally horizontal in winter, or near winter, because you're at pretty high latitude.

The first photo in the book, "Nant y Benglog at dawn," was the very first color photo I ever took. I grabbed it on a cheap Minoltina point-and-shoot. The third subject is a storm up on Glyder Fawr. Which is not very far from Castell y Gwynt, "Castle of the Winds." That's the place where if you spend a wild night up there alone, in the morning you're either crazy or a great poet. Take your pick. I met a guy there who tried it one night. I tried it several times myself, but I was never there under quite the right conditions. This guy was there under perfect conditions. He said he left before midnight and ran down so fast in the dark that he just touched a foot down now and then in order to steer. I said, "What made you run so fast?" And he just wouldn't talk about it. Having the wind sing in that place was quite an experience. The wild Welsh wind singing in those slates, up on that ridge out of Arthurian legend, where you're stalked by y Brenin Llwyd, "the Gray King," who disappears people.

You remember the cover of the book, this remarkable rock formation with snow on it? Philip was trying to get sort of toward the side of that, up on Glyder Fach, to photograph it from a certain angle. He slipped on some ice under this granular snow and went upside down, pinned by his pack between some rocks, and just at that moment, the sun, in the Welsh way, scanned across the ridge like a spotlight, and he grabbed the shot with his last frame. Upside down. That's a special thing he would always do: he would make fabulous shots on the last frame of a Kodachrome roll of thirty-six. In this case he was also upside down. He couldn't get up without help, and I was trying to get to him, across these icy rocks. Meanwhile he grabbed the shot. Philip and I had a little game we played. He would run out of film, score big on frame thirty-six, and then I would mysteriously produce another roll, so he could do another magnificent thirty-sixth shot.

By now I was at Merton College at Oxford.

What had happened was that in my second year at Magdalen I was running out of money again. After squash one day, my Indian squash partner, Sudhir Anand, and I were talking, and I told him I'm going broke, and I'd have to figure out something other than occasional physics consulting, which is how I'd got through college so far. And he said, "Oh, well, I've got this cushy post at Merton College, probably the oldest college and one of the richest. It's called a Senior Scholarship, which pays all your fees and gives you a stipend. It's good for two or three years. And since mine is expiring, they'll advertise it again, so why don't you compete for it? All they can do is say no."

So I did. And I found out partway through the shortlist interview that I was actually being considered for a much more exalted thing, kind of a postdoc faculty position called a Junior Research Fellowship, which happened to share the same application form. There was no box to check which one you were applying for. So they somehow assumed I was applying for the JRF. Which I wouldn't have considered doing, because they have about two hundred applicants a year, all with graduate degrees, and many of them with doctorates. And I didn't have any degrees at that point. Just a high school diploma. Anyway, I got the JRF, quite unexpectedly. It meant three years of being a don, and being given room and board *and* a generous stipend.

So when I was writing this book for Dave, I was a scrawny, nerdish twenty-one-year-old don with a big sunny room where I could lay out all the dummies for the book. I had these bits of poetry and prose and the images all laid out on these big sheets of paper folded into double-spreads. Whenever I walked by, something would want to move around to some other place. After a few months, they figured out where they wanted to be with each other.

Meanwhile Dave and I were doing various edits. He had asked me to write a long essay as the main text of the book, a case study of British national parks. Because this one, Snowdonia National Park, like all British national parks, is not internationally recognized. Because it's just a green line on a map. It's not legally protected. In fact, the main threat to it is the government, because parks tend to be in remote upland, impoverished areas, and the government tends to put industrial mega-projects there. This particular park had an old, giant slate quarry carved out of the middle of it like a hole in a doughnut. And the government had put a nuclear power plant in the southern part and an aluminum smelter just outside the northern edge, and later on they put a giant pumped-hydro scheme kind of in the middle. These things were sold on the basis that they could bring jobs.

In those days the big threat was Rio Tinto Zinc, the world's largest mining company at the time. RTZ wanted to strip-mine *Coed y Brenin*, "the King's Wood," in the middle of the national park, for copper and dredge the nearby and very beautiful Mawddach Estuary for gold. I thought that was a bad idea, and I wrote this eight-part essay about the national park and economic development and wildness.

I did about a third of the photography in the book, and Philip two-thirds. And then I did the text and layout. Sir Charles Evans, who had helped organize the first successful Everest expedition—a very distinguished mountaineer and rector at the University College of North Wales, up the road in Bangor—wrote the introduction. I tried to get the Prince of Wales, but I didn't know him at the time.

It's still some of my best writing. At the time, I was speaking a little Welsh and I was much immersed in the North Wales culture. They had a mature poetic tradition a thousand years before Chaucer. It's a remarkable place.

I'm very pleased now, when I go back, to hear just about everybody speaking Welsh. When I was first going there, Welsh was dying out. Cymdeithas yr Iaith Gymraeg, the Welsh Language Society, was burning English holiday cottages and trying to protest the decimation of the culture. Then Wales became semiautonomous and now has a parliament, and part of the deal was that they get to revive the language. *Yr Heniaith*, the Old Language, is now flourishing. Anyway, I had some of my poetry in the book. Some of it is haiku stanzas, but I use a Welsh device called *cynghanedd*, which means "binding," where you echo consonants instead of rhyming vowels.

So the book came out in 1971 and it got quite a lot of attention. In those days I wasn't yet skilled in aikido politics, and in parallel with the book I made a fairly hard-hitting documentary. Or *I* didn't make it, but a couple of terrific producers at BBC made it, and I was a consultant and advisor. It was called *Do You Dig National Parks?* The BBC show and the book, which Rio Tinto Zinc held up for a year with a threat of a libel suit—and that of course got it a lot more publicity—caused such a public uproar that RTZ gave up the project and went away mad. The copper's still there. But I may have saved them from going broke, because just as they would have been at the maximum outstretch of cash flow, the copper market collapsed. At the time they didn't take my efforts to help them quite as graciously as I think they were meant. In fact they were quite annoyed.

During the course of this writing, I was hanging out with Dave whenever he was in London, which was a few times a year, and absorbing the way he did things. I quickly learned, whenever I went to see him in London, that I better bring a passport and a toothbrush, because he was perfectly capable of saying, "Oh, by the way, we're on the four o'clock to Timbuktu. Or to Tashkent. And back in a week and a half." He would drag me off on short notice to all sorts of peculiar places. This was a style I was quite unaccustomed to. The trips were always interesting and worthwhile. We were rarely if ever disappointed. We rarely thought we shouldn't have come. Because he had a very good sense of timing and a huge global network.

So it was always an adventure. I had not dealt with somebody before who was so strategic and decisive. I think a lot of that came from his military background, but I only understood some of that a bit later. In those days, telephones, long-distance phones, were much too expensive for a student, or even for a don, to use much. In calling many countries, you often actually had to prebook when you wanted to call and for how long. And the phones didn't work very well. You could easily pay five or ten dollars a minute to call across the Atlantic. But Dave used the phone all the time. If he needed to talk to somebody to get something done, he would just pick up the phone and call. Of course, there were no cell phones in those days. It was all wire line with predigital stepper-switch rotary dialing, and switches at the phone-company switching center. I rather quickly realized how effective he was at figuring out what to do and doing it, thinking many steps ahead. And I've been much the same way myself ever since. It was a profound influence on my thinking about how to be effective and what to be effective about.

Eryri was quite a project. It took most of my time for a couple of years. By the end of that effort, when we won on the mining, I had become much more interested in who Dave was and what he did. The kind of issues that he cared about, I came to care about them too. Then, in 1971, Oxford wouldn't let me do a doctorate in energy. It was two years before the '73 oil embargo, and they said, "Energy? What's that? It's not an academic subject, is it? We haven't a chair in it! Pick a real subject." So I said, "Well, I'm sorry, but I think energy is going to be really important."

As I was leaving, they gave me a master's, by virtue of being a don.

Dave was the big catalyst in allowing me to realize that what I was doing in academic life was intellectually interesting but ultimately not that important. If we end up understanding mitochondrial membrane kinetics, or tertiary structure of proteins, which were two of the puzzles that intrigued me at the time, it would be important, but not as much as keeping the planet livable by solving energy problems, or preventing nuclear proliferation, or addressing climate change.

So I went to work for Dave. For the next ten years in London, I was British representative of Friends of the Earth in the United States. The British Friends of the Earth, which had been in formation since I first met Dave in 1969, was very sensitive about issues of colonialism, so I became sort of the ambassador from the United States branch of Friends of the Earth. Once I was working for Dave, starting in fall of '71, I would travel a lot more over the world with him, mainly in Europe.

I worked from my London base all around the world, chiefly Europe, and then I'd come back to the US to guide in the White Mountains each summer. The trips with Dave were learning journeys, working on a wide range of issues, increasingly about energy. A lot of the work was on nuclear energy and nuclear proliferation issues. Everything, you name it. I worked on the Stockholm Conference *Eco*. We hit most of the European capitals pretty regularly. Dave was paying me enough to more or less cover my phone bill. I would live by my wits for the rest by writing, lecturing, broadcasting, and consulting. In 1979, I married Hunter. It was kind of a nomadic hunter-gatherer existence. Hunter hunted and I gathered. We moved back to the States in 1981 and settled in Colorado in 1982.

My parents were disappointed that I had left a promising academic career. But I didn't realize that until twenty-odd years later. My dad finally told me. At the time, they very kindly gave me no intimation of their concerns. They were just completely supportive of whatever I wanted to do. Both my parents lived to ninety-seven. Their philosophy of child-rearing was love your children, support them, and get out of their way.

What I picked up from Dave was the importance of humor. And turn of phrase. And aesthetic principles—Dave was a consummate aesthetician. He was a great editor, and his aesthetic sense is in all his books. In 2010, I wrote a little recruiting essay for Rocky Mountain Institute, "On Whom We Seek." One of its eleven hallmarks of success in our work starts: "Do you strive to get the concept clear, the number right, the word precise, the image moving, the layout beautiful, the message compelling, not just because it works better, but because you have high personal standards? We do too."

That sense of duty to aesthetic standards is one of Dave's greatest gifts to me. That, and obviously the content of the work, the purpose of the work, the passion behind it. I started to learn from him what I would now call aikido politics. Because although, on the one hand, he was utterly uncompromising in pursuit of his high purpose, on the other he was never rigid or disrespectful in how he dealt with adversaries. This is what emerges so clearly from *Encounters with the Archdruid*. The way he interacted in that book with the dam builder, Floyd Dominy, and the developer, Charles Fraser, and the miner, Charles Park. "Narratives about a conservationist and three of his natural enemies," is the tagline on the cover. But Dave wasn't *inimical* to his enemies. McPhee catches that very well in the book.

It's respectful engagement. That has never left me. I think I'm now a lot better at it for understanding more of its roots in Taoism and Buddhism. It's transformed how I work. The more adversarial, classic conservation-battle stuff I did in the early days with Rio Tinto Zinc and others, I wouldn't dream of doing now. That had its time and place. And I'm glad that there are still people who do that, also in Dave's tradition—they fight the battles in the classic way, and that makes those of us who do it differently seem terribly reasonable.

There's another lovely piece of history to round all this out. More than two decades after the fight with Rio Tinto Zinc over copper mining in Snowdonia, I was asked by the Copper Development Association to come give them a talk about copper, electricity, and energy efficiency. Most things that you do to save electricity use more copper, and they wanted to sell more copper. Fatter wires, fatter pipes, better motors, better heat exchangers with bigger area, and so on. Well, several years later I ended up doing some consulting for Rio Tinto, as it's now called. It's still one of the top mining companies in the world. At Rocky Mountain Institute we have now done many engagements with Rio Tinto around the world, helping them redesign existing mines, or design new ones, or use renewable energy at their remote sites, in order to avoid the high costs and logistical risks of hauling fuel in. Rio Tinto is now leading the greening of the global mining industry.

So this has come full circle. Very few people in the company remember the history. Sometimes, when we've had a nice dinner after working together for a week on a project design, I will recount some of our early mutual history. We'll all have a good chuckle about it. I think it's the most delicious irony. One of our most valued and constructive relationships at RMI, in changing how industry works, is through the company whose initial efforts to build a bad mine brought me close to Dave's work, and into Dave's world, and into what I've been doing ever since.

Of course Dave had extraordinary leadership skills. You would know better than I how much of that came from mountaineering and how much from the war, or elsewhere. But he really knew the difference between leadership and management. I've had the privilege in the past decade or two to work with many flag and general officers in the Services, people of extraordinary personal and professional quality. They're about in Dave's league. I have no doubt that if he'd continued his military career he would have been a three- or four-star general.

I started to pick up some elements of leadership. As Dave and I were having a conversation, we would figure out whom we ought to talk to, and who ought to get an idea from a certain source at a certain time to cause him or her to behave in certain ways. He would get on the phone and call whomever it was around the world and start activating his social network to actually make things happen.

What he brought to his work was a detailed and exact knowledge of how things are connected. Nonlinear thinking. Strategic thinking informing tactics. Not simply doing what's right in front of you, but what's the bigger pattern that this supports and connects. I never knew him as a military officer, but I would think he was an exceptional one, and must have inspired great loyalty. He was fearless, and that rubbed off. His mountaineering would help in that, too. He wasn't foolhardy. He would take calculated risks and know what he was going to do if it wasn't working out. His climbing must have figured here: he was very aware that gravity is not an option; it's the law. Your gear must be in order, and you have to use it properly to protect yourself.

There were probably half a dozen times—not that I remember them anymore—where I would think he was wrong about the course of action that would bring about the result we want. But I would do it his way. Within one or two or occasionally three years, I would realize he was right. He just had more experience to bear on it. And I even told a number of people that, over the years, when they had a disagreement with him about what to do. I advised them my experience has been that he turned out to be right.

Neither of us took kindly to being micromanaged. When Dave was kicked out of Friends of the Earth, it became clear that I would be, too, unless I wanted to get micromanagement, and it was clear that would not be a good idea. So Hunter and I went and started our own outfit. We began Rocky Mountain Institute in 1982 with two or three people and ten thousand bucks out of our back pockets. It grew fairly steadily. For many years it held at around forty or fifty people. It briefly went a little over one hundred, and then back to about ninety, and it's been eighty or ninety ever since. I no longer know all the names, at this point. There are a few people at staff meetings I don't quite recognize. We're now getting our various business and people systems working a lot better. We grew a little too fast for a while, but we're now catching up with ourselves. We're attracting some terrific talent.

Which is another area where Dave had influence. I learned a lot of my hiring philosophy from Dave. He would hire largely on intuition, based on aptitudes and attributes, as opposed to the normal HR procedure of looking at the résumé and hiring on the basis of achievements and qualifications. That's how he got Jim Harding, who ended up doing decades of important work on electric utility policy. That hiring philosophy is a perpetual and healthy source of tension at Rocky Mountain Institute. Because I have very much the Brower philosophy. I've kept it because it has served us so well.

Occasionally Dave's intuition was wrong about someone. Sometimes mine is, too. I've hired several people who didn't work out. And then you have to recognize it and get gracefully out of it as soon as you can. But most of them have worked extremely well. The test that I keep challenging our HR director with is: If a young Amory showed up at your door, would you hire him? Based on your present criteria, probably not, because he doesn't have any degrees. It would be the same if the young Dave Brower showed up. No degree. Dropped out as a sophomore to go climb mountains. But made up for it with things he learned up there, didn't he?

Dave was a very smart guy. And not at all shy about learning new things. He delighted in continuous learning. He reminded me of that Confucian analect, "Learn as if you're chasing after somebody you can never quite catch up with." Nothing got past him. And your mother was like that, too. Absolutely nothing got past Anne. Very sharp.

I came out of experimental physics and a bunch of other mathematical disciplines, and I was always impressed and astonished that Dave would get the numbers right. If you didn't get the numbers right, he would spot it right away, doing the math in his head. You know, he's kind of like these financial guys who can glance at a spreadsheet and instantly know what's going on in the company. You don't normally think of him as a quant. But he had a very keen mind for numbers, which does not normally go with all of the right-brain genius. As long as I wrote clearly what the numbers were about, he would have a very good idea of what they were supposed to be. In the rare event of my making an arithmetic mistake, he would generally spot it before I did. That was impressive.

I think Dave's predilection for action over study really rubbed off on me in a big way. I've spent decades studying a lot of things, but I tend to learn them better by doing them. Dave would never have been effective in a think tank. He was very much a learn-by-doing guy. Occasionally I would ask him if he thought something was on the right track. He might say yes or no, and he might have a few sentences of koan-like encouragement. But he was very good about not telling me too much about how to do something. Because if I figured it out, then I'd really own it and I'd really get it.

He did have a way of attracting talent and inspiring action that was unique in my experience. I've had some treasured mentors over the years, but he was by far the greatest influence, especially in his leadership, his style of being and doing, and his ability to cause vast and lasting change.

I don't know if he was ever much exposed to Taoists. But he would have liked Taoism. He would have very much resonated with a lot of Zen.

I was just reading Huston Smith the other night, the great theologian who was here at Esalen a few weeks ago. Huston Smith describes his last conversation with Goto, a great Zen roshi in Japan. The roshi said, "Zen is simple. Simple! So simple: Infinite gratitude to the past, infinite service to the present, infinite responsibility for the future." That could have been a Dave Brower line.

Guanacos in the future Patagonia National Park

DOUG TOMPKINS

T HE HONEY-COLORED floors and desk of Doug Tompkins's office in Chile are of *manio,* a conifer endemic to the Lake Region. The tree, a podocarp, likes the heavy rainfall on the southern Chilean coast between 35 degrees and 42 degrees south latitude. The yellowish wood is straight grained and moisture resistant. The local tree imbues the room with a warm and honeyed light, an antidote to the gray, wet weather for which this coast is notorious.

Today the fine-grained expanse of the *manio* desktop was uncluttered, nothing there but Tompkins's MacBook, a phone, a mug stuffed with pens and pencils and scissors, and a black-and-white portrait of Kris Tompkins, his collaborator and wife. The multiple panes of the office windows looked out on sheep grazing the rehabilitated pastures of Reñihué Farm. There was something fake, something staged, about this flock. The scene was a little too pastoral to be true. There were too many sheep for the fields to remain so green—or so it seemed to the eye of the interviewer, educated in the dry rangeland of the American West. The secret lay, I decided, in this coast's 235 annual inches of rain.

"And the sheep are on intense, short rotational grazing," said Tompkins. "So they are in the fields only for a few days before being moved to another field. But you're right, the rainfall makes this green like Ireland."

The pastures end seaward in the waters of Reñihué Fjord, visited by southern sea lions, dusky dolphins, and whales, and they end landward in forests of pudu deer and pumas. This coast has huge tides, in excess of twenty-three feet. At high tideline, the glacier-carved fjord becomes a glacier-carved valley and rises through temperate Valdivian rainforest toward Volcán Michimahuida, an 8000-foot, glacier-flanked, snow-capped volcano.

The volcano is the centerpiece of Pumalín Park, a reserve larger than Yosemite, acquired in a series of purchases by Tompkins and his Conservation Land Trust, beginning in 1991. It is the pilot project for a network of national-parks-to-be that Doug and Kris Tompkins are creating in South America. At the moment Pumalín is being run as a national park, and someday it will be official, as the Tompkinses are now working on a plan to donate all of Pumalín to the Chilean government.

The ceiling of the Tompkins office is darker and rougher than the golden floor and has none of the luster. The planks up there are recycled siding pulled from a weathered barn that was falling to ruin when Tompkins bought Reñihué Farm.

"We use almost entirely demolition wood for the vast majority of our buildings in the parks," he told me. "Just this afternoon I was down inspecting a new campground in the future Patagonia National Park project. The wood in the cook shelters and the public bathrooms is all recycled. In the houses we use nearly 100 percent recycled wood for all furniture, interior beams and trusses, and flooring. It looks better, too. You've seen our California office, in Sausalito. That is almost all recycled wood. Quincey Tompkins Imhoff, my daughter, is responsible for the Sausalito office. A chip off the old block, I hope.

"I've been interested in recycled materials for a long time. When I was at Esprit, our big 110,000-square-foot headquarters building was also almost all recycled wood, when we rebuilt after the big fire that destroyed the original place. We have lots of experience with using demolition materials."

Tompkins is a high school dropout, expelled from prep school in his senior year for an accumulation of piddling infractions. His lack of any sort of degree or diploma has not impeded him much. He made his first fortune as cofounder of an outdoor-recreation equipment company, The North Face, and then a bigger fortune as cofounder of the giant clothing company Esprit. Spared the drudgery of university study, he spent his late teens rock climbing and ski racing in the Rockies, Europe, and South America. In 1964, at twenty-one, he opened The North Face, where he put his wilderness experience to work in the design of high-quality tents, sleeping bags, and backpacks. (It is largely thanks to Tompkins that your tent has no central pole, but rather an exoskeleton of bendable poles, which allows that dome-shaped, wind-shedding profile.) In 1968, Doug and his first wife, Susie, began selling women's dresses out of the back of a Volkswagen bus. In 1971 they incorporated as Plain Jane, a name later changed, at Doug's suggestion, to Esprit de Corps, which was then shortened to Esprit. By 1978, the company had formed partnerships in Germany, Canada, Australia, and Hong Kong, and sales were topping $100 million a year.

In 1989, Tompkins, increasingly troubled by the effect of fashion on the environment, cashed out, selling his share of Esprit's American branch to Susie, from whom he had separated. In 1990, he founded the Foundation for Deep Ecology, which funds environmental activism. In 1991, two years out of Esprit, he bought 17,494 acres in the Reñihué valley, including the degraded fields and forests of Reñihué Farm. He commenced restoring those fields and forests, and thereby established the pattern for the next twenty years of his life.

In 1993, Tompkins married Kristine McDivitt, the former CEO of Patagonia, Inc. He seems to be sweet on powerful female captains of the garment industry. This one, Kristine, at fifteen had met the great climber and piton-forger Yvon Chouinard, who not long afterward, as it happened, would set off with a climbing buddy, Doug Tompkins, on a fateful six-month expedition to Patagonia, where they pioneered a route on Mount FitzRoy, among other adventures. The teenage Kristine went to work part time in summers at Chouinard Equipment, which eventually grew into Patagonia, Inc., with Kristine herself at the helm. In 1984, on her watch, Patagonia launched 1% for the Planet, a group of companies pledged to donate 1 percent of sales, or 10 percent of profit, whichever was more, to environmental causes. (Patagonia, for its part, favored radical outfits like Earth First!) Upon retirement and marriage, Kristine's life path veered from Patagonia, the company, to Patagonia the place—the actual Andean landscape—where she took up residence on Reñihué Farm. The two entrepreneurs pooled their talents and resources. Kris, like her husband, began Book II of her career way down south on this farm.

The Tompkinses restored the pastureland, badly overgrazed and eroded and bordered by stretches of burned-out forest. They replanted that forest. They renovated the farm buildings, striving to retain the "vernacular" of the local architectural style. The main farmhouse, after two years of restoration, became a stellar example in the Chilote manner of the Chilote manor. The farms of the region use woodstoves for cooking and heating. The Tompkinses did not abandon that tradition; they expanded it. In the farm's two large organic gardens, woodstoves heat three greenhouses, which produce fresh vegetables year-round. The couple run sheep and cattle, as is traditional here in continental Chiloé, but they also have introduced worm composting, perennial agriculture, apiaries, and jam making. The before-and-after aerials of Reñihué Farm are stunning, like satellite images of two different planets—a desert world followed by a lush and green one.

The couple began buying more farms. Doug, a pilot, built an airstrip at the original spread, and by plane they monitored their growing domain. They first replicated the Reñihué Farm model elsewhere in Palena Province. They acquired and restored:

The 1216 acres of Pillán Farm, the geographic and administrative center of Pumalín Park and the production center for the organic honey and jams marketed by their enterprise, Pillán Organics.

The 526 acres of Rincón Bonito Farm, in a remote valley on the banks of the Ventisquero River, eight hours by horseback from the nearest village, farmed entirely by draft animals and human labor, a refugium for nineteenth-century agrarian life.

The 3710 acres of Vodudahue Farm, straddling the river in Vodudahue Valley, the dry inland extension of Comau Fjord. Here the Tompkinses breed a strain of rams adapted to local pasture and weather, and have established a native plant nursery, with a greenhouse germinating and nurturing two dozen species for reforestation.

The 855 acres of Hornopirén Farm, almost entirely fallow, only 15 percent of its acreage devoted to agriculture, most of the rest of it damaged forest regenerating on its own.

The Reñihué Farm model then jumped the Andes, crossing over to the Argentinean side. The Tompkinses acquired and restored: The 7,418 acres of Laguna Blanca Farm, in the Entre Ríos Province of northeast Argentina. The 24,157 acres of Ana Cua Ranch in Corrientes Province of northeast Argentina. The 50,458 acres of El Tránsito Ranch, also in Corrientes Province.

Even as their acquisition and restoration of farmland expanded, they instituted programs of wildlife reintroduction and recovery: huemul deer and pumas in Chile; the giant anteater and pampas deer in Argentina; and research toward conservation of Argentine jaguars, giant otter, peccary, and tapir as well. They launched a publication program of large-format books. They funded South American environmental activism.

They created parks.

In 1991, when he bought Reñihué Farm, Doug Tompkins also bought a 42,000-acre tract of rainforest—pristine, for the most part—higher up the Reñihué Valley. He endowed a foundation, The Conservation Land Trust, which acquired an additional 700,000 acres of contiguous country to form Pumalín Park. In 2005, Chile's president, Ricardo Lagos, made it official, declaring Pumalín a Nature Sanctuary.

As with the Reñihué model in their farm restoration, the Tompkinses replicated the Pumalín model in their park creation. Through their foundations, and with the help of associates, and sometimes with surrounding parcels thrown in by government, they acquired: The 726,448 acres and stunning ocean-to-Andes beauty of Corcovado National Park, in Palena Province of Chile. The 165,000 acres and twenty-five miles of Atlantic frontage that Kris's foundation, Conservación Patagónica, donated to the Argentine Park Service to form Argentina's first coastal marine park, Monte León National Park, in Santa Cruz Province. The 37,050 acres of El Rincón, on the flanks of the Argentinean Andes. The more than 400,000 acres they have so far preserved of the wetlands of Ibera, "Argentina's Pantanal." The 65,751 acres of Cabo León, near Punta Arenas in far-southern Chilean Patagonia. The first 195,285 acres of what they hope will be, when they are finished, the 650,000-acre Patagonia National Park, in the Aysén Region of Chile.

And so on, and so on.

To date, Doug and Kris Tompkins have preserved more than two million acres—in excess of three thousand square miles—of South American wilderness and threatened pastoral landscape.

I REMEMBER MEETING Dave in the early 1960s at Francis and Mary Farquhar's house in Berkeley. I went there a number of times in the years right after that, around the time when I moved down to set up The North Face on University Avenue in Berkeley, and then the store in San Francisco. I was just a young guy and I had stars in my eyes for your dad and the Farquhars and for the Sierra Club and so forth. Dave did not remember me from then, as I remember him—and there was no reason for him to remember, either. I was just another one of the thousands of his fans in those days, another fresh face. But I remember sitting in, like, a living room and listening. I was at the feet of the Archdruid and the anointed circle. I don't remember well, but I don't think your dad had white hair then, although I kind of have this lasting impression of the white hair. Maybe he did have white hair already.

We used to talk over lots of things. We would argue some, but I always knew I would learn something. I was not nearly as fluent then as I am today on the big issues, on the root causes of the environmental crisis, so I did not have the confidence I have now to be able to go toe-to-toe with someone on theory, epistemology, eco-ethics, and philosophy.

He was good at boiling down an issue. He could quickly see strategies to get policy changed, or stop something—an unwise dam, bad forest practices. In those days that was the Sierra Club's great strength. I think he was strong in standing up to the Club's conservative, less dynamic members and directors. He was good at standing on principle. He was stubborn, of course, and perhaps at times that stubbornness got him in jams, but it was also a strength, for he persevered, and kept the pressure on, and didn't give up, and hated to throw in the towel. He also seems to have been able to recognize big errors. And with all that he did over a long period of time, he made some, of course.

I think what he taught me, more than anything, was the power of images and books. One of his great legacies was the Sierra Club book program, from which I learned a lot and have used, as Dave nicely pointed out, as the inspiration for our own books. Books like *Wildlands Philanthropy* and *Patagonia Sin Represas.* I owe your dad all the credit for sowing that idea in my head. I thought that if the Sierra Club could do that for beauty, we can use that same process with ugliness to move people. *Clearcut. Fatal Harvest. Wildfire. Welfare Ranching. CAFO: The Tragedy of Industrial Animal Factories. La Tragedia del Bosque Chileno. Plundering Appalachia: The Tragedy of Mountaintop-Removal Coal Mining.* It has worked very well. We have new books coming out all the time, and I have not regretted any of them. I think about Dave when we put them together. We talk about whether he would like the next one we are working on.

I can remember some evenings of a little too many martinis. Tanqueray gin, that was the brand, wasn't it? We did hit a few bars around. There was one near the offices of Earth Island Institute when it was there on Broadway Street in San Francisco, and we went there often. I am almost totally abstemious myself so I was not much of a drinking buddy. I do remember I would have to go out and find the right kind of gin to have at home, Tanqueray, so when he came over I was ready. I never knew even how to make the drinks, but I remember having the right brands.

One little anecdote. Dave came swooping over to our place on Lombard Street and popped in all of a sudden, all revved up, with a videotape in his hand, one of those big VHS tapes from back in the '80s. It was titled *The Faceless Ones* and he was really excited about it and had just got it and wanted to show it. It was produced in Canada, in British Columbia, by Terry Jacks, who we worked with later on a similar film for *Clearcut. The Faceless Ones* is about all the world-wreckers who sit in huge anonymous office buildings—the corporate class—and are eating the world alive, bite by bite. The text is a great poem by Jack Whyte, narrated by a Scot with a great voice, and accompanied by pictures of all the worst environmental disasters there are. You have to see it. It's great. Your dad was head over heels over it.

Apparently he had seen it someplace else and had gotten it and did not have a machine to show it on, or his was broken, or it was not at Earth Island Institute. So he bounded up the path and I saw him coming out the window. He said he was running to the airport but wanted to show it to me before he left. Because he was going to have to leave it with whoever he was visiting in New York—some big muckety-muck there. So we sat down and watched it in the little office we had there. It was great, of course. Later we had the guy who made that documentary make another one for us, of similar style, for a campaign in British Columbia that had a huge impact on the outcome of provincial elections. I still have that and it is now on DVD. But I will always remember Dave being so hyped up on that little film, *The Faceless Ones*, which was a small masterpiece. It so fit his own critique of development that he was just tickled pink about it.

When he was getting up there in age, I could see that he was falling into the same kinds of habits of my dad, when he was getting older and reached about the same age. Like my father, he was big on one-liners and was working them all the time. Sometimes I thought they could have been better thought through. I remember one time having some Sunday morning waffles with your parents and thinking how much he was like my dad, and wondering if I, too, would be like that eventually. Of course, he was a forceful character, and took the spotlight and the microphone a little too much at times, but I think we all forgave him for that. You do earn those privileges when you have a life like Dave's behind you.

The other night Kris and I watched an episode of the Ken Burns series *The National Parks: America's Best Idea*, and saw a section featuring Dave and the Sierra Club fights back in the fifties and sixties. I thought of John Muir, and Aldo Leopold, and Thoreau, and Arne Næss, and Dave

Foreman, and of course Dave Brower, and how they blazed the trail for Kris and me in the park making we're doing down here. I thought how they all influenced me, and how I am really beholden to the luck I have had to fall under the spell of all those great minds. I've been fortunate that my life wound around to where I got close to some of them and they were my friends and colleagues. Which I can say about Arne, your dad, Dave Foreman, Jerry Mander, and many others.

We just have finished a retrospective of the ad campaign we have been involved with here in Chile against the big dams planned on the Baker and Pascua rivers, and Jerry Mander and your dad are part of that, for their kind of newspaper ad making has been one of those seminal ideas that we have updated only a little and put into action in South America. They're working!

Dave was very, very complimentary about both our wildlands work in South America and our activism, and it gave me great pride to have him say it so explicitly. Coming from him was an honor. By now you may take it all as a matter of fact, but your dad was a giant of twentieth-century environmentalism and there are literally millions and millions of people beholden to him, even though many will never realize it. I think his place in history will only get more important as we move into the future. He's a legend. What luck I had to have known him! What good luck you had to have him as your dad.

DAVE FOREMAN

DAVE FOREMAN operates his latest outfit, The Rewilding Institute, out of his house in Albuquerque. His office downstairs looks out on his tomato garden. His living room upstairs looks out on a big yard of sagebrush, piñon pines, mesquite, and New Mexico locust. Previous owners planted a little orchard, a half dozen fruit trees, along with some grapevines. Foreman in his own tenure has scattered water stations around the yard and has installed birdfeeders in three different places. "The birds definitely like the fruit trees," he told me. "They always get just as many cherries as we do. And pretty much we let them have all the grapes."

Foreman is vaguely Hemingwayesque in visage. He is markedly Hemingwayesque in build, grizzledness, affection for drink, combativeness, affinity for terse prose, and proneness to accident. A rough-and-tumble life has brought him into his sixties "all beat to hell," as he himself admits. He has a very bad back. One fall in Chile was particularly damaging. Foreman tumbled down the stairs at Doug Tompkins's place on Reñihué Farm, and this led to surgery and two fused vertebrae.

"I can't get out on hikes the way I used to," he said. "I can still do float trips. But I can't hike and I can't backpack. I haven't been able to backpack for ten years, and that's the thing I love most of all. So I've just really concentrated on turning my yard into good bird habitat. I've got a recliner chair that I probably spend most of my time in. Right out the bay window are all these bird feeders. I've had fifty-eight species of birds in my yard. As well as some really regular ones that I've gotten to know quite well."

It is a dispiriting image, the burly eco-terrorist watching birds from a recliner, washed up, like Napoleon in exile on Elba, or Man o' War turned out to pasture. But don't cry for Foreman, not yet. He still gets himself out occasionally on river or trail, and at home he has learned to let the wildness come to him. The last time we had met, two years before the interview, we both had given talks at the Western Wilderness Conference in California, where Foreman, for his theme, had selected five birds from among the visitors to his garden. He had deduced, from close observation, the temperament and worldview of each species. From each of the five he had distilled a moral—five lessons for conservationists from the kingdom of the birds.

BUSHTIT.

Tiny and drab, but loveable, the bushtit is "winsome in a way that overflows," or so it seems to Foreman from the vantage of his recliner. A score of bushtits will flock into one of his piñon pines and clean it of bugs and caterpillars, then sweep into one of his New Mexico locusts and do the same. These little carnivores, if they grew to the size of ravens, would be as scary as winged velociraptors, yet among themselves they do not squabble. No one bushtit is the identifiable leader of the flock. All these traits, said Foreman, make it the totem bird for grassroots conservationists.

LADDER-BACKED WOODPECKER.

Foreman once watched a ladder-backed woodpecker drill for thirty minutes into one of his trees before she got the grub she was after. This small woodpecker species, he told the audience, is the hardest-working creature he knows. It is a model of doggedness. Foreman turned to single Polly Dyer out of the audience. He knew where to look, for he had been sitting beside her before stepping up to the dais. Polly Dyer of Seattle, said Foreman, now in her nineties, had been defending the mountains of the North Cascades for sixty years. She was still at it, working to expand wilderness areas in her state. For pure doggedness, he recommended Polly Dyer and the ladder-backed woodpecker.

216

WESTERN SCRUB JAY.

The corvids—the family of the jays, crows, and ravens—are the smartest of birds, Foreman told us. A Western scrub jay has an elephantine memory and is able to recollect where it has hidden a thousand nuts and more. Researchers have verified a "theory of mind" in scrub jays. The jays recognize mindfulness in other creatures and demonstrate this by rehiding their nuts when they have been observed. Foreman has tested this himself, with peanuts, on the four jays resident in his Albuquerque yard. Jays think ahead. Conservationists must do the same.

CURVE-BILLED THRASHER.

Foreman marveled at the "loftiness and steadfastness" of the curve-billed thrasher. Over his morning coffee, looking down on the trays of sunflower seeds under his Albuquerque window, he had watched a single curve-billed thrasher displace all four of his resident jays. A single scrub jay, much less four of them, outweighs a curve-billed thrasher, and robins and doves outweigh them, too, but all these birds yield to the thrasher at Foreman's feeders. Curve-billed thrashers are tough. Toughness in a conservationist is indispensable.

MOUNTAIN CHICKADEE.

Nothing is happier than a chickadee, Foreman asserted. His evidence was the merriment in the bird's namesake call. He admitted that he chicka-dee-dees back at his chickadees, sometimes for fifteen minutes at a time. Mountain chickadees have a good time. Why, he asked rhetorically, do they have so much fun? It is because they live for themselves. They do not exist to provide entertainment for Foreman in his recliner, or for any other human being. They are here for their own sake. They don't need to justify themselves by any sort of service to Man. The mountain chickadee is an example not so much for the conservationist as for humanity at large: Wild things exist for themselves.

Foreman's audience at the Western Wilderness Conference that morning had not come expecting Aesopian fable from the eco-saboteur, I think. They had not come expecting a remake of Aristophanes' *The Birds*. But they were charmed. Animal tales are our first narrative tradition, or one of them, and Dave Foreman is, as much as anything, a storyteller. With his parable of the five birds, he had not simply held the audience in the palm of his hand that day; he had gripped them firmly by the short feathers for the duration of his speech.

For most of the 1970s, Dave Foreman worked for The Wilderness Society, first as Southwest regional representative and then as director of wilderness affairs in Washington, D.C. Toward the end of the decade, he became disheartened by changes in The Wilderness Society and in mainstream environmentalism as a whole. In 1978, the Society's executive director, Celia Hunter—a pioneering Alaskan environmentalist he much admired—was replaced by a businessman named Bill Turnage. Turnage's environmental credentials amounted to his successful marketing of the photographs of Ansel Adams. Within two years, he had purged almost all Celia Hunter's staff. Millionaire environmental dilettantes were invited onto the Society's council. The equitable salaries and democratic decision making of the Celia Hunter era ended.

The Wilderness Society was not unique in this shift. Many other environmental organizations began the same devolution in this period. It was a curse of success. Growing staffs, memberships, and budgets required better organization. Fire-in-the-belly activists lost out to managers. Often this meant a change of personnel; but sometimes, more chillingly, the shift came as a metamorphosis within the soul of the individual activist. The young firebrand, happy at first to work for a pittance, began to contemplate marriage, children, and a car that started on the first crank and did not leak buckets of oil. The specter of middle age loomed. As the full moon of the mortgage payment shined through his window, the firebrand, losing fire, began the frightening transmogrification into manager. In a number of organizations, MBAs became executive directors and CEOs. Corporate types flooded the boards of directors. The Bill Turnages proliferated.

For Foreman, a final blow came in 1979. The US Forest Service survey, Roadless Area Review and Evaluation (RARE II), came up with its recommendations: Of the sixty million acres that remained roadless in the national forests, only fifteen million would be protected as wilderness and spared from road building and logging. Despite the hard work of Foreman and other environmental lobbyists like himself, the best opportunity in the century for expanding designated wilderness was lost.

Foreman quit Washington and returned to his old job as Southwestern representative of The Wilderness Society. In April of 1980, hiking in the Pinacate Desert of Mexico with four friends—Mike Roselle, Howie Wolke, Ron Kezar, and Bart Kohler—Foreman had his epiphany, which came in the form of a phrase. "Earth first!" The planet first, and all other considerations secondary. No more suits and ties in Washington corridors. No more political compromise. No more making nice or moderation. In June of 1980 Foreman quit The Wilderness Society entirely.

His new "organization," if that is the word for Earth First!, was deliberately nonhierarchical. Foreman was the leader, or something like that, to the extent that the outfit had one. The Earth First! bible and inspiration was the novel *The Monkeywrench Gang,* by Edward Abbey. Abbey himself became patron saint of the movement. In the Abbey novel, a band of misfits dedicate themselves to blowing up Glen Canyon dam, the *bête noir* of all Western environmentalists in the 1960s and 1970s. Earth First! dedicated itself to similar sorts of guerrilla warfare. "Monkeywrenching" entered the language as the description of their basic approach.

Foreman founded and edited *Earth First! Journal,* in which he ran a "Dear Ned Ludd" column dispensing advice on sabotage techniques, and he eventually collected these tips in the book *Ecodefense: A Field Guide to Monkeywrenching.* The Foreman message was never pure recklessness. Under his editorship, *Earth First! Journal* became a forum for debate on monkeywrenching ethics. "Tree spiking," for example, a practice potentially fatal to sawmill workers when saw hits metal spike, failed to pass the test. There is little doubt, however, that Foreman occasionally took his own Ned Ludd advice and slipped off into the desert with cutting tools.

In 1990, Foreman was asleep in his Tucson bedroom when his wife Nancy was startled by loud banging on their door. As she moved to open it, four men shouting "FBI!" burst past her toward the bedroom with drawn guns. Foreman woke to unfamiliar voices shouting his name. Later there would be some disagreement in the media as to what passed through his mind when he opened his eyes to the .357 magnums trained on him. According to *People* magazine, the first thing he thought was of Allen Funt and *Candid Camera.* According to *Green Muckraker.com,* "He immediately thought of the murder of Fred Hampton in Chicago, expecting to be shot in cold blood."

Perhaps Foreman thought of both Allen Funt and Fred Hampton simultaneously.

Dave Foreman was one of five people arrested by the FBI in Operation Thermcon, by which the agency infiltrated an Arizona group, EMETIC, the Evan Mecham Eco-Terrorist International Conspiracy. An FBI undercover agent, Michael Fain, suggested that the group might like to bring down a transmission tower from the Palo Verde Nuclear Generating Station, and the EMETIC people were ready to oblige. Foreman was not directly involved in the attempted sabotage that followed, but was charged with conspiracy. In the end he pled guilty to a misdemeanor, the crime of having given two inscribed copies of his book *Ecodefense* to agent Fain, along with a $100 donation. He received a suspended sentence.

Even before the FBI and Operation Thermcom, Foreman was looking for another direction, and in 1990, quitting Earth First! and the counterculture, he turned to conservation biology and founded The Wildlands Project. "We seek to bring together conservationists, ecologists, indigenous peoples, and others to protect and restore evolutionary processes and biodiversity," he wrote in a mission statement. The Wildlands Project calls for establishment of systems of core wilderness areas, vast reserves linked by biological corridors. As founder and editor of The Wildlands Project journal, *Wild Earth,* Foreman made the case for really big wilderness.

In their present house in Albuquerque, Dave Foreman and Nancy Morton have converted an upstairs bedroom to a library of more than two thousand books on conservation. In Foreman's office downstairs, where he sat for our interview, were several hundred more, references for work in progress. Among these were: *Pleistocene Mammals of North America,* by Bjorn Kurten. *On Human Nature,* by E.O. Wilson. *Traces on the Rhodian Shore: Nature and Culture in Western Thought,* by Glacken. *The War Against the Greens,* by Helvarg. *The Sixth Extinction,* by Leakey. *This Land is Your Land,* by Shanks. *Driven Wild: How the Fight Against Automobiles Launched the*

Modern Wilderness Movement, by Paul Sutter. *The Population Bomb,* by Paul Ehrlich—five copies of this classic. (For some reason the Ehrlich book was having a population explosion of its own at Foreman's place.)

"These on the desktop are basically the books I need for the work I've been doing," Foreman told me. "I'm writing five books right now. It's for a series called The Wild Things. There's basically a giant manuscript that I've broken down into five more targeted books. The first one is my population book, *Man Swarm and the Killing of Wildlife.*"

On the office wall were several photos of Foreman standing in front of signs posting the borders of various wilderness areas. There was a gallery of posters from Foreman's lectures around the country. One advertised a joint talk with David Brower at the University of Vermont. Several others paired the same two Davids, the one serving as warm-up act for the other, or vice versa. Still other posters advertised Foreman as solo performer.

Over the years I had seen a number of Foreman's one-man shows. The posters brought the power of these performances back to me.

In 1988, I had followed Foreman around the Pacific Northwest, gathering notes for a magazine profile of him. We took turns at the wheel, driving from one speaking engagement to another. In the car, Foreman was generous with his ideas and affable enough, in a road-weary sort of way, yet always a little grave and self-contained. Then at each destination, whether auditorium or lecture hall, a different Foreman began to appear as he warmed to his talk. The new Foreman, inflating, would fulminate Earth First! fire and brimstone. Startling declarations like: "The blood of timber executives is my natural drink, and the wail of dying forest supervisors is music to my ears," for example.

To someone who has forgot his *Huckleberry Finn,* this homicidal raving might seem over the top. Indeed, when my Foreman profile appeared in the magazine *Harrowsmith,* a record number of readers cancelled their subscriptions. But there is always a Twain-like wink at the crowd in Foreman's performances. A segment of the American public is no longer able to detect it.

Not since the ever-changing speech that my father called "the Sermon" have I seen an environmentalist with such an effect on his audience. David Brower believed that if anyone in the new generation of conservationists would fill his particular niche, it would probably be David Foreman. Foreman ended each speech by howling like a wolf. Audiences understood this instantly as call-and-response, and he always left the stage to a thunderous howling.

"Thank God for Dave Brower, he makes it so easy for the rest of us to look reasonable," Judge Russell Train, head of the Environmental Protection Agency under Nixon, once said in a speech. My father was delighted by the compliment. Often in his own talks, after quoting Train, he would go on to say: "And thank God for Dave Foreman, he makes it so easy for Dave Brower to look reasonable. Now what we need is someone to make Dave Foreman look reasonable."

T HE FIRST TIME I met your dad was in 1978, at a reception that Friends of the Earth held for him in D.C., when I was working there for The Wilderness Society. But that was just to shake hands. When we *really* met, I believe, was at the first California Wilderness Conference, in Visalia. I gave one of my Earth First! talks, and then Dave gave a talk. That's where we hit it off. He was very complimentary. He said that he had learned his lesson, which was to never follow me at a talk. And then he did the bit of business that became his standard introduction of me, when we were giving talks together. And we gave quite a few together. It was Dave's riff on the Russell Train quote: "Thank God for Dave Foreman, because he makes Dave Brower look reasonable."

When we would show up for a joint presentation somewhere, I would talk to him about history. I'd ask about the old times in the conservation movement, trying to get things straight. I'd ask him about the books I'd read that go into the history. I don't think there ever was a single book I asked him about that he agreed with. Not one book where he was happy about how they captured the history. He always had quibbles with them.

He was much more particular about that stuff than I am. I think part of the difference is that your dad was an idealist, and I'm not. I'm a cynical realist. But I pretend to be an idealist. In public I do a lot of role-playing. That's not the real me, in some ways. And so I think your father expected more of people. He expected more of historians. Whereas I don't really expect a whole lot from other people. In that way I'm never disappointed—and sometimes I'm very pleasantly surprised. But I think your dad expected more, so he was disappointed when people didn't come up to that.

After our talks with college students, we went out and drank, and he always drank everybody under the table. I just never could keep up with him. Yeah, I have a reputation myself in this area. But your dad was the champ.

It's amazing, but over the years that we knew each other, in some ways I felt he really was younger. Younger than *me*, though in fact Dave was what, thirty-five years older? Just younger in his approach to life. In the sense of not being jaded, and of liking young people. He just never was an old guy. He really liked young people. He was always interested in new stuff. He was always hopeful, and everything. He just wasn't jaded and cynical at all, like I am. For me, the troubles at The Wilderness Society, after Bill Turnage came in and screwed up the organization, had soured me. But it's also just who I am. I've always been a misanthrope. In other ways, Dave was very much my senior. But in that one sense he really did seem younger.

One thing I learned from your dad was about organizations. What I realized was that he and I were fairly similar, in that we're visionaries, and inspirational, and tough, and fighters, and everything, but that neither one of us was terribly skilled at actually administering an organization. I helped start, and then was squeezed out of, a number of groups, but I never fought it. I saw Dave's battles with Sierra Club, and with Friends of the Earth, and I thought, *Why waste my time on that type of thing?* I'm never that wedded to the organization. I was only really tied to one organization, and that was The Wilderness Society. I loved The Wilderness Society, the lore of it, everything else about it, and when the Turnage thing happened, that just soured me. I never fell in love with another group. I was ready to leave Earth First! well before I did.

That's another part of my life. I've always just gone from this group of folks to another group. Maybe that's from being an Air Force brat. Going to thirteen different schools.

The people at Earth First! just changed. Most of us who started Earth First! were conservationists, folks from The Wilderness Society, Sierra Club, and Friends of the Earth. We considered ourselves as still being in the conservation business, and we knew a lot about it. But that didn't last for too long. We started Earth First! in '80, but even by '87, it was becoming very obvious that the kind of people that seemed attracted to Earth First! were not my kind of folks. They really weren't conservationists. They were animal rights people, or anarchists, or left-wing ideologues, and that type of thing. And I was eager to get out of there.

The irony is that the FBI framed me, and busted me, after I had quietly *left* Earth First! I was already gone. My arrest kind of put me back in the outfit publicly, but by about a year later, Nancy and I just didn't want to be associated anymore with Earth First! Not with the way it was going. It was turning into a bad version of the New Left.

I pretty well got squeezed out of The Wildlands Project, too. That's fine. I'm a lot better off just doing my own thing. Working with just a couple of people I can really trust. I always decided it was time to leave my organizations sooner, I think, than Dave decided it was time to leave.

I've got an organization now, of course. I'm like Dave; somehow I always have one. It's good to have an organization. Hell, I've jump-started so many! But what The Rewilding Institute really is, is "Dave Foreman, Inc." It's just for me to do my thing. And I don't want anything big anymore, organizationally.

Occasionally, Dave and I did talk strategy, a little bit. He was very supportive of what we were going to do with The Wildlands Project and *Wild Earth*, its journal. I do remember that Dave and I had a get-together at J.P. Morgan's place in the Adirondacks. Hah! We both thought that was wonderfully appropriate. And that was with Tom Butler and John Davis, who were editors at *Wild Earth*, and some other folks. We sat around this giant fireplace, and drank, and talked about the new conservation movement. New groups were emerging in the nineties, many of them started by people who had been in Earth First! They were in reaction to what was going on in mainstream environmentalism. We were calling it the new conservation movement, these new groups. A good example would be the Center for Biodiversity, and some of the other groups that have taken a very scientific but a very tough approach to things.

People, when they try to compare me and your dad, I tell them there's no way to do that. He was Mr. Conservation. He just really dominated the movement, and was the face of it, in the fifties and sixties, whether at congressional hearings, or through the ads, or the books, or whatever. There'd never been anybody who had that role. And there never will be anybody again.

That's partly because of the times. There weren't that many people in the movement back then. But he certainly also had the charisma, and he had the sense of drama. He made up a bunch of stuff that we take for granted now, strategies and approaches. It was something like me at Earth First! I became the face of Earth First!, not because I pushed other people out of the way, or undercut them, or anything. It was just that I had more charisma, I did better speaking in public, and that's just how it was. And I think that's the way it was for your dad and the whole conservation movement in the fifties and sixties. The only real competition he had was with Zahniser leading on the Wilderness Act, and then other people doing things like the Arctic Wildlife Refuge. But as far as overall, it was your dad.

The history of the movement has always interested me. I've been in it for forty years, so I've seen a lot of it firsthand. But I've also always sought out the older folks and talked to them. I talked to Bob Marshall's brother about his brother Bob. I talked to Aldo Leopold's kids about their dad. I talked to your dad. You know, the lore of the movement is really important to me. Well, it figures it would be; I *am* an historian. I got my degree in it. But that's also just how I am. I really believe that you need to know where you come from. And I'm so frustrated with the young folks of today's conservation movement, who really have no sense of the past.

I don't think I took anything specifically from Dave's Sermon. We had a different cadence and rhythm. But I loved watching your father talk. Even when it was the same talk I'd heard before, several times. But just the way he worked the audience.

I'm not a competitive person, but I did want to be the best public speaker I could be. I heard a lot of Southern evangelists when I was young, and that's certainly where my speaking style originated. But it was in the Earth First! roadshows in '81 and '82 where I really worked on my talks and my style. I suppose there's some common thread there with Dave Brower. We're the two people who weren't embarrassed to give a sermon. Other people are uncomfortable, I think, giving a sermon.

I don't know if he used some of the same techniques I do. But I try to pick out a few people scattered around the room, and consistently make eye contact with them. Dave needed feedback from the audience, and so do I. I hate to talk when the lights are on me and I can't see the audience. I want to see the audience. So I can feel how they're reacting. A great speech is in many ways a joint production between the speaker and the audience. If the audience really connects with you, you can feel the energy there. They're with you, and it just leads you to greater heights.

I think both Dave and I did sort of what Ronald Reagan did. Reagan had all these three-by-five cards that would help him remember some phony story or some other point he wanted to make. He would just re-sort those cards. I think your dad and I both had the three-by-five cards in our heads. We re-sorted them there, in our heads. You know, it's like, *Click, here's this one. Just go with it.* And then it's, *Okay, now they need this other one, or they need that one.* It's never the same speech. It's always different. And I always tried to figure out how to make it local, how to connect with the people there. Dave would do that, too. Being self-deprecating is something that really works, too. I probably did more of that than your dad did, but he did it, too.

One way I'm very much like your dad is I'm shy. If I'm not the star of something—if I'm not why people are there—then I'm basically a wallflower. And I noticed that in your dad, too. He was not real outgoing, except when he was onstage.

He was a master with words. He really could work the language well. I try to do that, too. I've been studying Old English lately, because it really helps me understand the English language better. And I think it's really important to know the language, to understand it, to be able to communicate. In *Man Swarm,* my latest book, I went for the Anglo-Saxon in a big way.

In an anthology I'm doing now, I have this long chapter, "Five Feathers for the Cannot Club." I go into how important bird-watching in my yard is for me. The "Cannot Club" comes from Aldo Leopold's first line in *Sand County Almanac.* "There are those who can live without wild things, and there are those who cannot."

Anyway, "Five Feathers for the Cannot Club." The five feathers are for five of the regular birds in the yard I have gotten to know well—the same five from my talk at the Western Wilderness Conference that Vicky Hoover put together a couple of years ago. You were there. Here are these five birds and the lessons they have for the conservation movement. And people just loved it, I think. It's little things like that that are the secrets of how you capture people. So many speakers, they might be able to give a perfectly workmanlike talk, but they don't know the magic that you do. Your father knew it. And I know it. Not so many other people do.

One thing Dave Brower brought to the movement was that he did stuff outside. All those climbs. All those first ascents. He actually knew something about wilderness, which is not always the case with the leaders of the conservation business these days.

There's this famous passage from Thoreau about his experience on Mount Katahdin. It's in his book *The Maine Woods.* In this passage, Thoreau is basically frightened. He writes about how Mother Nature talks to him on Katahdin. She says, "Why'd you come up here? I didn't make this place for you. I can only be a cruel stepmother here. You're supposed to be down in the valley." It's a very key passage for American attitudes towards Nature, as I think all the academics would agree. For understanding Thoreau, and for understanding real wilderness, it is the most important passage.

Well, there's a professor at Wisconsin, Bill Cronon, who has a certain degree of fame as one of the leading wilderness deconstructors. He has criticized the idea of wilderness as being romantic. Baird

Callicot is another example. These guys are prominent conservation historians or philosophers who have been influenced by postmodern deconstructionism and are critical of the wilderness idea. So Bill Cronon takes Thoreau's Katahdin experience, and writes about it, but he doesn't understand it at all. He says, "Surely no modern American backpacker would ever have this reaction." Which just completely blew me out of my chair. I thought, *Hey, have you ever been outside, man? I've had that reaction dozens of times. Out there with my cruel stepmother. All my friends have had that reaction. Who hasn't been frightened in the wilderness?* It just was an indication of how basically ignorant these academic critics of wilderness are. It was absurd. It indicated that Cronon had never had any serious wilderness experience.

I was nearly trampled by a musk ox last summer. And that was wonderful. This was on the Noatak River in Alaska—22 days, 375 miles. Oh boy, was I ever not in shape for that trip! Anyway, so this musk ox went for me. Afterward, one guy on the trip said, "I can't think of any more appropriate way or place for Dave to die." I thought that was really a fine compliment.

The musk ox was chasing me. I was trying to sneak up on it, but it had gotten closer to me than I thought. We saw each other, and we were about ten feet apart. Big old bull musk ox. He pawed the ground, started coming after me. Here I am, crippled, running around on the tundra trying to take pictures of it. It was pretty amusing. It actually was a very funny way to die.

And so I think that's one thing your father brought, *just being out there.* Being on the edge out there. And that's certainly something I've done, too. It's one thing to know the history, through making the history yourself, and through talking to the older folks, and through reading the books and the documents, and all that, but then you've also got to have the true, hard experience outside.

Randy Hayes, Monument Valley, Navajo Nation

RANDALL HAYES

THE OFFICE OF the World Future Council is at the corner of 7th and Pennsylvania, down the street from the White House. Randy Hayes's window looks down on a median strip of cherry trees and the Eastern Market Metro stop. "So from a mass-transit perspective, it's an ideal location," he said.

Perhaps, but from a humidity-in-summer perspective, and from a wide-open-spaces perspective, the corner of 7th and Pennsylvania falls far short of the desert vistas of the Four Corners country where Hayes began his career. He likes his present work, all the same. The World Future Council, which has its headquarters in Hamburg, is dedicated to the implementation of policies promoting sustainable living, an intact world, and the rights of future generations. Hayes has been director of the US Liaison Office since 2008.

His path to Pennsylvania Avenue began in the dusty streets of the Hopi pueblos, detoured down the rainforest trails of the Kayapo in the Amazon and the Iban and Dayak in Borneo, and then wandered the streets of San Francisco. In 1985 he founded Rainforest Action Network, which advocates for rainforest and the rights of indigenous peoples. He next tried his hand in city government, first as president of the City of San Francisco Commission on the Environment, and then, across the bay, as director of sustainability in the office of Oakland Mayor Jerry Brown. For a time he joined Jerry Mander at his San Francisco think tank, the International Forum on Globalization. Finally he headed east.

On his office walls in Washington are three Ansel Adams photographs: Grand Canyon, Glacier National Park, and a geyser in Yellowstone. Hanging there, too, is a blue silk "Save the Rainforest" flag with a jaguar and orchids emblematic in the middle. "What's interesting about the flag is that it flew at the North Pole," he said. "One of my donors was taking a trip to the North Pole and she had that made, and then had a picture taken of it at the North Pole. 'Save the Rainforest' at the North Pole! After that I took it with me to Woodstock '94. There was a huge rainstorm and wicked mud, just like at the original Woodstock. Our flag just got trashed. I had it dry-cleaned, but if you look closely you still see Woodstock mud in it."

On the wall, too, was the logo of Friends of the Hopi, the first organization founded by Hayes. "It's a peace symbol of the Hopi," he explained. "A circle with a cross inside. It means many different things, but here the circle represents the wholeness of Nature and the great cycles, like the hydrologic cycle. The cross can mean human ingenuity, even engineering technology. What the symbol says is that it's okay to rearrange things, but only within the circle of Nature, only within the cycles of Nature. It's a story I use in a lot of my talks. The symbol is essentially calling for an Age of Appropriate Technology. The cross is not outside the circle. The cross is *within* the circle. It's okay to have technology, but the technology needs to be in sync with the great cycles of Nature.

"The Hopi symbol inspired the original Friends of the Earth logo. Not the new logo, but the old one used when Dave was running Friends of the Earth. The old logo was also a circle with a cross inside. Within three of the quadrants marked off by the cross were the letters *F, O,* and *E,* and in the fourth was a leaf. The idea to borrow the Hopi symbol came from Gordon Anderson, FOE's Southwest representative. Most Friends of the Earth people never knew it came from the Hopi."

Among the books on Hayes's shelves were: *Overshoot, the Ecological Basis of Revolutionary Change,* by William R. Catton, Jr. *Deep Ecology,* by Bill Devall. *Let the Mountains Talk, Let the Rivers Run,* by David Brower. *What I*

Learned from the Rainforest, a confessional by a Mitsubishi executive written after Hayes and his Rainforest Action Network boycotted that company.

W HILE I WAS working on the Four Corners film, I rented a desk at the Friends of the Earth office down on Sansome Street in San Francisco. I had heard about Friends of the Earth in the Southwest from Gordon Anderson, the Southwest rep. I liked the attitude of FOE, the gutsiness, so I rented a desk there. That's where I met Dave.

The film is called *Four Corners: A National Sacrifice Area?* It's a documentary on the ecological and cultural impacts of uranium and coal mining in the Navajo and Hopi country. Three of us, Toby McLeod, Glenn Switkes, and me, were the coproducers. We all three got our masters' theses from that film. For the other two, it was a master's thesis in broadcast journalism at the University of California at Berkeley. For me it was a thesis in environmental planning at San Francisco State University.

Well, I had another project in mind called The Peoples of the Earth Directory, and Dave got interested in that. It was going to be a directory of support groups for indigenous peoples around the world. This was on the heels of ten years where I spent a lot of time with the Hopi elders and I lived on and off out at Hopi. So I explained my project to Dave, and he thought it was a clever idea. It ended up morphing into Rainforest Action Network. I found I could raise money around indigenous people as soon as I started talking about saving the rainforest *and* indigenous people. It was easier to raise money. One thing about Dave was his willingness to help with new ideas. His words of encouragement to entrepreneurial types was a major part of his brilliance.

My great-grandmother was a Blackfoot Indian in West Virginia, of all places. We don't know how she wound up in West Virginia—she wouldn't talk about it much. So I was always fascinated with American

Indians. Lots of kids like to think they are partly American Indian. In my case, I actually was.

Well, in my senior year of college, at Bowling Green State University in Ohio, I took a yoga class and a meditation class. The meditation teacher was a former Hell's Angel from California. "You were a Hell's Angel and now you're teaching meditation?" I asked him. And he said, "Yeah, I'm just a person of extremes. After seeing too many of my friends in the emergency room for motorcycle accidents, I decided to go to the other extreme." And later this same teacher, in a kind of prophetic tone—and I liked the sound of it—he said, "I see you going West, working with the American Indians."

And, interestingly, this was about a month after Gary Snyder had come to campus to do a poetry reading. I didn't know anything about Gary Snyder, but a buddy of mine, who liked poetry, said, "Come on! Come to this poetry reading with me." And I was captivated by Snyder's presence and poetry. He was from Northern California. I thought, *When I graduate I'm gonna go West.* I had a free place to stay in Sausalito.

So I move to California. I take another meditation class, and there's a guy in my class, a former Marine, an interesting, squirrelly little guy, who taught yoga himself. He was doing his master's thesis at UC Davis on cross-cultural prophecies. We became friends. He said, "Hey, I'm going down to Arizona, near the Grand Canyon, out in the desert, to meet with these elders in this tribe, this very old tribe, an American Indian tribe. I'm going down for several days, you want to go with me?" You know, I'm footloose and fancy-free, I just graduated from college and moved to California. I thought, sure, why not? So we left Sausalito at midnight and drove all the way through the night and got to the Grand Canyon by sunset the next day. We watched the sunset over the Grand Canyon and then we drove at night into the Hopi villages.

Well, there's a dirt road that goes to the oldest village, Old Oraibi, in Arizona. We could hear drums and we could see light, fires, so we know a ceremony is going on. We drive down the dirt road toward the village and we come across this big sign that says, WARNING, WHITE MAN.

BECAUSE YOU CANNOT OBEY YOUR OWN LAWS, LET ALONE OURS, YOU ARE HEREBY PROHIBITED FROM ENTERING THIS VILLAGE.

Oh, shit. So we sat there, it's early evening, and the Indians would come screaming by in their pickup trucks, blowin' dust on us. We were doing yoga postures, hoping someone would realize our pure spirit and invite us in. Which did not happen. So we finally rolled out our sleeping bags and slept by the side of the dirt road that night.

The next day, we go over to the next village, Kykotsmovi. My ex-Marine friend had done his homework, and he did know who the elders were. We went actually right to Thomas Banyacya's house, and that led to the next ten years of my life. From 1973 to 1983, hanging out with the Hopi and making the Four Corners film with the Hopi, and so on. I was just ready for it. At Bowling Green, my major had been in psychology and my minor in sociology, but by my senior year I figured out that my calling was ecology and Nature. And yet I was interested in indigenous peoples, as I said, from my great-grandmother days. Phoebe Smith was her White name, in West Virginia. A Blackfoot among the hillbillies of West Virginia.

The Hopi, there's a real singsong nature to their voices. And there really is sort of poetry to their life and a philosophy of long-term ecological sanity and sustainability. It's woven into their myths. They believe that this present civilization is the fourth highly evolved civilization that's been on Earth. In the first three, the technologies got out of sync with the cycles of Nature. In the last cycle, things were destroyed by flood. Thomas Banyacya's message was one about reverence for Nature, and about living in sync with the ways of Nature.

I ended up becoming essentially a secretary and chauffeur to the Council of Elders for that ten years. That's largely what I did. I wasn't trying to be a shamanic understudy, or anything. Lots of people were interested in that, in terms of the Hopi. But that wasn't my orientation. Mine was more around ecology and sustainability and lifestyle stuff. I stayed with the Banyacyas or I camped in my hippie van. We started a support group called Friends of the Hopi, and I would do little benefits to raise money when they needed tickets to go to the United Nations, or things like that.

Dave was interested in the Hopi. They represented kind of a model society, in the sense of long-term sustainability, and being farmers in the desert, and being peaceful people. Dave found that particularly interesting. When Thomas Banyacya was in town, I would sometimes get them together to sit and chat.

At one point, when Dave was scheduled to speak at the United Nations, the Hopi wanted to speak there too. It was kind of an interesting episode. The Hopi had their prophecies, their instructions, and one was to go to the UN and knock on the door three times. In other words, to speak at the UN, or seek help from the UN, three times. Thomas Banyacya was Coyote Clan, one of the elders asked to go out and talk—coyotes are barkers—and he was to address the United Nations about the Hopi message of peace and sustainability. But on one of those three times they knocked at the UN door, they weren't on the agenda, so they weren't allowed in to speak. But Dave was on the agenda. I'd introduced him to the elders. He offered to read their statement, which he did.

My ten years in Hopi were great. But, you know, desert life has got its pros and cons. I mean, I come more from the forests of West Virginia and the banks of the Ohio River. And then I lived for a while in central Florida out in the swamps, especially from age eight to sixteen. In 1958, my dad uprooted us on an adventure, and we moved to central Florida and the swamps, and I had pet alligators and everything. It was just paradise. In the late '50s, central Florida had nothing destroyed yet by Disney World or anything else. There was so much beauty down there, even in the orange groves, and such. Lakeland, Florida, was the town. We had all these spring-fed lakes. Central Florida is the aquifer recharge area. That's where you get Crystal Springs and Weeki Wachee Springs, coming out of the swamps. You have these beautiful, crystalline springs bubbling up out of these swamps and cow pastures.

You don't get that in the Four Corners, with the Hopi, not out in the desert.

The sunrises and sunsets in the Four Corners are just so stellar. But there's a kind of sensory-deprivation-tank thing, too. That simplicity of the desert. You got white sand and blue sky. There's cultural complexity, of course. You know, if you've ever been to any of the Hopi ceremonies, I mean there's a cultural complexity. It's like the opera and ballet combined, but with this sort of ancient, guttural, pantheistic thing, too. It was a great era, from '73 to '83, to hang out at Hopi. And it was such an honor, to sit at the feet of the elders. To be their secretary and chauffeur. But at the end of that, I wanted a kind of an ecosystem shift. I'd been ten years in the desert. So, in finishing up the Four Corners film, which is all about coal and uranium mining on Hopi-Navajo lands, I rented that desk at Friends of the Earth. And shifted to rainforest. The work was still about indigenous peoples, about fragile environment, and about insensitive corporations, but just in a different place.

It's an interesting little sequence. When I first met Dave Brower, at my rented desk, my thinking was around this indigenous people's directory, The Peoples of the Earth project. But David Chatfield ran the international program for Friends of the Earth, and Chatfield had gotten interested in rainforest issues. John Seed from Australia came to visit Chatfield. John is founder of the Rainforest Information Centre in Australia, and he was in the United States on one of his roadshows. So I met John Seed. John is very infectious. I mean, he really is a Johnny Appleseed, sowing seeds of hope: "We can get out there and support native peoples and save the rainforests." The very next day, Seed was going up to the Sierra foothills to see Gary Snyder. Snyder, you know, is like an archetype of the humanity we need on the planet. I said, "Oh, my God, can you get Gary to do a poetry reading for a rainforest benefit? A benefit that I will organize, with Dave Brower speaking and Gary Snyder reading poetry?" The money was to go to Seed's group, the Rainforest Information Centre. And John Seed said, "Sure. I'm happy to ask him."

Lo and behold, John Seed called me the next day from Gary Snyder's house and said that Gary's agreed to do it. So I went and asked Dave if he would speak. And then Dave Foreman and Mike Roselle of Earth

First! were coming into town, because Earth First! was doing its own very first national roadshow. This period was also kind of the beginning for Earth First! So we had Dave Foreman speak, and Dave Brower speak, and Gary Snyder read poetry, and it was like a sellout at the Unitarian Church on Franklin Street in San Francisco. Beforehand I went to North Beach and just peppered every coffee shop with flyers, just plastered every laundromat, for a solid three weeks. It was such a great event.

I proposed to Friends of the Earth that they set up a rainforest department and hire me to head it. But that was right when the big internal battle at Friends of the Earth was brewing. It was the struggle where eventually the gang from the D.C. office persuaded the board to vote to shut down the San Francisco office and consolidate in Washington. The coup, so to speak. So it just wasn't in the cards for my rainforest project to happen. Finally, Mike Roselle and I, at my rented desk, after hours, we were the only people there. We'd go get a six-pack of beer and put our feet up. One day we said, "This is going nowhere, getting Friends of the Earth to set up a rainforest department. So let's just set up our own organization." Well, at the very next desk was Monica Moore of Pesticide Action Network, PAN. She also rented a desk from Friends of the Earth. And at PAN she was worried about the rainforest, too. So we decided we'll become RAN, Rainforest Action Network. Roselle, who was always artistic, got some press-on type, and we took some photocopy paper out of the copy machine, pressed the letters for "Rainforest Action Network" on the top of the sheet, and xeroxed fifteen copies of it. And that became the birth of the Rainforest Action Network.

In November of 1985 we had a three-day strategy session at Fort Cronkhite, at what was called the Yosemite Institute at the time, out at Cronkhite Beach in Sausalito. And that's what we consider also the founding strategy conference of Rainforest Action Network. I asked Dave to give the keynote introductory speech. That was right on the heels of a prayer by a California Indian elder by the name of Coyote. Fred "Coyote" Downing, from the Wailaki, a California tribe—a wonderful, inspired, wise old Indian. Because we were on Native American lands here in California, we wanted to have a Native American prayer at the beginning of the Rainforest Action Network. And then Dave gave his keynote speech. And then we had three days of strategy sessions. Brent Blackwelder, who later became president of Friends of the Earth, was there, and Winona LaDuke, the Chippewa-Jewish environmentalist. She would be the Green Party candidate for vice president in 2000. And John Trudell, the Native American–Mexican author and poet and actor, a real heavyweight in the Indian world. We had a who's who of environmental activists from around the world: people from Borneo, activists from Japan, Africa, the Amazon, and Europe, and most all of the major environmental groups. One of the best things I did was just asking Dave Brower to give the keynote.

In the early Rainforest Action Network days, I'd set up these house parties to raise funds, and nobody turned up. Then when Dave offered to come and speak at them, it was not hard to garner a crowd of twenty or forty. At the first house party with Dave Brower, we raised a couple hundred dollars. Or a couple thousand dollars, I don't quite remember which. And that was our humble beginnings.

So, at the very first Rainforest Action Network was a Friends of the Earth project. Then the coup happened. I had started raising money from these house parties with Dave's help, and lo and behold, Jeff Webb, Jeff Knight, the whole gang who made the coup, they froze the assets. I never did get that money back from Friends of the Earth. Dave had previously set up Earth Island Institute. So after the coup, when Friends of the Earth froze my money, Dave proposed to make Rainforest Action Network an Earth Island project and asked me to join the board of directors, which I gladly did both.

That evening when Roselle and I did our press-on-type "Rainforest Action Network" letterhead, the coup was brewing already at Friends of the Earth. The rule was that because I rented a desk there, whenever I used their photocopy machine, I had to write the number of copies down on a little chart on the wall, so they could bill me later. But by now Roselle and I were pissed off at the people that were trying to throw Dave out of Friends of the Earth. So when we went into the copy room and we photocopied the first fifteen sheets of letterhead that said RAN at the top, we very consciously didn't write the "15" on the chart. That was our little protest. Maybe I was anticipating that they were going to freeze my funds.

Herb Gunther, at Public Media Center in San Francisco, was a real fan of Dave's. Herb said there's no real strategy without a media strategy. Public Media Center took on helping me with an inexpensive national media campaign on the rainforest. There were numerous meetings with Dave Brower, Herb, and me sitting down and plotting out a media strategy for the Rainforest Action Network that Public Media Center implemented.

The organization really took off. Civil disobedience was the key. Earth First! was doing civil disobedience, but it was around domestic wilderness areas and issues, whereas Rainforest Action Network was focused on the Amazon and the other rainforests of the world. We stayed focused for the first two years on Burger King and the World Bank. We had "Five Reasons to Boycott Burger King." Burger King was importing cheap beef from tropical countries where rainforest was being destroyed for pasture. We launched this campaign, using the grassroots fighting force of Earth First! across the country, because Earth First! also cared about the rainforest and they were happy to do demonstrations at Burger King. I have a great picture of Dave and some high school students at a Burger King protest in '85. In Cleveland, I think it was.

And then we did the first civil disobedience ever at the World Bank, in September of 1986. World Bank, of course, funds bad, environmentally disastrous projects everywhere. So in our first full year of operation, that fall, we organized the first Citizens Conference on the World Bank, Tropical Forests, and Indigenous Peoples. And one of the things we did—it wasn't common at all in the mideighties—was to connect environmental issues and indigenous peoples on an international front. There weren't close alliances between environmental groups and indigenous peoples back then.

The campaigns over the World Bank and the Amazon really got us going. You are never again going to have an annual meeting of the World Bank where there isn't a group of indigenous leaders there speaking on their own behalf in several different places about these issues, about the projects of the World Bank. And we did well, too. After fifteen years, the Rainforest Action Network had a budget of one and a half million dollars a year and a staff of twenty-five. In the course of it I got thoroughly arrested. To this point I've been arrested about eighteen times in various civil disobediences—Burger King, Scott Paper Company, Home Depot, Mitsubishi, the World Bank, Citibank. I never did a single night in jail. It was always a signed release after five or seven hours locked up.

In Brazil the big fight was around hydroelectric dams in the Amazon, particularly the Altamira Dam. That dam proposal is back again now under a different name, but it's in the same Kayapo Indian Reserve on the Xingu River. We stopped the Altamira Dam. One of the things that happened was that we invited two Kayapo chiefs to come to our Save the Rainforest Conference in Miami, Florida. We started doing a series of conferences across the country. We did one in Boulder, Colorado, one in Miami, one in Cleveland, and one in Seattle. A conference virtually every year for the first five years. And the one in Miami, we invited these two Kayapo chiefs. They were so powerful, through their interpreters speaking to the crowd, that we passed the hat and raised enough money to get them up to Washington, D.C., and then the D.C. activists took them, literally, into the World Bank. They just railed on these bank officials, "How dare you finance a dam that would flood 70 percent of our ancestral territory?"

There was so much publicity around it that when those two chiefs went back to Brazil, the Brazil government arrested them. They arrested them as *foreigners* interfering with the sovereign affairs of Brazil, because the status of a Native person in Brazil back then, they weren't regular citizens. They are now, but they weren't then. And so Rainforest Action Network, when the two chiefs were arrested and came to trial, we just helped to get CNN and Turner Broadcasting involved. We created what Ralph Nader called the Dracula Strategy, as he explained it to me back then. He said, "Think of a Dracula movie. Some things are so bad that just shining the light of day will kill them." This hydroelectric dam that the World Bank wanted to finance for Brazil was so bad that just bringing it to the light of day was fatal. The fact that Brazil arrested two Kayapo chiefs as foreigners over the dam, that was so bad that shining the light of day on it could kill the project, and it did kill the project.

Dave Brower was a big dam killer himself, of course. That's how he got famous. He would talk about the hydroelectric dams at the Rainforest Action Network house parties where we raised funds.

I was railing on the World Bank and various corporations at some point, and Dave had some advice on that strategy. And it's a story that I've told probably two hundred times in speeches over the last fifteen years. Dave said, "I hear you criticizing the World Bank and these corporations, and you're right, they're terrible. But think of it this way. If there was a boat in the middle of the lake that was on fire, and it was full of people, and the people couldn't swim, and you're on shore screaming, 'Get out of that boat! Get out of that boat!' you're just not going to get a lot of cooperation. But if you pull up next to that boat with something else for them to get onto, and you say, 'Get out of that boat!' you're going to get a heck of a lot of cooperation."

He told me that story more than once, because I was a little thick and I would keep carrying on my negative rant. But it really emerged as a philosophy that solidified the Rainforest Action Network. Which is, there are simply two things you need to do to save the rainforest—or to save the day, or to save the world. Stop the bad and start the good. As simple as that advice is, it came from Dave's story about a burning boat in the middle of a lake.

There's another Dave story that I use a lot. It's one he told in his speeches: the great ecological U-turn. The story was pretty simple. If you're standing on the edge of a precipice, he'd say, and you're about to fall off, and the consequences are cataclysmic, sometimes the solution is relatively simple. Turn around and walk in a different direction. You know, as theater, if you're making this point in front of an audience—and I do that a lot—you can physically act like you are standing on the edge of a precipice, looking down. That's how dire things are. Then, "Well, turn around and walk in a fundamentally different direction." That's the great ecological U-turn toward a more socially just and ecologically sustainable society.

After the Earth Summit down in Rio, I went over to Japan for the Kyoto Protocol meetings. The Kyoto Protocol looked at the level of greenhouse gas emissions in the year 1990. It said that, on average, we want to get 7 percent below those levels by 2012. If you visualize it on a linear graph, the rising emissions, in leveling off and then dropping back to 1990 levels and below, well, the line is making a U-turn. We haven't accomplished that, but at least conceptually that was what was passed at Kyoto. It would be a great ecological U-turn. It gave people a lot of hope. At least it gave them the *shape* of a fundamentally different direction. And that U-turn is still the assignment.

I closed some bars with Dave, of course. Who didn't? In one of the bar closings, we were talking about economics. I don't remember what particular bar. It strikes me that it was Specs in North Beach. But this is where Dave explained to me that he'd come to understand that the most important environmental policy was economic policy. And I didn't really get that at first. But I've so come to believe that it's true that I'm now setting up a new think tank called Foundation Earth, which will specifically look at what is the economic model for long-term sustainability.

In this work we all suffer—and Dave worried about this as well— from a sense of incrementalism in our careers. That's what Dave was talking about when he quoted Tom Hayden: "All I have been able to do in my career is to slow the rate at which things get worse." We don't want our lives to be just about slightly slowing down the rate at which things get worse. So there we are at the bar, Dave and I, talking economics. You know, as Dave got older, it was no longer two martinis, it was just one, followed by a glass of wine. And then towards the very end he would just skip the martini and do the glass of chardonnay. But there we were, closing down bars again, and he's talking about how the most important environmental policy is economic policy. To this point, I'd been thinking more in the classic environmentalist way: We need to protect more wilderness areas, and we need to get around the toxicity in the industrial manufacturing process, and so on. But I was not thinking of it in terms of economic policy. Dave was right, though. And for me now it all boils down to the question, Can we ecologize capitalism? The Herman Dalys and the Hazel Hendersons of the world have been talking about ecological economics, but that talk seems to stay mostly in the academic world. That night Dave and I talked about what would it mean to *campaign* for an ecological economics. Can we ecologize the economic model? Capitalism is the economic model right now. If we can't ecologize it, then we need to come up with a new "ism." But that's no easy feat. At the very least, even if we can't fundamentally ecologize capitalism, we can do a hell of a lot of damage control, and buy us some time, which is not unimportant from the strategic standpoint.

Dave was a man of language. The most important advice I got from him, maybe, was, "You've got to come up with ways to explain your concepts. You've got to refine your linguistic representation, how you talk about issues." One of those refinements was his adage that the most important environmental policy is economic policy.

The current model is just "Cheater Economics." It's a model that does not account for pollution externalities in any systematic way. The reason Walmart can sell cheaper is that they squeeze their suppliers to externalize their labor costs through sweatshops, or by dumping their pollution into the river. They cheat the larger system. Right? But if you did it properly, with a *true* accounting—an accounting that included environmental costs, the real costs to the planet—then the ecologically cleanest manufacturing should be the cheapest. If you internalize the real pollution costs, say to produce cotton for a T-shirt—if your accounting recognizes all the pollution run-off in the Mississippi Delta that creates a dead zone out in the Gulf, and so on—then organic cotton is cheaper than toxic cotton. Organic food is cheaper than toxic food. Dave really helped me to get onto this—the principle that the cheapest is cleanest and, conversely, the cleanest is cheapest. It was the fruit of one of those long, lingering conversations, heading towards two in the morning, closing down the bars. This new think tank of mine, Foundation Earth, will fight for "True-Cost Economics."

We did get outdoors. It wasn't all cities and nightlife and bars. I remember one time Dave and I went up to Canada together. Dave had set up this alliance between Brian Staszenski and other Canadian environmentalists, on the one side, and US environmentalists on the other. This grew out of his global orientation across boundaries, on pollution issues and such. From time to time he would go up to Alberta and meet with Brian, and one time he invited me to tag along. It was a gathering of some Canadian First Nations people on the Kootenay Plains between Banff and Jasper in the Canadian Rockies. They'd set up a tent camp for a week and there were a couple of teepees and a sweat lodge. The sweat ceremony was conducted by a Sioux group. There were meetings held between the indigenous peoples and the Canadian environmental activists and US environmental activists. Just around how to collaborate on the work. One day we decided to go climbing in the mountains. It may have been one of the last mountain-climbing things your dad did. It was not a technical climb, but it was up in the jagged high Rockies. I remember how astute your dad was at watching the change in weather patterns and the clouds. Because a storm started to move in, and he noticed, and said, "Well, maybe we should be headin' down. We're about to be in a storm on the side of a mountain."

Dave had flaws, naturally. One that struck me was his way of picking members of his own boards of directors. He seemed to do it out of a sense of camaraderie. Did somebody care about the right things, and were they affable enough to hang out, and talk about it, and enjoy life in the midst of dealing with the serious, tough issues? I imagine this was true at the Sierra Club, and I know specifically that it was true at Friends of the Earth, but a number of the board members that turned on him were people that he'd asked to join the board himself. He admitted this. He told me once that he was not nearly discriminating enough when he picked his board members.

He could have maintained bridges with his board better, I suppose. He could have schmoozed better. But I wonder. That's an odd dynamic, actually, because it strikes me that there was a fundamental honesty with Dave that would sometimes overtake diplomacy. If he thought somebody was wrong, he'd be willing to tell them very directly. And do you really want to change that?

In the beginning, when I rented that desk at Friends of the Earth, I'd seen Dave around the office. I remember asking a staff member, Angela Gennino, "What makes this guy tick?" I didn't know much about him then. Angela said, "Well, he has a vision. He is a visionary, and he can articulate that vision." That's exactly right. Dave did that well.

Nancy Skinner
Photograph courtesy of K to College

NANCY SKINNER

THE PANORAMIC WINDOWS of Nancy Skinner's district office in Oakland look eastward to the long ridgeline of the East Bay hills, the high country of her domain. Westward, unseen—the assemblywoman has no windows in that direction—are her wetlands and bay waters and the low country of the 14th District. The office is spacious. Against the north wall is a sofa, with an American flag beside one armrest and the California flag beside the other. Against the south wall rest two gold shovels. One broke ground for the connector between Bay Area Rapid Transit and the Oakland Airport. The other started the dig for the fourth bore of the Caldecott Tunnel under the Oakland hills.

"Which, of course, many of our environmental colleagues really, really fought," said Skinner, studying the second shovel. "And I have a mixed opinion of it. But when you look at the miles of cars that just sit there idling, bumper to bumper, for an hour every morning and an hour every night…"

On the wall above the shovels is a large poster titled "Rookie of the Year," showing Skinner in a baseball cap, carrying a mitt, and wearing some sort of oversized trench coat belted in at the waist. "Photoshop," she explained. "This is my head on Madonna's body. Madonna was in that baseball movie, *A League of Their Own.* We made this in Photoshop after my first year in the Legislature. There is a blog called *Capital Weekly*, and they monitor all the dealings of the legislature and the governor. At the end of that year, they rated the legislators. They said, 'Here are the legislators to watch,' and they named me the rookie of the year."

The rookie of the year is now in her third season. She was in the news on the day of the interview, for a pet bill of hers had reached the desk of Governor Brown. Two years before, in early February of 2009, after just a month in office, Skinner had introduced what she called her "E-Fairness Legislation," Assembly Bill 178, which would close the loophole in California tax law that allowed out-of-state companies to avoid collecting California sales tax. This morning's papers had reported the protests of the online sellers.

"Amazon.com is wielding the ax," ran a headline in the *San Francisco Chronicle*. "The Goliath of Internet retail sent out an email to its estimated 10,000 California 'associates' on Wednesday afternoon, saying it will end their relationship should Gov. Jerry Brown sign the online sales tax bill passed by the Legislature." The governor, according to this account, had given no indication whether or not he would sign.

"My interest in e-commerce started with concern for bookstores, and then I got very involved in the issue," Skinner told me. "I started realizing, first off, if we take Amazon, for example, they sell everything now. Everything! So, while bookstores may have been the first collateral damage, every single retailer, no matter whether middle sized or small, whether you were a sporting goods store, a hardware store, or whatever, you were all being affected. Camera store, electronics, it doesn't matter, you were being affected. You'd have customers come into your brick-and-mortar store and say, "Will you please demonstrate for me camera X or camera Y, or this computer or that computer?" And the salespeople would get out all their different models. You'd test them, you'd play with them, and then you'd think, *Great, now I know which one I want to buy.* And you'd walk out of the store. Because you get a 10 percent discount if you go and order it online, in a place that doesn't collect sales tax. So I really got into how it was impacting every kind of California business and retailer. It was just unfair."

It turned out that the governor, even as Skinner and I spoke, was signing her bill into law.

Assemblywoman Skinner is a politician without the slightest trace of Boss Tweed or Chicago Machine in her. She has the look and manner of your favorite librarian. Her political career began in a successful race for the Berkeley City Council while she was still a university student—the first and only student ever to serve on that body. She has been a rookie of the year from the start.

WHEN I WAS an undergrad, you already had environmental groups being very strong against nuclear power, but not taking any kind of stand on nuclear war. The environmental movement was being absent and silent on the issue of war. Dave Brower was one of the first prominent environmentalists to say that war is an environmental issue. I was at Cal, a student in conservation and natural resources, so I was an active environmentalist, but I was also a very strong peace activist. I didn't define myself as an environmentalist only. I sort of felt like there was no home for me, if you know what I mean. The Sierra Club then seemed too much about people who only cared about Yosemite. And some of the organizations that were more into peace and social justice, they seemed to care only about those things. For people like me, who wanted a home that was more multifaceted, there didn't seem to be one.

But then Friends of the Earth, under Dave's leadership, really staked out some very clear and much broader positions around social justice issues, and peace and war issues, as well as what we might consider our more typical environmental issues. And I thought, *Ah! A home for me!*

So Dave lived in Berkeley, and I lived in Berkeley. He came to events on campus, or to events at the Sierra Club offices, or things in Berkeley at the Ecology Center. In those days all those were really close to campus, so I would attend them. I got to interact, to hear him speak, to hear him debate these issues. It was more than just having read about him; I got to see him in action, face to face.

So I felt this great affinity. And not only affinity, but I really felt like someone, Dave, through his work with Steve Rauh and others, had made a home for environmentalists like me, who also cared about these other issues. Right away I became a member of Friends of the Earth. Then in the late seventies I became involved in a variety of local community issues around garbage and around energy.

On garbage, I think it's funny—it's a case of that old "What goes around comes around"—but Jerry Brown was governor then, as he is now again. In his first term he set up the Office of Appropriate Technology. California was really looking at appropriate technologies; what were the new, innovative technologies to get us off fossil fuels and put California on the cutting edge? Meanwhile there was a statewide waste commission—I forget exactly what it was called—but it was concerned with solid waste. There was this effort in Berkeley around garbage, and they took the signal from this appropriate-technology effort and kind of fell for what I call "incinerator logic."

Corporations had got smart. They realized, all right, just calling it a "garbage burner" is not the way to sell this. We need to market our technology in a new way, so we'll talk about "waste energy." We're taking this stuff nobody wants, this junk, this *waste,* and we're turning it into energy. Three Mile Island had happened, and we had the Carter energy crisis, and all of a sudden there was this "waste energy" move. For me, the irony was that people who might otherwise have been skeptical about such technology were jumping onto it. They were thinking, well, of course, waste is just…useless. We should burn it and make energy! So Berkeley, interestingly enough, was slated to be the first city in California with a waste-energy plant.

But there were some of us who got hooked by Barry Commoner's Four Laws of Ecology. One of them being the idea that there's no such thing as *away.* Everything goes somewhere. No such thing as free lunch. Plus, there were some of us who pointed out that the word *waste* was originally a verb. In the twentieth century we turned it into a noun. In the original usage, nothing could be waste, unless it was wasted. We didn't view "waste" as a thing. We viewed it as materials you might otherwise be able to utilize or recover that were being wasted. We didn't view burning them and turning them into energy as being a positive thing.

So we started a campaign to try to stop the garbage incinerator, the waste-energy plant. But there were many environmentalists—good, respected environmentalists—who were for it. And so all of a sudden we found ourselves in this old conundrum of, well, is this environmental or isn't it? Dave, to his credit, immediately figured out, probably by looking at the science, that when you indiscriminately burn whatever people throw into the garbage, you're burning dioxin. And from an entropy point of view, it's not the highest and best use of the resource. So we interacted with Dave and he took a position against the waste-energy plant. He was one of the few environmentalists who did. A group of us met with him; we organized an initiative to stop the plant. Dave was supportive of it.

Then, in 1981, people who were involved in that campaign, and in a campaign we had done around recycling, recruited me. They said, "Well, Nancy, you should run for the City Council." They felt I would be a good candidate because I was a student, and I could help bring the student vote. Also I was very involved with these issues around recycling and such, so I had a broader constituency than a normal student would have. The trouble was that most of the groups with clout, groups that make a candidate viable, they just thought, *Nancy Skinner! How could she ever win?*

Nancy Snow, who worked for Congressman Dellums at that time, and who was close to David, too, she said, "Nancy, we should go and sit down with David Brower. We should see what he thinks of your candidacy." I was doubtful. Yes, I had met earlier with Dave, and yes, he was supportive of our trying to stop the waste-energy plant. But I just thought, lowly me, why would David Brower ever get involved in a situation like this? Nancy Snow arranged the meeting, and I sat down with David, and we had a *wonderful* conversation. He just said, "Nancy, of course I would support you! You are trying to do exactly the kind of efforts I'm trying to do in Friends of the Earth, and you're doing it right here in my own community." What I learned later was that some of his neighbors were quite upset. Berkeley is pretty polarized, and there were these two coalitions, the conservative ABC, and the progressive BCA. Some of his neighbors were quite, you know, "How dare you support one of those BCA people?" At BCA we were for rent control. We were for these awful, awful things. But he said, "No, I stick by it. Nancy is very good."

For me it was huge. To feel that someone of Dave's stature and caliber would put his trust in me. That helped *me*, because of course you doubt yourself, and you have to have a lot of confidence to run. But it also helped inform the people who might not know me fully. To have names like his, and Congressman Dellums also endorsed me, to have that kind of affirmation, was just really, really significant.

Where do my politics come from? It's a good question. I tried to explain it to some students the other day. The only thing I can think is that my family was Catholic. I went to Catholic school. When I was in elementary school, there was what we now call "liberation theology," though I don't think it was called that back then. And there was Vatican II. The tumult in our society in the sixties was reflected in the church. In the priesthood, and amongst nuns, there were people who were questioning certain things. That happens to have been the order of nuns that taught at my school.

Here I was in this very conservative suburb of Los Angeles. My father was a very strict Republican. He loved Nixon. He was a very strong supporter of the Vietnam War. But here we also had these nuns. I mean, the nuns were very careful not to sit there and say, "Oh, the Vietnam War is wrong." But they raised questions about war in general, and about killing, and about whether it was ever right.

As a child, I thought, *No, killing's not right. War is not right.*

Meanwhile, my family subscribed to both *Look* magazine and *Life* magazine. Very heavy visual images, right? Both those magazines had little text, mostly images. And those images were so powerful. For me as a little kid, having this stuff come into my house, the pictures of the civil rights movement, for example. We didn't have any African American neighbors, but here were these pictures on the cover of *Life*, White police officers with huge fire hoses hosing down Black people. You're taught that all people are equal, right? So how could somebody hose them down? Or sic dogs on them? And then pictures of the My Lai Massacre. And pictures of kids in Vietnam running down a pathway with the napalm burning on their backs. You know, when you're a kid, things are right or wrong. There is no gray. It's developmental; kids don't see shades of gray. It's either right or it's wrong. And those things were wrong.

One of my father's reasons for being a strong Republican was that he was a small business owner. He felt that Republicans protected small business, and that we Democrats didn't care. He was born in 1909 and he lived to be eighty-six. In the last five years of his life, he concluded that the Republicans really weren't protecting small business people anymore. He was crushed. He also concluded that the Vietnam War was the biggest mistake we had ever made.

But when I was in high school! My goodness, did we ever debate it! My father would look at me and he would say, "Nancy, you would argue with the pope." Of course if you're Catholic the pope is infallible. And I'd go, "Yes! If I thought the pope was wrong, I *would!*"

After I was elected to the City Council, there were many issues I worked on with Dave. When I introduced the ban on Styrofoam, for example. My law banning Styrofoam in Berkeley was the first in the United States. David was a big supporter. When you're doing something as controversial as that, you want a lot of prominent people to weigh in. Alice Waters also weighed in. And others.

Then when David formed Earth Island Institute, he and Steve Rauh and others started these Fate and Hope of the Earth Conferences. The point of them being that you had these emerging countries like Nicaragua, where a new government had come in, and they were writing their constitutions. The hope was that these new constitutions might reflect more integration of good principles of environmental and economic sustainability, and of peace. The US Constitution, as good as it is, with its embodiment of individual rights, doesn't address that same kind of protection for the Earth. It doesn't address the idea that other living things also have rights to protection. So these Hope and Fate of the Earth Conferences started. The second one was in Nicaragua. I not only helped plan it, but I attended. Steve Rauh and I were going to be the core staffing to design it, then some other work I was doing interfered. But I did help in inviting people to participate on the panels, and I was on a panel myself. And Dave was the inspiration for it.

At the time, Reagan was president. There was this ongoing effort by the United States to undermine the Sandinista government. A duly elected government of the Nicaraguan people, right? The US, through CIA and military efforts, was trying to destabilize Nicaragua. One day a large group of the American attendees at the Fate of the Earth Conference, including your dad, went to the US embassy in Managua and we marched at the embassy to express our dismay at the ongoing US involvement in trying to destabilize Nicaragua. Of course, the embassies always have cameras, so we were well photographed, and we waved.

Dave was a force, too, in preserving the East Bay shoreline. In Berkeley and the East Bay, our bayfront, when it was still underwater, was owned by the Santa Fe Land Development Corporation. These train people! The railroads! I don't know how these people got so brilliant. Way back when, they figured, great, someday this bayshore is going to get filled. It's going to be really valuable land! We're going to make a ton of money. So the City of Berkeley filled it with our garbage, it became viable land, reclaimed land from the bay. Santa Fe said, wonderful, now that it's good land, we want to build on it. Had they been able to build what they had in mind, we would not have the beautiful public access that we do have now.

When I got on the City Council, it came to a critical head. Because for the first time the Santa Fe Land Development Corporation put forward a development proposal. Before that, it was a notion, but they had never actually gone to the city to try to get a permit. Here once again we had to be very smart legally, and also smart politically. There were people in the community who felt that development made sense, that we needed the revenue. It's the same fight you always have when a Walmart comes into a community. But there were some of us who felt, *No, that's treasure that you can never replace. How are you ever going to reclaim the bayfront if they build on it?*

We ended up, the Sierra Club and others, going for a ballot measure. We felt it was the strongest way. The City Council's action was going to be good, but independent of that we needed a way to really cement it, and that was by a vote of the people. Dave was again one of the pivotal supporters of that measure. And that measure, that initiative, even though it said nothing about Eastshore State Park, and even though it dealt with Berkeley's waterfront only, it was the thing that really cemented all of our efforts—Citizens for Eastshore Parks, Save the Bay, everybody—to form Eastshore State Park. And Dave was a pivotal part.

So far my work in Sacramento would please David, I think. My first year, I got a bill passed, AB 758. What it is, in effect, is RECO and CECO. Berkeley has these two ordinances that I helped write when I was on the City Council, RECO and CECO, which are energy-efficiency retrofit ordinances for our existing building stock. For the homes and commercial buildings built before California's really good energy code was enacted, RECO and CECO allow those buildings to be brought up to a better energy efficiency. When I was running for the assembly, people asked, "Well, what do you want to do in Sacramento?" I said that I wanted to be able to do RECO and CECO for the whole state of California. And I did! It will help bring efficiency to all of our older, aging buildings, whether a home or business.

And I'm also coauthor now on Senator Alan Lowenthal's bill to eliminate Styrofoam food packaging. This is, again, just bringing some things that Berkeley started to the state as a whole.

Another thing was that I raised the cap on what is called "net metering." Crazy names! But what net metering addresses is this problem that if you have solar on your house, it's generating electricity during the daytime, when the sun's shining, but you may not be home using electrical appliances. Your ability to access that electricity is through net metering. While your solar rooftop array is generating the electricity, it's moving your meter backward. That's net metering! When you come home later and you're using electricity, you get credit. It was very controversial. When it first went into play, they capped it. They allowed only 2.5 percent of total electricity generation in the state to go on net metering, which amounted to an artificial cap on how many solar rooftop arrays you could have. And in the PG&E territory, when I got elected, we were already just about at the 2.5 percent. So I wanted to remove the cap. The utility fought that really hard, but I managed at least to get it doubled. So now the cap is at 5 percent.

Joining the board of the David Brower Center was an easy decision for me. What I love about the whole effort around the Dave Brower building is that for me it really does reflect what attracted me about Dave Brower's leadership. The complex is not just a wonderful green building that's housing organizations concerned with the environment and sustainable development. Because half of the project is affordable housing right there in the middle of our downtown, near rapid transit. So there's that social justice component. It fulfills that problem of how we lower our carbon footprint, how we become more sustainable. We have to provide housing for people. We want to give them opportunity to not have to have a car. We want to give them places where they can gather and interact with great environmental thinking. That facility, that complex, with the affordable housing feature, and the restaurant, and the conference room, and the office space, it really, really does it.

One little anecdote. It's a posthumous David Brower story.

Because of my work with my project Cities for Climate Protection, I attended all of the international climate negotiations. There was one in the Netherlands. Not in Amsterdam, but in that other big city. What is it called? The Hague. The negotiations were held in the Hague, right at the time when Dave passed away. I learned of his death just before I arrived. When I got there, as I got out of the train station, the first thing that I saw was this huge display put up by Friends of the Earth. It was their demand that all the countries that showed up for this international negotiation had to do the right thing by climate change. Many years had passed since David left Friends of the Earth, of course, and many of the activists there from Friends of the Earth International might not have known who David was, or even that he had started it. So I went over and started talking to them. I said, "Do you know that your founder just recently died, and do you know what he represented?" There were a few who did. I had this long conversation with these activists from all over the world that were there for Friends of the Earth.

Then I left, and I was walking down the street to go to the conference, when I ran into a friend of mine from Louisville, Kentucky, who had also just arrived for the conference. He was a city official from Louisville. I asked, "How are you doing?" And he goes, "Oh! I just got off the plane, and I read the most amazing book!" So I asked, "Well, what did you read?" He said, "*Encounters with the Archdruid.*"

So on the plane to the climate negotiations, my friend from Kentucky had been reading John McPhee's great book on Dave. This all happened within the same couple of hours in the Netherlands! Dave had just died, but really not. He was still with us there on the streets of the Hague.

Paul Hawken

PAUL HAWKEN

I N 1965, at the age of nineteen, Paul Hawken worked as press
coordinator with Martin Luther King, Jr.'s staff in Selma, Alabama, in
preparation for the March on Montgomery. Hawken registered and
issued credentials to the press—a kind of security officer, in effect, given
the danger of the times. After serving as marshal in the march, he traveled
to New Orleans to work as a staff photographer for the Congress of Racial
Equality, covering voter-registration drives in Bogalusa, Louisiana, and the
Florida Panhandle. In Meridian, Mississippi, he photographed the Ku Klux
Klan after the murder of the civil rights workers Chaney, Goodman, and
Schwerner. He was seized by the Klan, but escaped thanks to FBI intervention.

In 1966, at the age of twenty, Hawken took over a small retail store in
Boston, Erewhon, named after Samuel Butler's utopian novel by that name.
(Erewhon, the fictional land of the book, is an anagram for "nowhere," but
was based on Butler's experience of New Zealand. In Erewhon, machines
are banned as dangerous. Butler, a Darwinist, was the first to suggest that
machines might develop consciousness.) Paul Hawken, an asthmatic, was
drawn to natural solutions, and he turned the little store Erewhon into a
natural-foods wholesaler, Erewhon Trading Company. With this transformation, he discovered his life's work, which has been to harmonize the
relationship between business and environment.

With Dave Smith, he founded the Smith & Hawken Garden Supply Company, which grew into an empire of fifty-six stores. With the biologist Janine Benyus, he founded Biomimicry Technologies. He is the founder, too, of PaxFan, which borrows from geometries found in Nature to increase the efficiency of industrial fans and turbines. Most recently he founded the Natural Capital Institute, a research organization based in Sausalito, California, where he lives. Hawken is author of *The Next Economy* (Ballantine 1983), *Growing a Business* (Simon and Schuster 1987), *The Ecology of Commerce* (HarperCollins 1993), and *Blessed Unrest* (Viking, 2007). With Amory Lovins he wrote *Natural Capitalism: Creating the Next Industrial Revolution* (Little Brown, 1999).

For Hawken, as for David Brower, the Sierra Nevada—in particular the east side of that range—was formative. Both men attended, a generation apart, the University of California at Berkeley, both left without degrees, and both did well in spite of dropping out. They served together on what the enlightened industrialist Ray Anderson, founder and chairman of Interface, the world's largest manufacturer of modular carpet, called his "Brain Trust."

I MET DAVID AT Tuolumne Meadows in the late fifties. He was the tall, handsome, mountain man. He was wearing shorts, a hat of some kind, Austrian looking as I remember, leather boots, shorts, tan legs, very elite. I felt like a mouse next to him.

Dave's large-format books had a huge impact on me. My father was a member of the Sierra Club and these books were prominent on our coffee table at home. My father was a photographer, as was I, and he had studied with Ansel Adams in Yosemite in the 1930s. From the time when *In Wildness Is the Preservation of the World* was published, we looked forward to each succeeding book, as if they were a serial. I had of course read Thoreau by then, but had not been aware of Eliot Porter. I was ecstatic. I must have gone through that book dozens of times. There had never been a book where photography and literature had come together so successfully, and I think it remains the all-time best in that category. *The Population Bomb* was not as influential, because by the time it came out I was acutely aware of resource and population issues, but I was so grateful it did come out. At the time, it caused a huge hullabaloo in the media and academia. It was the best pot stirrer we had seen until the publication of *Limits to Growth* four years later.

David's influence was very significant in my book *Natural Capitalism*, and in *Blessed Unrest* even more so. Not so much in *The Ecology of Commerce*, yet it was that book, *The Ecology of Commerce*, that brought us closely together, after the fact. He carried so much water for that book in his talks and travels! I have a picture someone sent me of him holding it up at a lectern. I couldn't believe my good fortune to have David being my biggest booster, along with Ray Anderson. It seems to me he did talk more about economics after *Ecology of Commerce* was published. I think it validated what he had, and had not, been saying about money as determining use value.

I think it's too early to tell his place in the history of the environmental movement, because the movement is morphing and growing in so many diverse ways. History is a perception modeled in the present, and we will be living in a radically different world, one augured by Dave's pronouncements, concerns, and predictions. When the time comes, will the messengers that were often shot at in their life be honored in hindsight? Hard to say. No single person created more ways and means for people to become active and effective with respect to the environment than David Brower. That is sure.

He loved young people and vice versa. He didn't get rigid. He was beyond generous to those who sought him out, whether on the road or at home. He was an elder that stayed close to the ground. He made young people hopeful, and fiercely protective of the Earth. He seemed to be a new and different David Brower every decade. He aged superbly. He got funnier, more relaxed, and kinder in all ways.

I remember when we were on a panel at Interface, and he was in his eighties then, and someone was perorating on something, and he turned to me straight-faced and asked, "What is the name of that disease you get when you are older?" I cracked up laughing and he looked back to the audience with complete innocence. His sense of humor made him human and compelling, and, in many ways, more credible.

I also remember a time when I was in my forties and he was in his eighties. I was invited to speak to a big environmental get-together in Mendocino on a Saturday and I turned it down because I was on the road earlier in the week and wanted to get home and rest. David was going to speak there. While I was on the road, I heard that he had been rushed to the hospital to get a pacemaker for his heart. I got in touch with the organizers, the Mendocino Environmental Center I believe, and sent them an email that I would be happy to speak after all, since David couldn't make it. Never heard from them. A couple weeks later I saw David and told him I offered to cover for him, and he said that he did the event himself. He had incredible stamina and drive.

Mainly I just remember his goodness now.

David Cornelius Brower and David Brower, Carmel Valley
Photograph by Sara Harkins

DAVID CORNELIUS
BROWER

DAVID CORNELIUS BROWER is named for his two grandfathers. One was Cornelius Owens of Jefferson County, Arkansas, who eventually became a deacon but spent his young manhood in the Depression picking cotton, gambling, and hopping freights to get where he wanted to go. The other, four years younger, was David Ross Brower of California, who spent much of the Depression in the Sierra Nevada as a climbing bum, though that term had yet to be invented. Both men loved locomotives and the sound of that mournful whistle blowing. Both had prematurely white hair. But for the most part their lives were very different. The first grandfather found Christian faith late, the second lost it early. The two spoke divergent forms of English. In their complexions, for sure, they were like night and day.

Cornelius Owens never met this grandson, having died ten years too soon. David Ross Brower was luckier and lived through the first fourteen years of his namesake's life. The two David Browers were big mutual fans, each the apple of the other's eye.

There is a telling photo of David the Younger at three years old, a snapshot taken by his grandfather, or perhaps by me, from the backseat of my parents' car, a bronze 1980 Toyota station wagon. My son grips the steering wheel—we are parked, obviously—and he looks back impishly at the camera. He is wearing his grandfather's Tyrolean hat. If any possession of my father's was talismanic for me, it was this dark hat, which he had worn for most of his career in the mountains. It was covered with pins and enameled badges from various mountaineering and skiing associations, all beautifully made, and it was ragged and full of holes from long use. The hat was so charged with significance for me as a child, spoke so eloquently of countless miles of trail, and a thousand climbs, and the fraternity of climbers who gathered sometimes at our house for dinner, that I myself would have hesitated to put it on. David wears it very comfortably and humorously, though of course it is many sizes too large for him.

One evening the next year, when David Brower the Younger was four, the family gathered at the house of David Brower the Elder, on Earth Day, to watch a new PBS television documentary, *For Earth's Sake: The Life and Times of David Brower*, which included old footage of my father's first ascent of Shiprock. Midway through, we realized that the smaller David was missing. He had slipped away. In the backyard grew a tall incense cedar that my father had transplanted from the Sierra Nevada fifty years before. When we found him, Davey, inspired by the film, was halfway up the tree, self-belayed with a dog leash around his neck.

David Cornelius was a risk taker, a jumper from garage roofs, an explorer of Peralta Creek behind our Oakland house. He learned to ride bikes shortly after learning to walk. There were never training wheels or any learning curve; he jumped on the first bike he saw and took off at a high rate of speed.

David Cornelius grew to exactly the height that David Ross did, six feet one and three-quarters inches, or, as we like to round it off, six feet two. He is the best athlete we have had in our family since his grandfather, good at martial arts and football, but specializing in basketball. At Bishop O'Dowd High School, after several high-scoring games in a row, he made "Athlete of the Week" in Oakland, not an easy job in that tough town. In a poll for his senior yearbook, his classmates picked him for Best Physique, Best Lips, and Best Car. A trifecta, except that the school forced him to pick just one. He chose Best Car. It was his Grandfather Cornelius's '66 Malibu, the vehicle in which Cornelius, toward the end of his life, ferried old ladies to church and senior centers—a deacon's car, yes, but one which David successfully tricked out and gangsterized.

David began college playing Division I basketball at Fresno State and ended graduating from the University of California at Berkeley with a degree in environmental sciences, policy, and management. He is now twenty-five and works at ICF International as a project manager in an energy efficiency program for the City of San Francisco.

On the day his interviewer dropped in with his tape recorder, David gave him a tour of the spare bedroom. He had just assembled a crib, which he thumped to demonstrate its sturdiness. This was progress, as David spent his own first few weeks of life in the half-open drawer of a dresser—a tradition in rural Arkansas, apparently. Today, around the newly assembled crib, baby things that Shannon had collected at her shower were piled, bibs with little neckties painted on them, and that sort of thing.

The baby was known to be a boy. It was to be the interviewer's first grandchild of any gender. The scheduled arrival date was three weeks away, but there were signs it might be sooner. The name was still being debated. There was considerable talk of another "David." That would mean a succession of three David Browers interrupted only by me. This present David was confident that a "David" would definitely be in the name somewhere, maybe in the middle. There was also some talk of "Mason" as a first name. Mason? As in bricklayer? Or as in the order of the Masons? The secret order of the Masons with all their silly symbolism, as on the dollar bill, that spooky eye above the pyramid?

Ill-advised, don't you think?

As the manuscript for this book goes to the publisher, the baby is biding his time in the womb and the matter of the name is still up in the air. A resolution will have to await the sequel.

I DON'T REMEMBER the actual episode of me climbing the incense cedar. But I do remember seeing old movies of Grandpa rock climbing with what looked, to me, like stuff that I could use.

Stuff I could go find myself and climb on my own. It looked like just a regular rope—not some kind of bungee or anything. I thought, *I can do that.* And I think that's the time I went up in the tree, climbed up in the cedar and almost hung myself.

I just remember Grandpa's demeanor, more than anything. And I remember his, kind of, *presence* more than anything. I mean, he's the same height as me now, but he seemed like such a bigger person than I am right now. Even bigger than his own height suggested. I remember kind of broad shoulders. And a kind of similar walk to—this is kind of weird—but a similar walk to that of Phil Jackson, the Lakers coach. I remember a little bit of the same kind of bowlegged, rolling walk as Jackson's. I thought Grandpa was the size of Phil Jackson. Which is six foot ten. Grandpa's presence! He would command the table at dinner. Sometimes drifting off in his own thoughts. Moments of silence when he was in his own thoughts, but when he talked, everyone listened. And everyone kind of looked up to him. Looked at him like there's something about him.

Having the same name, that's been something. For one thing, it's immediate credibility, which is nice. But at first people obviously never make a connection. Me being Black. No one ever thinks that I'm mixed. So they don't necessarily think that there's a relationship there. They just think, "Oh, wow, you have a famous name." If in fact they know the name. It's always the same thing: "Did you know that you have the same name as…?" And I'll say, "Well, yeah, I do know. He's my grandpa." And then it's always a skeptical look. "Yeah, sure."

Just like that guy last month at the birthday party. So we're having martinis for Grandpa's ninety-ninth birthday—or what would have been his ninety-ninth birthday—at the David Brower Center. And I have a name badge, "David Brower." So this strange, thin guy comes up—and I forget the guy's name, it's probably good that I forget his name—but he's the son of a Nobel Laureate. So I introduce myself, "Hi, I'm David Brower." He frowns and kind of laughs. It's one of those "Yeah, sure" laughs. I tell him, no, really, I am David Brower, and I point to my name badge. I'm laughing now myself, because this happens so often. He still doesn't believe it. So I say, "Actually, I *am* David Brower. This is Ken Brower, my father. Kenneth David Brower. David R. Brower was my grandfather." Now I guess the guy halfway believes me. But he's still sort of puzzled, and he doesn't quite like it. And then he says, "Are you in contact with your mom?"

So weird stuff like that happens all the time. But, I mean, it's also pretty cool, because it's nice to know that people remember. It's strange to see the type of people who actually know the name. I mean, it's eleven years since Grandpa's been dead, and most of the stuff he did— his big wins—were more or less in the fifties and sixties and seventies. I wouldn't think that people my own age would necessarily know the name. Of course, lots of people don't know it. But I'm surprised at how many people do.

Just last year, on the interview for my job at ICF, this guy, Nick, they had him sit in on the interview. Nick's my friend now. He had already been hired, and he was brought in to give more of a same-age, peer sort of input to the interview. He was reading *Encounters with the Archdruid* at the time, and he's incredibly impressed with Grandpa. But he didn't make the connection. It was in that interview conversation that he found out. He looked at my résumé and he said, "Oh, 'David Brower.' I'm reading a book about a guy with the same name. A really cool guy, a great environmentalist." I said, "Yes, that's my Grandpa." Nick gets all excited. "No shit! Oh, man, we gotta hire you. You gotta take this job." I said, "Yeah, I mean, I'd love to. But I have to get hired first." Nick starts reciting one of his favorite quotes of Grandpa's from the book—I wish I could remember what it was. It wasn't the "boldness" quote, but I can't think what it was. And he says, "Your grandfather's favorite drink was martinis! That's my favorite drink, too!"

One of my two best teachers at Bishop O'Dowd, Tom Tyler, found out the first day of class—Earth Science—when he called out my name on the roll-call list. It was the same thing as always. Mr. Tyler starts with the letter *A*. Who were the *A*s in that class? I don't know, Tommy

271

Arnold might have been one of them. "Tommy Arnold," Mr. Tyler says. "Here," says Tommy. So Mr. Tyler reads some more As and Bs, and then, "David Brower?"

"Yeah, I'm here."

"Wow, did you know that you have a really famous name?"

Well, sometimes you got to have fun. So I say, "Oh, yes. Isn't he an environmental guy, or something like that?"

"Yes! He's one of the most influential environmentalists. He's probably the most important conservationist in the second half of the twentieth century." And so on, and so forth, blah, blah, blah.

"Oh, yeah," I said. "*That* guy! He's my grandfather."

Everyone in the class laughed, because they already knew. I'm playing it off, being the class clown. It was so funny. Tom Tyler laughed. He also kind of looked at me, you know, like, *Oh, great, is he going to be one of these kind of kids?* I don't really know what he was thinking. It was great.

Bishop O'Dowd has a David Brower Memorial Garden—the Living Laboratory—and it was there before I ever came to the school. It's a living laboratory to create awareness of Nature and for educational purposes for the students of O'Dowd. It's a chance for them to get credit—to do an accredited course—while being outdoors. Out gardening. Out learning all about native plants. Incredible view overlooking the bay. When I came to O'Dowd the garden was already being developed by Annie Prutzman, with some help from Tom Tyler. Two great teachers. Shout out to them!

I didn't tell Annie Prutzman who my grandfather was. Someone else told her. I think Tom Tyler told her. I just remember her being really, really excited, and she thought it would be great for the Living Laboratory. She was such a huge fan of Grandpa. And that's what I mean about the immediate credibility. She immediately liked me. So of course I immediately liked her. She was so into it. She's like, *Oh, that's great! Here's another opening! David's an athlete, so we can get all the athletic kids to jump into the Green Movement.* She didn't *say* that, but I could see it in her face. Her whole thing is getting people to come out and enjoy. Because she knows that once people come out, they'll love to be out there. And that was the case. Each year more people came to the garden.

Then when I was a sophomore they started the David Brower Memorial Award. Which is an award for two people in the graduating class for outstanding work in the garden. Either in the garden, or in other environmental endeavors. But it was mostly for the garden, for taking leadership of the garden, and organizing days for people to come out and garden and do work on this big plot of land. They put in a pond. One of the kids won the David Brower Memorial Award because he'd spent tons and tons of extra hours digging a pond. There are all kinds of toads and frogs, all kind of native species in there. And so they get the award every year. For three years I've presented that award to classes at O'Dowd. Once in my graduating class, in '04, and earlier in '03, and then I came back in my freshman year of college to present it for the '05 award.

It's never really bugged me, having the same name. But, I don't know. I've thought about this a lot more, now that I have my own little boy on the way. This question of naming him. Whether to name him David. Everyone asks about my name, is there pressure? No, it's never pressure, but you do often get put into a category. It works out for me, because I am interested in the environment, and I do like the outdoors. I don't mind the connection. But what if you weren't interested in those things? I could see how it would get to the point where it could be a little annoying.

I don't feel like I'm being pushed in a direction by the name, because my direction was basketball my whole life, until my junior year of college. So not necessarily pushed, but maybe kind of *shaped*. When I had Mr. Tyler for Earth Science, I never had a class where it was so focused on Grandpa. We had tests that would test us on...*Grandpa*. It was just weird for me to actually have other people in the class being taught that. So I said, Man, this is something special. Maybe I should think about this a little more. Think about becoming green. And then in college, you have these general education courses where you get exposed to everything, math, econ, all these different fields, and none of the other stuff sounded as interesting as environmentalism. And the fact that I already had something of a head start also made it, you know, a lot nicer and more desirable.

I don't read that much. I spend most of my spare time making music. That also could be attributed to Grandpa. A lot of times when we came up to the house, he'd be playing the piano. Never reading any scores. Just something he would do to soothe himself. I would get my toy from Grandma. She'd always somehow magically have a toy up in the middle room waiting for me. And Grandpa was always playing the piano. Uncle Bobby, too, sometimes I would sit in his lap while he was playing the same piano.

When I was four, for Christmas, Grandpa got me that tiny little keyboard. I had no musical training, but it was fun to play on that thing. And eventually it progressed into something that's really a big hobby for me. If I had never gotten that keyboard, it's possible I would never have discovered it. Later on, another Christmas, you bought me a bigger keyboard that I still have, the Yamaha. You got that for me when I was twelve, and it's still working, thirteen years later. But for Grandpa to buy me that little keyboard, I must have shown some interest. There's what I think is an interesting photo. There's Katy, and Erik, and they're drawing or something on the living room table. I'm completely turned around, and I'm staring down at Grandpa's big piano.

The only thing I remember about that Tyrolean hat is what you told me. That it had all those climbing and skiing medals on it and he wore it on all his climbing and backpacking trips in the Sierra. For some reason that hat always makes me think of his yodeling. And how impressive his yodeling was. And about how he would call you guys back when you were out in the mountains, or in Tilden Park or wherever, by yodeling.

The bronze Toyota. I remember leaving Sinbad's Restaurant in San Francisco and following the bronze Toyota station wagon going back into the East Bay. I can still picture this so clearly. We're in our Volvo and Grandpa's in the Toyota. He's eighty years old and he's going, like, ninety-five miles per hour back to the East Bay. And you're behind him. You're pissed off, because you're always telling him to drive slower. He's already had a martini or two back at Sinbad's. And he's just bombing across the bridge, and you have to weave in and out of the bridge traffic to keep him in sight. You're so pissed. You're saying, "I'm going to drive up to the house, and I'm going to tell him, 'You can't drive that way anymore.' " He was *drivin'*. Man, he was going fast.

Another Sinbad's story. This is about four years ago, so about six years since Grandpa has died. Shannon and I, we're at Sinbad's. I'm giving her this whole spiel. Yeah, this is my grandfather's favorite restaurant. We should come here all the time. Really good seafood. The windows are right on the water, right on the bay. Grandpa used to count pelicans going by—one hundred seventeen pelicans was the record, or whatever it was. So here I am, twenty-one years old, and when we got there, they asked, "Would you like anything to start?" We said we'll have some wine. And naturally, because we're pretty young-looking, he said, "Oh, can I see your ID?" I give it to him.

He reads the name, and he says, "You know, a guy by the same name used to come in here. A really great, great man. He was an environmentalist, saved the Grand Canyon. It's really interesting that you have the same name as him." And I said, "Yeah, it's my grandpa." "Nooooo!" he says. And then it's, "Hold on, sir, I'll be right back." *And he takes my ID.* So he comes back with the general manager. "Oh, my God," says the manager. "You're the son, the grandson, what's the relationship?" I say I'm the grandson. "The grandson of David Brower! That great man. Wine is complimentary! On the house! What else would you like?" I'm like, Yeah! This is the first time Shannon's ever been there. I'm sitting there bragging about this place, and we have this special treatment. It couldn't have gone any better.

To me, he was my Grandpa, so he seemed like the patriarch.

Even though he was this big, powerful figure, he was still at the same time gentle. I just remember he had a gentle voice. And that's what made him seem like a grandpa. It seemed like what a grandpa should be. This big, big figure with a gentle voice.

John de Graaf

JOHN DE GRAAF

FTER STARTING HIS career in radio in Minnesota, John de Graaf moved back home to the West and into television. For the past twenty-nine years, he has been an independent producer of documentaries in association with KCTS-TV in Seattle. Fifteen of his documentaries have been broadcast nationally in prime time on the Public Broadcasting System, among them: *Affluenza,* a critique of American consumerism. *Escape from Affluenza,* the sequel. *Running out of Time,* a study of overwork and time pressure in America. *Visible Target. The Motherhood Manifesto. Circle of Plenty. Beyond Organic. A Personal Matter: Gordon Hirabayashi vs. the United States. Silent Killer: The Unfinished Campaign Against Hunger. It's Up to Us: The Giraffe Project. For Earth's Sake: The Life and Times of David Brower.*

To date he has won three regional Emmy Awards, and there is now an award in his name, the John de Graaf Environmental Filmmaking Award, presented annually at the Wild & Scenic Film Festival.

De Graaf is coauthor of the book *Affluenza: The All-Consuming Epidemic* and he is the editor of *Take Back Your Time* and the children's book *David Brower: Friend of the Earth.* At the time of the interview, his book *What's the Economy For, Anyway?* was about to be released. He is the national coordinator of Take Back Your Time, an organization dedicated to ending time poverty and overwork in the United States and Canada. He serves on the board of Earth Island Institute, David Brower's last organization.

De Graaf's preoccupation lately has been Gross National Happiness. The concept began in the Himalayan Kingdom of Bhutan, whose monarch, His Majesty Jigme Singye Wangchuck, declared in 1972 that "Gross National Happiness is more important than Gross National Product." In 2008 the new king, Khesar, the fifth Druk Gyalpo of Bhutan, repeated, in his coronation address, the sentiments of his predecessor: "Without peace, security, and happiness, we have nothing. That is the essence of the philosophy of Gross National Happiness." The first Gross National Happiness Conference was held in Bhutan. De Graaf attended the second, which was held in Nova Scotia. He reported as a journalist from the fifth, held in 2009 at Iguassu Falls in Brazil, where the delegates discussed the latest in "Happiness Science." (Iguassu, the biggest waterfall in the world, seems an appropriate spot, in that waterfalls, like coniferous forest and the seashore, swarm with the negative ions that impart, they say, a sense of well-being.)

As national coordinator of Take Back Your Time, de Graaf is particularly interested in the intersection of work—or overwork—and health and happiness. At the Gross National Happiness Conference in Brazil, he made the case that shorter working hours, especially in rich countries, are key to happiness, health, and long-term sustainability. "Not surprisingly," he said, psychologists and sociologists "have found that beyond a certain minimum level of income, greater happiness comes from strong and plentiful human connections, a sense of control over one's life and employment, meaningful work, good health, basic economic security, trust in others and in government, and other opportunities less directly connected with monetary remuneration."

De Graaf is codirector of the Happiness Initiative at Sustainable Seattle. He and his colleagues are trying to create a national model for measuring and improving well-being in the United States.

THERE WAS A fair distance between my first encounter with Dave and my next one. My first was meeting him at the University of Minnesota, Duluth, back around 1972, when a couple of us got together and were able to collect an honorarium for him to speak there. I'd been a fan of his for a long time. I'd read all the Sierra Club books. I was in the Sierra Club at least nominally when I was a teenager. Dave's name was so familiar to me. I remember even seeing it in the logbooks, whatever those things are—the registers—on top of Sierra peaks when I was climbing them in my teens. In those days there were still names in those registers from the thirties, because not that many people had climbed these peaks.

My buddy John Ellsworth and I, we loved the Sierra. John lives now in June Lake, and he just retired after thirty years in the Forest Service in Lee Vining. From the time I was about ten years old, my dad took us on little backpacking trips. By the time I had finished my freshman year of high school, my parents trusted me enough, and John Ellsworth's parents trusted him enough, to let us go backpacking on our own in the Sierra. So in 1961, my dad drove us up to Yosemite Valley and dropped us off. We backpacked up to Tuolumne Meadows, climbed Mount Dana and kind of hiked around the area, then hitchhiked back down to Yosemite Valley, spent some time in the Valley doing trails there. Two weeks later, John's dad picked us up.

After my sophomore year, we got a couple of other kids involved from my high school, and we went for six weeks. When I was a junior, we went for four weeks. Then after my senior year of high school, John and I worked the first half of the summer just to earn a little money for college. I was going to go to the University of California. It wasn't that you needed much, because there was no real tuition in those days, and my parents, of course, were going to help out some. So we worked for the first half of the summer, saved some money up, and then in mid-July we went back up to the Sierra and we spent six weeks just doing the range from north to south. Mount Lyell. Banner Peak. We screwed up on Ritter. We didn't get to the top of Ritter. We did several other peaks on the way down. We got to the Palisade group, and we hiked over Bishop Pass, climbed Mount Agassiz, and then went down cross-country into the Barrett Lakes, and we climbed North Palisade.

North Palisade was the toughest. It's a three-thousand-foot climb. It's pretty exposed. We didn't do it with a rope. If you stay on the LeConte Route, you don't have any trouble. And we did stay on it. You get off that route, I think you could be in terrible trouble, if you don't have a rope. Because it's very exposed. Dave's name was in the register on top.

Then we did Junction Peak and Mount Muir. Finally we spent the last night on top of Mount Whitney, where we got blazingly drunk, because someone had left a whole bottle of champagne about a hundred yards from the top of the mountain. And there was no one there, period, but us, staying overnight. The two of us almost never drank anything before, and here we are at 14,500 feet and we downed this bottle of champagne. Oh, my God. In the morning John really didn't want to get up. I had said that I was going to get up and see the sunrise from Whitney, so I dragged myself out of the sleeping bag and got some pictures.

It was a great trip. It probably felt a little like Dave's 1934 trip. Except for the champagne. I do remember seeing Dave's name in the register on North Palisade.

So, as I say, my first meeting with Dave was when I invited him to the University of Minnesota, Duluth, in 1972. Then in about 1980 I started thinking about doing a film on him. Having already thought of him as kind of a hero. I contacted him about that, and we got together in '81 and started shooting the film. We went up to the Sierra, and we shot some stuff. But I had just gotten into filmmaking at that time. I was a real rookie. I'd only really made two films up to that point, and I couldn't get the money to finish the film. Or even go further with it. I dropped it. I felt really guilty about that, but I wasn't able to follow up.

Then about 1986, a woman named Carolyn Gates, a friend of mine from Seattle, started working with Earth Island, and she told me I should really try again to make this film work. She connected me with Huey Johnson, who also encouraged me to do it.

I was a little hesitant even about talking to your dad, at that point, because I had so dropped the ball. But I was in Berkeley, and I just thought I'd give him a call. He answered, and I said, "You probably don't even remember me, but I'm the guy who wanted to make the film." He said that yes, he did remember. I said, "I don't know if you'd consider this, but I'd kind of like to try it again." And he said, "Sure. Where are you?" I was in Berkeley, at the Berkeley BART. He said, "I'll be down and pick you up in ten minutes and we'll go down to Spenger's and talk about it. He bought me lunch. It was such a gracious thing, after I felt like I'd so failed.

So we began figuring out how to try this again. I got some other people involved who had a little bit more clout. And by then I also had a number of other national PBS documentaries under my belt. So it was a little bit different story. So this led to our doing *For Earth's Sake*. Huey Johnson helped out. We did a kind of fundraiser at Dave's seventy-fifth birthday party, with Huey as the master of ceremonies.

We went to Vail and did some shooting in Vail, interviewing Dave in Vail. Then in July of '88, we went up to the Sierra again, and shot more material with Dave and your mom. We went to the Grand Canyon and did a short trip with Dave and Martin Litton. I finished in '89, and in 1990 PBS broadcast the film nationally in their twentieth-anniversary-of-Earth-Day broadcast.

During the making of *For Earth's Sake*, Dave and I didn't talk about filmmaking techniques, as such, but we did talk about video. By then Dave was into doing videos himself. We were videotaping him while he was videotaping things at Mono Lake.

I do remember telling him what a fan I was of many of those films that he did do. I thought that they were quite remarkable films, and quite effective, for the times. I thought he was a good filmmaker. He made films that made a difference. The one that I particularly showcased in my film was *The Wilderness Alps of Stehekin*, which I loved. I used a lot of footage from that.

I've taught documentary filmmaking, off and on. In class I would show parts of that film and just talk about some of the techniques. People seeing the film nowadays, they kind of chuckle at parts of it. It's got this really sappy boys' choir singing "America the Beautiful," and it intones this sort of fifties flavor. But what I've been saying to filmmakers is, you can laugh now, but this was hugely effective at the time. Dave knew his audience. He knew who he was trying to reach. This film was shown to a hundred members of Congress and it helped pass the bill for a North Cascades National Park. That kind of patriotism, that kind of music, the way Dave narrates it over "America the Beautiful," and all that kind of stuff, it was very, very persuasive filmmaking. The whole way the film was done, as sort of personal story. You know, you're in it, and your brothers and sisters are in it. The way he told it as a personal story, all of that was extremely effective.

He wasn't like me. I mean, I can shoot fifty times as much video as I use in the film. I have lots of opportunity to get just the perfect shot. But he was using *film*, and he didn't have a lot of money. His shooting ratio was probably three to one. He was using probably about a minute of film out of every three he shot.

In *For Earth's Sake* I also used shots from his Shiprock film and from his winter mountaineering on Bear Creek Spire film. I used shots from his film *Skyland Trails of the Kings Canyon Park*, which helped inspire Kings Canyon National Park and has a lot of beautiful footage—really, really nice stuff. That was made in, like, 1940. I also used shots from Cragmont Rock in Berkeley that he did, and shots from Yosemite. I used clips from his Hetch Hetchy and Dinosaur National Monument films and from *Wilderness Alps of Stehekin*.

One thing I thought, as I got to know Dave, was that John McPhee did a very, very good job of capturing Dave's personality in *Encounters with the Archdruid*. McPhee was very observant. Another thing that struck me is that the people I talked to had two quite different feelings about your dad, depending on whether they'd ever been with him in a bar. The people who had just met him in formal settings, after he'd given a talk, many felt he was kind of cold and distant. That he came across as superior. McPhee got that. And so did Dave. He said to me once that he was more comfortable talking to a thousand people than to one person he hadn't met before. What came off to people as coldness, I think was shyness. I honestly think he had to go to the pub and get a Tanqueray in him in order to break that down. And then he could be such a good listener and questioner and companion. Young people who actually got to spend a little time with him in the bar, or in some setting of that sort, they all came away feeling like this guy is so personable, he really cares about us. Exactly the opposite feeling that I heard from some of the people, friends of mine, whose only connection with him was in a formal setting.

He always had a great sense of humor. There was always wit in his conversation, and of course there were the one-liners. "What do the Bible and environmentalists have in common? *No humor.*" He would always say we should thank Richard Nixon. We never thanked Richard Nixon for the Environmental Protection Act. We know how to criticize, we environmentalists, but we don't know how to thank people for doing the right thing. Your mom came to the Sierra with us, and your mom, of course, was funny. She was even funnier than he was. Her humor was dry. One one-liner after another. She gets most of the laughs in the film.

In our narration we say that they shared a small office at the UC Press, when they worked as editors there. Then comes the war, and he goes off to Camp Hale with the Tenth Mountain Division to train troops in climbing techniques. We say that after only a short correspondence, David proposed. "And since I had never kissed him, it seemed a little abrupt," your mom says. But she accepts. "We went to our first movie when we had been married two weeks. That was our first date. So I married a total stranger, actually."

Then, later on, the film talks about Dave's being hired in 1952 as executive director of the Sierra Club.

"I was delighted," says your mom. "Because he spent so much of our evenings and weekends on Sierra Club matters, I thought that now, as an employee, with a nine-to-five job, he certainly isn't going to want to do this in his evenings and his weekends. I was quite mistaken."

We went up to do some shooting in the basin behind Saddlebag Lake. I knew that area really well. I thought this is a really great place where we can get a really alpine look, but rather easy, because we take the little water taxi across Saddlebag, and just walk up to Greenstone Lake and beyond. Not very far, but it feels so alpine. Dave was animated up there. He points up to North Peak, and he says, "This is North Peak. It was not named after Oliver North." He kept telling us these stories. He'd find lessons. He'd look at these fairy circles, where the grasses form a rim, expanding out into wider and wider circles, as they exhaust the nutritional value of the earth inside the circle. He said, "Even before people started wasting the Earth, the grasses were doing it."

Your mom said that when David gets out here, he's just like a little kid. He becomes a little kid. And one thing Dave himself said is that he didn't get out nearly enough. He said that his life wasn't really about the mountains—not about mountains like this anymore. It's really about being surrounded by mountains of paper.

I also remember, from making the film, the great testimonials by people who were touched by your dad. People like Mark Terry. Mark told me that all he did at some conference was to mention that there should be a book about environmental education. And your dad said, "Yes, and you're going to write it." He talked Mark into it, and it became the book *Teaching for Survival*. And people like Harvey Manning, who told me, "Yeah, Dave came up to Seattle and he said, 'Harvey! We need a book about the North Cascades, and you're going to write it, and I need it in thirty days.' "

I also remember a little interview I did with your dad and Ansel Adams together in Yosemite Valley in 1981, just a couple of years before Ansel died. It was nice, because after all that hard feeling that had come between them in the Sierra Club fight, they had clearly gotten beyond that, and they both appreciated each other. Ansel made a comment to the effect of, "We got to know who the real enemies are. We've got James Watt to deal with. We've got to be together."

Your mom said that she was the one who couldn't forgive people for what happened at the Sierra Club. She said your dad got over it really quickly, and was willing to make friends again, but she had trouble.

I'll tell you the story that stands out, and this is probably a painful one. Might be painful for you to hear this one. But the story that stands out for me most, maybe because it's the last story, was that a week before Dave died, Michael Ableman and I visited him at Alta Bates Hospital. We were chatting with him in his room. You could tell that he was not feeling real positive, obviously, about the future. But he was still game, still talking about, "I've asked for another twenty-year extension," and this kind of thing. But when we left, I said, "Bye, Dave. I hope that the next time I see you, you're back out of here and fighting the good fight again." Some kind of cheery thing like that. I don't remember my words. I remember *his* words precisely, though. He looked at me and he said, "I don't think that's in the cards. But it's been a great eighty-eight years."

Kenneth Brower
Photograph by Barbara Brower

ABOUT THE AUTHOR

K ENNETH DAVID BROWER is the oldest son of the pioneering environmentalist David Brower. His first memories are of the Sierra Nevada and the wild country of the American West. His father drafted him into service as an editor at nineteen. Under the general editorship of David Brower, he wrote or edited fourteen volumes in the Exhibit Format Series of photo books produced by the Sierra Club and Friends of the Earth. In his midtwenties he departed his father's shop to become a freelance writer, and has written for *The Atlantic, Audubon, National Geographic, Canadian Geographic, Paris Review, Reader's Digest, Smithsonian, Sierra, Islands,* and many other magazines. His emphasis has been environmental issues and the natural world. His work has taken him to all the continents. He is the author of *The Starship and the Canoe, Wake of the Whale, A Song for Satawal, Realms of the Sea, The Winemaker's Marsh, Freeing Keiko,* and many other books. He lives in Berkeley, California.

THE PUBLISHER wishes to thank the following donors for their contributions to this book. We are especially grateful to Judy Avery, Nik Dehejia, Troy Duster, Guy Lampard and Suzanne Badenhoop, and Michael McCone for their exceptional generosity.

Suzanne Abel

Stephen Becker

Ralph Benson

Lance G. Brady

Nancy Bye

Steven B. Chiem

Edward Church

Steve Costa and Kate Levinson

Christine Crawford

Bill Curtsinger

Shelly Davis-King

Donald Day

Christopher Dean

Mark Evanoff

James T. Fousekis

George Frost and Marilee Enge

Deborah Garcia

Patrick Golden

Nicola W. Gordon

Loni Hancock and Tom Bates

Leanne Hinton

Susan Ives

Alan La Pointe

John Muir Laws and Cybelle Renault

David Loeb

Jonathan Katz

Matthew Kelleher

Marty Krasney

Malcolm Margolin

Adrienne McGraw

Joe and Lynn Medeiros

Michael Mitrani

Annie Moose

Charles Pelton and Jacqueline Frost

Bob and Susan Rosenberg

Tom Rusert

Gail Canyon Sam

Thomas Schmitz

Victoria Shoemaker

Paul Smith

James Swinerton and Clarissa Cutler

Cynthia Hart Tapley

Lisa Van Cleef and Mark Gunson

Azile and Marcus White

James and Belinda Zell

HEYDAY
into California

About Heyday

Heyday is an independent, nonprofit publisher and unique cultural institution. We promote widespread awareness and celebration of California's many cultures, landscapes, and boundary-breaking ideas. Through our well-crafted books, public events, and innovative outreach programs we are building a vibrant community of readers, writers, and thinkers.

Thank You

It takes the collective effort of many to create a thriving literary culture. We are thankful to all the thoughtful people we have the privilege to engage with. Cheers to our writers, artists, editors, storytellers, designers, printers, bookstores, critics, cultural organizations, readers, and book lovers everywhere!

We are especially grateful for the generous funding we've received for our publications and programs during the past year from foundations and hundreds of individual donors. Major supporters include:

Acorn Naturalists; Alliance for California Traditional Artists; Anonymous; James J. Baechle; Bay Tree Fund; Barbara Jean and Fred Berensmeier; Joan Berman; Buena Vista Rancheria; Lewis and Sheana Butler; California Civil Liberties Public Education Program, California State Library; California Council for the Humanities; The Keith Campbell Foundation; Center for California Studies; City of Berkeley; Compton Foundation; Lawrence Crooks; Nik Dehejia; Frances Dinkelspiel; Troy Duster; Euclid Fund at the East Bay Community Foundation; Mark and Tracy Ferron; Judith Flanders; Karyn and Geoffrey Flynn; Furthur Foundation; The Fred Gellert Family Foundation; Wallace Alexander Gerbode Foundation; Nicola W. Gordon; Wanda Lee Graves and Stephen Duscha; Alice Guild; Walter & Elise Haas Fund;

Getting Involved
To learn more about our publications, events, membership club, and other ways you can participate, please visit www.heydaybooks.com.